D1249183

AN ECONOMIST'S PROTEST
Columns in Political Economy

AN ECONOMIST'S PROTEST
Columns in Political Economy

MILTON FRIEDMAN
The University of Chicago

Thomas Horton and Company New Jersey

Editing and Production: **Nat LaMar**
Design: **Barbara Ellwood**
Cover: **Rafael Hernandez**

Library of Congress Cataloging Data
Friedman, Milton, 1912–
    An economist's protest.
    Chiefly columns originally published in *Newsweek* Magazine, 1966-72.
    1. United States–Economic Policy–1961
Addresses, essays, lectures. 1. Title.
HC106.6.F75   330.9'73'092   72-7120

Manufactured in the United States of America

Published by Thomas Horton and Company, 22 Appleton Place, Glen Ridge, New Jersey 07028.

15 14 13 12 11 10 9 8 7 6 5 4 3 2 1

Chapter One
NIXON ECONOMICS

When President Nixon came into office, he faced three major economic problems: inflation, balance of payments deficits, and spiraling Federal government expenditures. His announced policy for dealing with *inflation* had three elements: (1) fiscal restraint, (2) monetary restraint, and (3) reliance on private markets to set prices and wages. In fiscal and monetary policy, the administration stressed "gradualism," the importance of slowing down gradually to ease the transition without imposing abrupt shocks on the economy. The announced policy for dealing with the *balance of payments* was to reduce direct controls on foreign investment and lending and to rely on the ending of inflation to expand exports and reduce imports. The announced policy for dealing with *spiralling Federal government spending* was to produce fiscal restraint primarily by holding down government spending rather than by raising taxes.

The actual execution of policy falls into two sharply demarcated parts: before August 15, 1971 and after August 15, 1971.

Before August 15, 1971, there was no change in stated policies, but the actual execution of policy departed from the stated policy. The departure was least in fiscal policy: Federal government spending rose less than 7 per cent a year from 1968 to 1971—a sharp reduction from the more than 13 per cent a year rise from calendar year 1965 to calendar year 1968. The departure was significant in market policy. The President engaged in some "jawboning," notably by establishing a productivity commission and by having the Council of Economic Advisers issue "inflation alerts." More important, in construction, the President, after temporarily suspending the Davis-Bacon Act, accepted an arrangement involving the setting up of joint management-labor councils to police wage agreements in the construction industry. The departure was greatest in monetary policy, where the "independent" Fed stepped too sharply on the brakes in 1969 and too sharply on the accelerator in the first seven months of 1971.

I strongly agreed with the stated policies of the President, though I was repeatedly disappointed with their execution, particularly in the monetary area. That disappointment is reflected in many of the columns in Chapter 3 dealing with monetary policy. On the other hand, the columns in this chapter before August, 1971, mostly support the general direction of policy and defend it against what I considered to be unjust criticism. The last of this series, "Steady as You Go" (July 26, 1971), praises the President for sticking to his policy of gradualism despite the great pressure on him to "do something."

My praise proved premature. On August 15, 1971, under pressure from an international monetary crisis, President Nixon changed course drastically. I heartily approved his actions in closing the gold window—indeed my initial column in Chapter 5 on international monetary policy, dated May 15, 1967, recommended precisely the action that the President belatedly took. I equally heartily disapproved of his domestic actions in freezing prices and wages, and then subsequently establishing a pay board and a price board. Though these measures were an understandable reaction to strong political pressures, they seemed to me then—as they still do—a major economic mistake. Most of the remaining columns in this chapter develop that theme.

The departure from a free market policy on wages and prices was shortly followed by a departure from fiscal restraint—a development that I saw coming in my columns "Why the Freeze is a Mistake" (August 30, 1971) and "Will the Kettle Explode" (October 18, 1971). But in those columns, I expected Congress to be the prime actor in departing from fiscal restraint. Congress has more than done its part, but the President has given spending a further major boost: the budget he submitted in early 1972 recommends that Federal spending in calendar 1972 as a whole rise more than 13 per cent over spending in calendar 1971 and by an even larger percentage in the first half of 1972. The budget calls for deficits exceeding any except those incurred during World War II.

The actual outcome is turning out to be very different from the budget forecast. Tax receipts were much higher in the first half of 1972 than anticipated—thanks to a multibillion dollar mistake by Internal Revenue that led to massive overwithholding of taxes. Federal expenditures did not increase as rapidly as anticipated. The result was that the Federal deficit for the fiscal year ending June 30, 1972 is the astronomical sum of over $20 billion instead of the superastronomical sum of nearly $40 billion forecast in the budget.

However, this has merely postponed rather than eliminated either the spending or the red ink. The tax overwithholding in 1972 means large refunds in 1973; and the spending programs will gain momentum. It is therefore almost certain that government spending will increase rapidly through at least 1973. The exact size of the deficit is less certain, since continuing economic expansion will raise tax receipts, but the deficit will nonetheless be substantial at best.

AFTER THE NEW ECONOMICS
December 9, 1968

The Nixon Administration will confront major economic problems in three areas: inflation, balance of payments, and the government budget. In each area, there is a stark contrast between John F. Kennedy's inheritance from the Eisenhower Administration and Richard M. Nixon's inheritance from the Kennedy-Johnson Administration. In each area, the New Economics has managed in eight years to turn a comfortable, easy situation into a near-crisis, to squander assets and multiply liabilities.

Inflation

KENNEDY Consumer prices rose at the average rate of 1.4 per cent per year from 1952 to 1960. More important, the price rise had been slowing down. A burst of inflationary pressure in 1956 and 1957 was surmounted and replaced by essential price stability. As a result, widespread fears of inflation were converted into expectations of price stability.

NIXON The consumer-price index is currently rising at a rate of 5 per cent per year. The creeping inflation that started in 1964 has turned into a trot. Expectations of substantial further inflation are nearly universal.

The New Economists argue that Eisenhower bought price stability at the cost of heavy unemployment. Yet unemployment during the Eisenhower years was only fractionally higher than during the Kennedy-Johnson years: 4.87 per cent vs. 4.85 per cent. The time pattern was different: unemployment was higher at the end of the Eisenhower years than at the beginning, when the Korean War boom was in full blast; unemployment was higher at the beginning of the Kennedy-Johnson years than at the end when the Vietnam war is in full blast.

Balance of payments

KENNEDY The balance of payments deteriorated somewhat in the final three years of the Eisenhower Administration. The gold stock declined roughly $5 billion and there was a minor run on gold in 1960. *But*, the gold stock was still a healthy $18 billion, sales of goods and services abroad exceeded purchases by $4 billion, this trade surplus was growing rapidly, and, most important, there were no controls on exchange transactions, no concealed devaluation, no financial gimmicks to make the figures look better.

NIXON Eight successive years of substantial deficits in the balance of payments have reduced the gold stock from $18 billion to less than $11 billion. An "interest equalization tax" on purchases of foreign securities was levied in 1964 as a "temporary" measure—a concealed devaluation of the capital dollar that is still with us. Direct controls were imposed on foreign lending by commercial banks and on foreign investment by businesses—first on a "voluntary," then on a compulsory basis. Ingenuity has run wild in creating financial gimmicks to hide the true situation—beginning with the so-called Roosa bonds (which some of us dubbed subrosa bills). And withal, the surplus on trade account has essentially disappeared for the first time in many years. The recent improvement in published figures simply reflects a shift of capital funds in reaction to the disturbances in France and the invasion of Czechoslovakia.

The New Economists leave Mr. Nixon scant reserves; even worse, they leave him a mess of controls and a set of cosmetic measures that must be eliminated before he can even guess the real size of the problem.

The government budget

KENNEDY In 1960, the Federal government spent $94.7 billion and took in $98.3 billion—a cash surplus of $3.6 billion. Expenditures were 32 per cent higher than in the final year of the Truman Administration, receipts 38 per cent higher.

NIXON In the first six months of 1968, the Johnson Administration spent almost as much as the Eisenhower Administration in all twelve months of 1960: $92.1 billion compared with $94.7 billion; but took in much less, $86.4 billion compared with $98.3 billion. Despite the 10 per cent surtax and the reduction in expenditures legislated by Congress, the budget continues in deficit, and spending continues to grow.

And this is not all. Many programs have been started on a small scale but call for large increases in expenditures in later years. It will be a major achievement just to keep spending from growing at a rapid pace.

Many a New Economist may well have secretly sighed in relief when the election results were in. What a mess to have to straighten out! What a legacy to leave the opposition!

UNEMPLOYMENT FIGURES
October 20, 1969

Few figures are watched with more fear and trembling than those reported each month on the percentage of the labor force unemployed. The jump from 3.5 to 4 per cent reported last week has been seized on by some as the first real sign of success in the battle against inflation, by others, as a portent of economic collapse.

Yet few figures are more misunderstood and misinterpreted.

The unemployment percentage is currently 4 per cent. This corresponds to roughly 3.2 million unemployed. Does this mean, as one might suppose from most news stories on unemployment, that more than 3 million families are wondering where the next paycheck is coming from?

Who are the unemployed?

Not at all. Roughly 1 million unemployed are teen-agers, about half of whom are looking for their first job. Of the remaining unemployed, half are females, many of whom are not regular earners. Of the million unemployed males 20 years and older, only about half are married men.

More important, unemployment is mostly a brief period between jobs—or between school or housework and a job. Nearly two-thirds were either working in the prior month, or not looking for a job. Only slightly more than a million were unemployed.

Put differently, fewer than half of the currently unemployed have been unemployed for as long as five weeks; only 5 per cent—about 150,000—for as long as six months. This is the hard-core group that leaps to mind when we talk about "the unemployed." Their plight is certainly serious—but 150,000 persons in that position is a far cry from 3 million.

Many persons are unemployed by choice. Some quit one job to look for a better job—more than a third of those who leave jobs in any week do so voluntarily; others have refused a job offered in the belief that a better one will be along; still others left an earlier job some time ago to go to school, or to make a home for their husbands, or to have or raise children and have only just re-entered the labor force. A rise in unemployment may be a good thing as well as a bad thing—if it means that people have so much confidence in finding another job that they do not hesitate to leave one they do not like.

In some ways, a more meaningful figure than the number of persons unemployed at any one date is the average length of time that persons who become unemployed remain unemployed—the average time between jobs for those who change from one job to another, or the average time it takes to get a job for those who go from school or home to the unemployment rolls. Until the most recent jump in the unemployment rate, that average has been about five and a half weeks—hardly a period long enough to cause acute distress.

What this meant was that each week about 530,000 people started to look for work—because they left or lost a job or because they had just entered or re-entered the labor force. Simultaneously, about 530,000 people each week found jobs or stopped looking. Of the 530,000 people who started to look for jobs each week, about one-fifth found a job within a week; about three-quarters, within a month; and all but about 1 per cent, within six months. During a year as a whole, not 3 million people but around 20 million separate individuals were unemployed at some time or other—the bulk for trivial periods.

Time between jobs

Cries of horror go up when it is suggested that the slowing down of the economy as a by-product of policies to stop inflation may mean a rise from 3.5 per cent to around 4.5 per cent in the unemployment percentage. What, it is said, throw more than a million additional people out of work?

In fact, the number who each week start to look for work would be raised very little—from 530,000 to perhaps 560,000. But these job-seekers would spend on the average an extra week or so finding an acceptable job—the average duration of unemployment would go from about five and a half to about six and a half weeks. The most serious effect would be to raise the number of persons unemployed at any time for more than six months from 180,000 to perhaps 300,000.

These changes are not desirable. But they are not a major catastrophe. They do not spell acute distress. And their avoidance does not justify letting inflation run rampant—which would in any event only postpone higher unemployment temporarily. We badly need less hysteria and dogmatism and more perspective, proportion and balance in judging these matters.

ECONOMIC PERSPECTIVE
December 22, 1969

The current flood of talk about inflation is marked by an extraordinary lack of perspective. Instant coffee, instant tea, instant solutions to instant problems—that is the flavor of the discussion. In near-hysterical tones, we are told over and over that monetary and fiscal restraints are not working, that price inflation continues unabated, that new and more drastic steps must be taken.

Let me try to inject a sense of proportion into this discussion by answering some questions it raises.

Are we on schedule?

Q Has there been monetary and fiscal restraint?
A Yes, indeed. Since December 1968, the rate of growth of money has been slowed down sharply: from over 7 per cent per year to less than 4.5 per cent until May 1969 and to about zero since then.

The Federal budget was in *deficit* to the tune of $25 billion in the year ending June 30, 1968, but ran a *surplus* of $3 billion in the year ending June 30, 1969.
Q Has inflation been stopped?
A No. Consumer prices are still rising—at about 5 per cent per year.[1]
Q Doesn't that mean that anti-inflation policies have failed?
A No. When you come home to a cold house and turn on the furnace, has the furnace failed because the house does not warm up instantly? In the same way, it takes time to restrain inflation.
Q Are there any signs that restraint is working?
A Many. Until a few months ago, prices were not only rising, they were rising faster and faster. The acceleration has stopped and it looks as if the rate of rise has even eased a bit. The house is still pretty cold but it has stopped getting colder and is beginning to warm up.

[1] Subsequent figures show a rate of rise of about 6 per cent.]

Q How long does it usually take for restraint to make itself felt?

A On the average, six to nine months. That is the average lag between a change in the monetary growth rate and in the rate of growth of spending. Of course, sometimes it takes only three months, sometimes twelve months or longer. A change in spending, in turn, shows up first in output and only later in prices.

Q Isn't restraint taking unusually long this time?

A There is no sign as yet that it is. Inflation during most of this year was the usual response to the rapid monetary growth in 1968. It now looks as if total spending will grow less in the final quarter of 1969 than in the third quarter. If so, the turn in spending will have come six to nine months after the turn in monetary growth. Industrial production reached a peak in July and has been declining since. That is a lag of seven months—just about on schedule.

Q How long will it take to eliminate inflation?

A That depends on how much restraint is imposed. Inflation has a momentum of its own. Prices and wages are being set today for months or even years in advance. The only way to stop inflation in short order would be to engineer a real economic collapse. The better policy is to taper off slowly—and that is the policy of the present Administration. It may take several years of moderate restraint to achieve really stable prices, but we should get some results sooner. Chances are good that the price rise will be down to 3 per cent per year by mid-1970.[2]

Is present policy right?

Q Is the present degree of restraint about right?

A No. I think monetary restraint is too severe. The quantity of money should be permitted to grow at about 3 to 5 per cent per year, not held constant as it has been.

Q Can't we eliminate inflation without an economic slowdown?

A I do not know of any case in history in which that has been done. It seems paradoxical that output must be slowed down in order to stop prices from going up. Yet that is the only way to reduce the pressure of demand.

Q What about direct wage and price controls?

A Diocletian tried them in the Roman Empire. They didn't work for him. They have been tried since again and again—always without success, though sometimes, when controls have been accompanied by sufficient monetary restraint, inflation has been stopped despite them.

Q Will there be a recession in 1970?

A A major contraction on the 1929-33 scale is just about impossible. A minor recession on the 1960-61 scale is just about unavoidable.[3] A more severe recession on the 1957-58 scale is possible, even likely, if the Fed continues its present unduly restrictive policy.

[2This was overoptimistic. The rate of rise in consumer prices was around 5.0 per cent.]

[3This is about what occurred.]

HOW MANY TIMES?
November 30, 1970

For the second time in less than two decades, we are experiencing the cost of stopping an inflation. We paid the cost once—and then threw away the prize. We are paying the cost again—and in danger of again throwing away the prize. How many times must we go through this process?

The first inflation

Prices rose rapidly during the Korean war, then subsided, then rose again. The rise was small by recent standards—less than 3 per cent per year from 1955 to 1958 in consumer prices—but large by our own peacetime record. To stop inflation, the Fed adopted a restrictive monetary policy; the Eisenhower Administration, a restrictive fiscal policy. An inevitable by-product was unemployment averaging 6 per cent from 1958 through 1961. This was a high cost. But it stopped inflation. It disabused workers, employers and investors of the notion that inflation was inevitable. It created a climate favorable to price stability.

As a result the economy was able to expand from 1961 to 1965 without inflation. However, expansion was slow. From 7 per cent in early 1961, unemployment did not get down to 4 per cent until late 1965. The New Economists were dissatisfied. They wanted more rapid expansion. So taxes were cut in 1964 and government spending was increased. The monetary authorities cooperated by increasing the rate of growth of the quantity of money—except for a brief interval of tight money in 1966, which, however, was followed by an even higher rate of monetary growth.

The second inflation

The result was to throw away the favorable climate gained at such high cost. Prices started to rise more and more rapidly. The tight money of 1966 produced a temporary slowdown of inflation in early 1967. But then resumed monetary growth was followed by resumed inflation. As inflation accelerated, people came to expect still further inflation. These expectations got built into wage contracts, price lists and interest rates: inflation reached more than 6 per cent by the end of 1969 and interest rates reached levels not seen for more than a century.

Once again, policies were adopted to stop inflation: the 1968 tax surcharge, and, more important, monetary restraint in 1969. Once again, the initial impact was on output and employment. In late 1969, unemployment began rising and is now 5.6 per cent. In early 1970, inflation began to taper off. Consumer prices are now rising about 4 instead of 6 per cent a year.[1] Inflation is not yet licked but it is on the ropes. Moreover, the economy seems to have hit bottom and to be starting a mild expansion.

[1 Subsequent figures show a somewhat higher rate of rise.]

The third inflation?

Unfortunately, the election campaign and the results of the election threaten a repetition of the mistake that was made from 1964 to 1968. It is being said on all sides that Mr. Nixon *must* achieve both full employment and stable prices by 1972 to win a second term. Few are asking whether any economic policy can assure this outcome.

The only way to be *certain* of ending inflation by mid-1972 would be to step really hard on the monetary and fiscal brakes. But that would almost certainly start a renewed and sharper economic decline. Since the effect on unemployment would come earlier than on prices, this path fortunately has no political appeal.

The only way to be *certain* of reducing unemployment to a rate of 4 per cent by mid-1972 would be to step really hard on the monetary and fiscal accelerators. But that would almost certainly mean renewed inflation. However, the favorable effects on unemployment would come earlier than the unfavorable effects on prices, and the effects on prices might even be delayed until after 1972. Hence, this path has great political appeal.

It also has enormous economic dangers. The benefit to the unemployed will be temporary; the harm to them and to the rest of us, lasting. High employment achieved under forced draft cannot be maintained for long. The resulting inflation would inevitably produce still another attempt to stop inflation. And the attempt would very likely involve even higher costs in unemployment than this time, because the public would have become even more persuaded than they are now that inflation is the wave of the future.

The wiser policy for all of us is to steer a middle course that can achieve both full employment and stable prices not merely for a few months but for many years. It may be that such a policy will succeed by mid-1972. But if it does not, better patience than another round of go-stop.

NEEDED—MORE OF THE SAME
February 15, 1971

President Nixon's economic rhetoric has clearly changed. Talk about stopping inflation has given way to talk about stimulating employment. Talk about nonintervention in prices and wages has given way to jawboning. Talk about "gradualism" has given way to talk about "activism."

Is the change in rhetoric a response to a failure in economic policy? Does it portend a drastic shift in policy? I believe that the answer to both questions is "no."

President Nixon came into office facing the most serious inflationary spiral in U.S. history except in time of major war. The rise in consumer prices had accelerated from an annual rate of 2.3 per cent in the first half of 1967 to nearly 6.5 per cent in the first half of 1969; in wholesale prices, from 0.8 per cent to 6.3 per cent. This spiral had to be stopped.

It was stopped and then reversed. In the second half of 1969, consumer prices rose at the annual rate of 5.9 per cent; in the first half of 1970, at 6 per cent, and in the last half of 1970 at 4.9 per cent—still high but a great improvement. Wholesale prices reacted more sharply—to rates of rise of 3.4, then 3.3, then 1.4 per cent.

The moderation of inflation was accompanied by a recession that raised unemployment to 6 per cent. This was unavoidable: I know of no nation at any time that has been able to stop a serious inflation without a recession, and generally a severe recession. Yet the recession, which I believe is now over, has been one of the mildest in U.S. history.

What produced this outcome? The critical element was monetary restraint, instituted by the independent Fed with President Nixon's full approval. In 1967 and 1968, the quantity of money narrowly defined (currency plus demand deposits) grew at an average annual rate of over 7½ per cent; broadly defined (including also commercial-bank time deposits other than large CD's) of nearly 10 per cent. In 1969 and 1970, the average rates of growth were cut nearly in half—most sharply in the latter half of 1969. Wisely, restraint was eased in time to prevent a deep recession.

Great expectations

Monetary restraint was reinforced by fiscal restraint. And both were permitted to work without irrelevant jawboning or arm twisting. All in all, a courageous, farsighted, wise policy.

With inflation on the run and with a recovery in prospect, this country needs more of the same. We need moderate monetary expansion to match increasing output without fueling renewed inflation. We need fiscal restraint to keep in check the fraction of our income absorbed by government, and we need to let the market system work. That is the preferred way to combine further moderation of inflation with gradual reduction in unemployment and with productive efficiency.

Unfortunately, rhetoric and politics combine to threaten this policy. The Administration made the mistake of promising to halt inflation without a recession. This promise raised expectations that could not be fulfilled and put the Administration on the defensive. The result is that a highly successful policy is regarded as a failure.

Fortunately, the change in policy is likely to be less sharp than the change in rhetoric. In the crucial area of monetary policy, the Fed is now using monetary growth rather than the behavior of interest rates as its primary criterion of policy. As a result, it is unlikely to let monetary growth get out of control as it did in 1967 and 1968.

As one of the inventors of the concept of a full-employment budget, I heartily approve its use—as a device for fiscal discipline, not as an excuse for higher spending. In my opinion, a budget deficit is "expansionary" only if it is financed by creating money. If it is financed by borrowing, its effect is primarily to raise interest rates. But for those who believe otherwise, a deficit created by reducing taxes is just as expansionary as a deficit created by increasing spending. And reductions in taxes would be far healthier for the country than increases in spending.

If inflation continues to slow down, there will be less and less occasion for jawboning. Perhaps the occasion will disappear entirely before we have gone very far down the slippery slope toward compulsory wage and price controls. In that case, jawboning will have confused the issue and miseducated the public but will have done no lasting harm to our system.

In short, I regret exceedingly the new rhetoric but remain hopeful that the old policy will prevail. If it does not, the sky is the limit.

WHICH CRYSTAL BALL?
July 5, 1971

Another test is developing between two competing economic theories—the Keynesian theory that stresses the effect of taxes and government spending on the course of the economy, and the modern quantity theory that stresses the effect of changes in the quantity of money.

Keynesian economists, most notably the New Economists of the Kennedy-Johnson Administration, are forecasting that the current recovery will remain weak unless taxes are reduced promptly and government spending increased sharply. Further, they forecast that such a stimulus would affect mainly output rather than prices.

The monetarists—a smaller though growing group—are forecasting a vigorous expansion with or without further fiscal measures.[1] We believe that the real danger is an expansion so rapid that it will reignite inflation.

The recent record

The Federal budget is now running a deficit of more than $20 billion a year. However, this deficit reflects mainly the recession. The so-called full-employment budget—what expenditures and receipts would be if the economy were operating at full capacity—is in rough balance. The New Economists believe that a large full-employment deficit, which means an even larger actual deficit, is needed for a vigorous expansion.

[1The forecast was not realized. However, the new economic policy introduced by Mr. Nixon on August 15, 1971 changed the ground rules drastically. It remains an open question whether that development—not allowed for in this forecast—may not have aborted a vigorous revival. See "Last Readings on the Old Game Plan" (September 27, 1971) and "First Readings on the New Game Plan" (November 8, 1971).]

The quantity of money grew from February 1970 to January 1971 at the annual rate of 5.5 per cent for M_1 (currency plus demand deposits), 10.1 per cent for M_2 (currency plus all commercial bank deposits other than large CD's). Since January, there has been a veritable monetary explosion—to 13.6 per cent for M_1, 18.3 per cent for M_2. Monetary acceleration in February 1970 was followed by an end to the recession nine months later—about the usual delay. The recent monetary explosion will start showing up later this year. That is why monetarists forecast a vigorous recovery.

This is the fourth such test in the past five years.

In 1966, the Fed sharply slowed monetary growth, while fiscal policy was expansive. The New Economists forecast continued expansion in 1967; the monetarists, a slowdown or recession. A "mini-recession" did occur in the first half of 1967.

In mid-1968, a temporary 10 per cent surtax was enacted to stem inflation. The Fed, fearful of overkill, proceeded to expand money rapidly. The New Economists forecast a slowdown in the first half of 1969 and a recovery in the second half. The monetarists correctly forecast continued boom into 1969. Then, when monetary expansion finally slowed in early 1969, they forecast the end of the boom by late 1969. Inflation reached its peak at the end of 1969 or early 1970.

In late 1969, the New Economists forecast continued expansion. Ebullient Pierre Rinfret—a New Economist in approach though a sometime Nixon adviser—proclaimed confidently, "There ain't gonna be no recession." The monetarists, impressed by mild retardation in monetary growth in the first half of 1969 and severe retardation in the second half of 1969, correctly forecast a recession in 1970.

Score so far: New Economists, 0; monetarists, 3.[2] The next six to nine months will provide another tally.

I hasten to add that this evidence alone justifies little confidence in the monetarist views. Three swallows do not make a spring. Moreover, proponents of neither view claim anything like infallible ability to predict. All recognize that forces other than fiscal and monetary policy have an important influence on the course of events.

Science and the Fed

However, this is far from all the evidence. Scholarly work on the relation between changes in the quantity of money and in economic activity covers more than a century of U.S. experience, as well as experience in many other countries. My own confidence in the importance of the quantity of money rests primarily on this evidence, not on the recent episodes. However, these

[2] For my own forecasts, see my NEWSWEEK columns, "Inflationary Recession," Oct. 17, 1966; "Taxes: The Hard Sell," May 13, 1968; "The Inflationary Fed," Jan. 20, 1969; "Economic Perspective," Dec. 22, 1969.

episodes are newsworthy and dramatic. As a result, they have probably done more to promote acceptance of the monetarist view by the public at large than more basic scholarly work.

The fiscal and monetary authorities have made an important scientific contribution by their erratic policies. They have provided four successive experiments for our edification. But scientific knowledge has been bought at heavy cost—a mini-recession, an inflationary spiral, a real recession and now, the danger of renewed inflation. As a scientific observer, I am grateful. As a citizen, I am indignant. Why must the Federal Reserve swing so erratically from side to side? We urgently need a steady course.

STEADY AS YOU GO
July 26, 1971

My title is taken from the title of an important but little-noticed talk made in Chicago some months ago by George P. Shultz, director of the Office of Management and Budget.

It is also an apt description of the policies that President Nixon has been following—not only in economic matters but also in Vietnam and other aspects of foreign and domestic policy. In every area, he has taken the long view, set long-range objectives and policies, and sought to steer a steady course.

This is a major achievement for which the President has not received the credit he deserves. Washington generates an atmosphere in which it takes great will power and moral courage to look very far ahead, to sacrifice transitory gains for long-term advantage. The horizon is at most two years—the period between Congressional elections—and generally much shorter—tomorrow's headlines.

A threefold policy . . .

The major defect in the economic policy of the prior Administration was the tendency to swing too far from one side to the other, to follow a go-stop policy as a result of trying to fine-tune the economy without the requisite knowledge, understanding, and tools. Impatience with steady but undramatic improvement in the economy in the early 1960s produced a series of highly expansionary measures (tax cuts, spending increases, rapid monetary growth) that started an accelerating inflation. The early stages of the inflation produced a sharp over-reaction by the Fed that caused a credit crunch in 1966 and a mini-recession in 1967. Overreaction to that mini-recession set us off on the accelerating inflation of 1967 to 1969. Fine-tuning with a sledge hammer!

Mr. Nixon adopted a threefold policy to slow inflation without a severe economic decline: (1) moderate fiscal restraint, (2) moderate monetary restraint, (3) preservation and strengthening of free markets. The first and third elements required cooperation of Congress; the second, of the independent Federal Reserve.

His aim was not complete steadiness, but more severe restraint initially and, as the initial restraint slowed down inflation, an easing off to a path that could be continued indefinitely.

In the main, Mr. Nixon has stuck to this policy. The full-employment budget moved to a surplus initially and then to rough balance—too much spending for my taste, yet not the wild gyrations of earlier years. The most unsteady element has been monetary policy—the area least subject to control by the President. Yet even here, except for the recent monetary explosion, hopefully now being corrected, policy has been steadier than in earlier years. There has been mild jaw-boning yet no extensive intervention into price and wage decisions.

. . . That has worked

And the threefold policy has worked. Inflation has slowed, although less than all desired and many expected. There was a recession—but it was one of the mildest in U.S. history. The recession is now over and the economy is again expanding. The expansion, like the recession, is moderate, but it is solid and widely based. Moreover, moderation is desirable so that continued tapering off of inflation can go along with reduced unemployment. As Mr. Shultz said, what we now need to complete the treatment is "time and the guts to take the time, not additional medicine."

Just when this policy is producing demonstrable results, there is increasing pressure on the President to alter course—to recommend lower taxes, higher spending, and even more rapid monetary growth, to establish a wage-price review board, or to freeze wages and prices. Unabashed by their own failures, the fine-tuning Kennedy-Johnson economists are in effect saying, "We produced an accelerating inflation, why shouldn't you?"

Mr. Nixon has not given in to the pressure. Instead, he has announced that he is sticking with his policies. Once again, he has shown the vision and the courage to pursue long-run stability rather than short-term gains.[1]

Mr. Shultz ended his talk: "Those of you familiar with sailing know what a telltale is—a strip of cloth tied to a mast to show which way the wind is blowing.

"A captain has the choice of steering his ship by the telltale, following the prevailing winds, or to steer by the compass.

"In a democracy, you must keep your eye on the telltale, but you must set your course by the compass. That is exactly what the President of the United States is doing. The voice from the bridge says, 'Steady as you go'."

[1] Unfortunately, this tribute was shortly demonstrated to be premature, when on August 15, 1971, Mr. Nixon reversed his policies.]

WHY THE FREEZE IS A MISTAKE
August 30, 1971

I applaud President Nixon's proposed reductions in both taxes and Federal spending. I applaud also his action in ending the fiction that the dollar is convertible into gold. But I regret exceedingly that he decided to impose a 90-day freeze on prices and wages. That is one of those "very plausible schemes," to quote what Edmund Burke said in a different connection, "with very pleasing commencements, [that] have often shameful and lamentable conclusions."

Cosmetic, not therapeutic

Freezing individual prices and wages in order to halt inflation is like freezing the rudder of a boat and making it impossible to steer, in order to correct a tendency for the boat to drift 1 degree off course. The "price level" has been rising at something like 4 per cent per year, or one-third of 1 per cent per month, or 1 per cent in 90 days. Surely, you will say, preventing so minor a rise can do no harm. Why the outcry? Because the 1 per cent is the average of changes in literally millions of individual prices, some rising 10 or 20 per cent or more, others falling 10 or 20 per cent or more. These price changes reflect changes in conditions of demand and supply affecting particular goods and services. They are the way that we steer the economy. Preventing them leaves the economy rudderless, yet it does nothing to alter the basic force producing the average 1 per cent rise in prices. That basic force is a more rapid rise in money demand for goods and services than in the physical supply.

Of course, individual price and wage changes will not be prevented. In the main, price changes will simply be concealed by taking the form of changes in discounts, service and quality, and wage changes, in overtime, perquisites and so on. Even 60,000 bureaucrats backed by 300,000 volunteers plus widespread patriotism were unable during World War II to cope with the ingenuity of millions of people in finding ways to get around price and wage controls that conflicted with their individual sense of justice. The present, jerry-built freeze will be even less successful.

But to whatever extent the freeze is enforced, it will do harm by distorting relative prices.

Shifting the buck

The freeze has reminded me forcefully of a personal experience during World War II, when I was working for the U.S. Treasury Department. In the course of a presentation to the House Ways and Means Committee on the need for additional taxes to prevent inflation, I was interrupted by one member who exclaimed, "Why do we need to worry about inflation in considering taxes? We have just passed General Max [the measure that put a ceiling on all wages and prices]. It is now up to Leon Henderson [director of the Office of Price Administration] to control inflation." I had barely embarked on a learned discourse about how General Max would not work unless it was reinforced by measures to reduce purchasing power, when he interrupted me again. "I understand that," he said. "Mr. Henderson may fail, but we have discharged our responsibility by giving him the power. Now it's up to him."

Similarly today, every proponent of more government spending who had been restrained by fear that the spending would be inflationary will breathe a sigh of relief and say, "Full speed ahead. The price freeze will hold back inflation." The proponents of tax cuts, and even the Federal Reserve Board, which deserves most of the blame for producing the inflation, will react similarly. The result is likely to be more inflationary pressure, not less.

Appearance vs. reality

Whatever happens to the *actual* cost of products to customers or of labor to employers, *stated* prices and *stated* wages will be largely frozen. These are the prices and wages that enter into officially computed index numbers. These numbers will therefore show a dramatic improvement—and depart increasingly from reality. If the freeze were simply ended after 90 days, the indexes would spurt, even though the prices actually charged and the wages actually paid did not. This will create a dilemma for Mr. Nixon. He has a tiger by the tail. Reluctant as he was to grasp it, he will find it hard to let go. The outcome, I fear, will be a further move toward the kind of detailed control of prices and wages that Mr. Nixon has resisted so courageously for so long.

How will it end? Sooner or later, and the sooner the better, it will end as all previous attempts to freeze prices and wages have ended, from the time of the Roman emperor Diocletian to the present, in utter failure and the emergence into the open of the suppressed inflation. Fortunately, as Adam Smith once put it, "There is much ruin in a nation."

LAST READINGS ON THE OLD GAME PLAN
September 27, 1971

By now, most sophisticated observers of the economic scene recognize that economic activity today reflects monetary and fiscal actions of many months ago, and that today's actions will have their major effects many months from now. Accordingly, the course of the economy over at least the next six months depends more on the old game plan for restoring prosperity without inflation than on the new one unveiled by the President on August 15.

However, this fact will not keep the public at large from attributing whatever occurs during the coming months to the new game plan. And they will be encouraged to do so by the news media, with their almost hysterical emphasis on the immediate, their short-time perspective, and their craving for the dramatic.

Before this process goes very far—it began minutes after Mr. Nixon finished speaking—it may be worth recording what we now know about the state of the economy before Mr. Nixon spoke, as the last unambiguous evidence on the old game plan. This evidence belies the doom-and-gloom prophecies that did so much to force Mr. Nixon's hand.

Inflation

Was it true that "no" or "negligible" progress was being made against inflation?

In July 1971, the consumer price index rose at the rate of 2.4 per cent per year—lower than in all but three months in the past three years, and two of those months were also in 1971. Of course, one month may be misleading, so here are the annual rates of price increase during the first seven months of the past five years:

1971	3.8 per cent
1970	5.7 per cent
1969	6.1 per cent
1968	4.8 per cent
1967	2.6 per cent

One must go back to 1967 for a slower rate of price increase.

The more comprehensive index used to deflate the GNP tells the same story. For the second quarter of 1971, it records prices rising 4.1 per cent per year, the lowest rate for any quarter in nearly three years.

Output

The GNP estimates for the second quarter of 1971 show output growing at 4 per cent per year—still too slowly to absorb unused resources rapidly but a clear improvement over the 2 per cent average rate for the final quarter of 1970 and the first quarter of 1971 (it is best to combine these two quarters to avoid the distorting effects of the GM strike). Except for the post-GM-strike quarter, this is the highest rate in almost three years.

Other indicators confirm the impression that the economy was accelerating from a recession to a vigorous expansion. In the first seven months of this year, industrial production rose at the annual rate of more than 2 per cent, after declining at the rate of 5 per cent during the prior fifteen months. Housing, always an early starter, has been booming. In the first seven months of this year, housing starts were almost 50 per cent higher than in the same months of 1970.

Consumer spending

There has been much wailing and gnashing of the teeth about the supposedly reluctant consumer, who was allegedly insisting on stashing away
his income instead of spending it—not a bad thing, incidentally, particularly
for interest rates. Yet in the second quarter of 1971, total consumer expenditures rose at a rate of more than 10 per cent per year. Retail sales have been
even more buoyant. In the first eight months of this year, they rose at the
rate of more than 14 per cent per year. Apparently, there is no satisfying
some people.

Unemployment

Unemployment is always slow to decline in a recovery and highly erratic
from month to month. Yet even so, unemployment, which reached a peak of
6.2 per cent in December 1970, and again in May 1971, was 5.8 per cent in
July and 6.1 in August (the unemployment survey was completed prior to
the President's talk).

Putting it all together

The evidence is entirely consistent with my forecast in this space several
months ago of "a vigorous expansion with or without further fiscal measures
. . . [T]he real danger is an expansion so rapid that it will reignite inflation"
(NEWSWEEK, July 5).

Mr. Nixon's abandonment of the old game plan was forced by the international monetary crisis and by the widespread though mistaken belief that the
economy was in serious trouble. It was not called for by the state of the
economy. The old game plan was working. It will continue to produce a
vigorous expansion despite the dust being thrown into the wheels of the
economy by the freeze.

WILL THE KETTLE EXPLODE?
October 18, 1971

The most serious potential danger of the new economic policy is that,
under cover of the price controls, inflationary pressures will accumulate, the
controls will collapse, inflation will burst out anew, perhaps sometime in
1973, and the reaction to the inflation will produce a severe recession. This
go-stop sequence, though not inevitable, is highly likely.

The freeze and the phase-two controls outlined by the President are like
putting a brick on top of a boiling kettle to keep the lid from blowing off. If,
simultaneously, the flame under the kettle is turned down, the brick may

prevent the lid from blowing off. But if the flame is turned up, the pressure will build until the lid blows off or the kettle explodes.

Practically all economists, even those most favorable to price and wage controls, would accept this analogy. Disagreements are about what the flame consists of—whether, as I believe, primarily of monetary expansion, or, as many other economists believe, also of government deficits and union and business power. These disagreements are important for some purposes but they do not affect the analysis of this column, since all agree that money is part of the flame.

Congress passes the buck . . .

One thing is crystal clear. The new economic policy means larger deficits. The President wisely recommended an equal reduction in taxes and spending. But Congress has already moved to cut taxes more, and spending less, than he recommended. The pressure for economy is off. Price, wage, and now also interest, dividend, and profit controls are there to handle inflation. Congress can forget about it. The deficits that were looming before the President spoke on Aug. 15 will become even larger. This flame is surely being turned up.

If monetary policy were also to be highly expansive, the controls would collapse, as they always have under similar circumstances. The repressed inflation would become open inflation. Index numbers of reported prices would start rising rapidly—no matter what happens to actual prices.

I cannot believe that the American public would accept rapid, open inflation without a vigorous reaction. It would demand that something be done. The only possible courses of action are the reimposition of controls, this time far more widespread, detailed and stringent; or sharply deflationary monetary and fiscal measures. The first would at best be a temporary expedient that would severely strain the economic and social structure; the second would produce a recession. Moreover, the recession would have to be more severe than in 1970 in order to stem inflation. The belief that inflation is the way of the future would be held even more strongly, and the rate of inflation would be even higher.

. . . to the Federal Reserve

The only hope of preventing this dismal outcome rests with the Federal Reserve System. We are clearly not going to have fiscal restraint. If the flame under the kettle is to be turned down at all, it will have to be by monetary restraint. If monetary growth could be held to something like 5 per cent per year for the next two years, it might be possible to dismantle the controls without unleashing a new burst of inflation.

One encouraging sign is that the quantity of money has grown slowly for the past several months, after exploding earlier in the year. However, this lull may prove temporary. Whenever non-monetary forces are lowering interest rates, the Fed tends to expand the money supply less than it intends. That was the case these past few months. Whenever non-monetary forces are raising interest rates, the Fed tends to expand the money supply more than it intends. That was the case earlier this year. Despite the new controls, it is likely to be the case again in 1972 as vigorous expansion and a large Federal deficit combine to raise interest rates.[1]

This behavior of the money supply reflects the Fed's continued attempt to ride two horses at once—interest rates and the money supply. There have been signs that the Fed was mending its ways and putting more stress on the money supply. But now, in naming Arthur Burns to head the committee on interest and dividends, the President has sharpened the Fed's dilemma. Burns may be able to twist the arms of commercial bankers to hold the prime rate. But he and the Fed can keep market rates down only by rapid monetary expansion—and even then only temporarily. If the Fed follows this route the kettle is certain to explode.

FIRST READINGS ON THE NEW GAME PLAN
November 8, 1971

I ended a recent column (Newsweek, Sept. 27, 1971) by saying. "The old game plan . . . will continue to produce a vigorous expansion despite dust being thrown into the wheels of the economy by the freeze."

All in all, I am of that opinion still, yet the first data on the performance of the economy since Aug. 15 suggest that I was too optimistic—that the dust has done more harm than I expected.

Third-quarter slowdown

The most dramatic single bit of evidence is the recently released estimates of the gross national product for the third quarter. These show annual rates of growth of 6.3 per cent for dollar GNP, 2.9 per cent for real GNP (corrected for price changes) and 3.3 per cent for the price deflator. The corresponding figures for the second quarter are 9.0, 4.8 and 4.0. Inflation tapered off further, but real growth declined even more sharply.

Other data confirm the impression given by the GNP figures. Industrial production in September was lower than in July, though higher than in August. Unemployment was roughly unchanged—6.0 per cent in September compared with 6.1 per cent in August. Retail sales appear to have been rising more slowly than earlier in the year—clearly so, if automobiles, which

[1 This is what has happened so far in 1972. In the first three months of 1972, monetary growth speeded up sharply.]

are benefiting from the proposed reduction in the excise tax, are excluded.

Like the GNP deflator, consumer prices have been rising more slowly—at the annual rate of 2.4 per cent in September, compared with 4.8 per cent in August and 3.8 per cent in the first seven months of the year. That improvement largely reflects declines in food prices not under the freeze, so must still be regarded as primarily a legacy of the old game plan.

Of course, one or two months is a very short period from which to draw any firm conclusions. Economic activity varies erratically from month to month as a result of all sorts of short-term influences, and the numbers that we use to measure economic activity can vary even more erratically.

But the figures are consistent with the effect that the new economic policy might be expected to have at this stage. The measures intended to promote expansion—the investment-tax credit and the other tax reductions—have not yet been enacted. The larger deficit and the more rapid monetary growth that I fear will emerge under cover of the wage-price controls have not yet done so, let alone had time to affect the economy. The one real change has been the freeze itself and the talk about phase two.

These have introduced increased uncertainty. The businessman is not sure what prices he will be permitted to charge or what wages he will be permitted to pay. He does not know how the Pay Board and Price Commission will operate or what criteria they will establish. He sees the prospect of controls on interest and dividends and, in the President's reference to "windfall profits," the thin end of the wedge of controls on profits. The natural reaction is to hold back, to play safe, to wait until the uncertainties are resolved. This reaction may very well have produced both the slower rate of expansion and the recent reaction of the stock market.

What now?

How long will the slowdown last? Not very long, I believe. Once an expansion gets under way, as it did at the end of 1970, it has enormous inertia. There are very few examples in our economic history of abortive expansions that got started, proceeded for several quarters and then relapsed into contraction. Increased uncertainty may slow the current expansion temporarily but is not likely to reverse the basic forces fueling it. The uncertainty will decline, if only because businessmen will quickly learn how to get around the controls. I, therefore, expect that the pace of expansion will shortly speed up again.[2]

Over a longer period, the controls will introduce distortions into the economy and lead to a waste of resources. However, monetary and fiscal expansion are likely to do far more to foster a boom than these distortions will do to halt it. What they will do is rather to reduce the gains in real

[2 This occurred in early 1972.]

output during the boom. Hence, I remain persuaded that the basic danger from the new economic policy is an accumulation of inflationary pressure that will produce a collapse of the controls and a resumption of open inflation.

That is the prospect for 1973 and beyond. But for the present, the irony is that the President's departure from long-held principles has postponed and weakened the economic expansion that he so ardently desires.

Chapter Two
FALSE CURES FOR INFLATION

Wage and price controls were imposed on August 15, 1971, largely in response to widespread dissatisfaction with the slow rate at which inflation was tapering off. That dissatisfaction reflected an even more widespread misunderstanding of the sources of inflation—the erroneous belief that inflation reflects the power of trade unions to raise wages and of producers of goods and services to raise prices. This belief was manifested in a crude and simple-minded form already in 1966 in a flare-up of protest movements by housewives who blamed supermarkets for rising food prices and sought in vain to drive prices down by boycotting the supermarkets. The first column in this chapter analyzes these boycotts.

The belief was manifested in a more sophisticated form in proposals for wage and price guidelines or controls considered in the remaining columns in this chapter. Unfortunately, the issues raised by these proposals are so complex that it is not possible to deal with them satisfactorily in a brief column. Hence the reader of this book will not find an adequate explanation of the reasons why I believe that unions and monopolies, which do immense harm to society in many ways, are largely innocent of causing inflation. Mostly they simply respond to inflationary pressure coming from Washington, though they may increase the difficulty of tapering off inflation and may lengthen the transition from a higher to a lower rate of inflation. But even in these respects I believe that their role is minor compared with the part played by governmentally imposed obstacles.

Most discussions of price and wage controls have dealt with their economic consequences. But controls have also disturbing political and ethical consequences. Indeed, my opposition to them derives even more from their political than from their economic consequences, as I made clear in two columns that I contributed to the Op-Ed page of the *New York Times* in October, 1971 and that are here reprinted as a single entry.

The final column in this section demonstrates that the widespread dissatisfaction with the tapering off of inflation that encouraged the imposition of controls was not justified by the record. Despite the repeated claims to the contrary, inflation reached its peak in early 1970 and subsided appreciably by August 1971. This column overlaps some of the columns in Chapter 1, and could as well have been in that chapter.

BOYCOTTS AND PRICES
November 28, 1966

Housewives who are boycotting supermarkets are in an ancient if misguided tradition. "When the price of a thing goes up," wrote the British economist Edwin Cannan in 1915, many people "abuse, not the buyers nor the persons who might produce it and do not do so, but the persons who are producing and selling it, and thereby keeping down its price . . . It certainly would appear to be a most extraordinary example of the proverbial ingratitude of man when he abuses the farmer who does grow wheat because other farmers do not . . . But have we not all heard the preacher abuse his congregation because it is so small?"

Today, too, the boycotters are attacking the wrong culprit, and their boycotts will be as ineffective as all previous boycotts.

Who sets prices?

Ask a supermarket operator, "Who sets your prices?"

"I do," he will probably reply.

"In that case, why don't you double them?"

"Don't be silly, I would have no customers."

Press him on the other side, "If you want more customers, why don't you halve your prices?"

"What do you think I am," may be his indignant response, "a philanthropist? If I halved my prices, I would go bankrupt—unless I could get the Ford Foundation to back me. And then they would go bankrupt."

The supermarket operator does not set prices. He simply records the prices that are set by forces outside his control. Blaming him for high prices is like blaming a thermometer for the fever it records. Boycotting him is like breaking the thermometer to cure the fever.

What effects, if any, do boycotts have on the basic forces of demand and supply?

When boycotters spend less at supermarkets, this does impose pressure on supermarkets—witness the rash of lower posted prices, not all of which are sales gimmicks. But if boycotters simply transfer their custom to family grocers, the other side of the coin is a greater demand at those stores and higher prices there. The boycotters lose—because they pay the higher prices at family grocers—and the nonboycotters gain—because they benefit from the lower prices at supermarkets. End the boycott, and you end the temporary stimulus to both the lower and the higher prices.

If boycotters spend less on food by emptying their pantries, there is no current offset to the lower supermarket prices. But when they restock, they will boost demand, which will lead to higher prices then. On the average, they will only have rendered supermarket operations more erratic and costly.

If they spend less on food by eating less and instead spend their money on other items of consumption, their abstinence will reduce the upward pressure on food prices. But the higher demand for other goods will increase the pressure on other prices.

If they spend less in total on all forms of consumption and put the difference in savings and loans, the extra funds available for mortgages will tend to stimulate the building industry. The upward pressure on consumer prices will be less but on construction prices more.

To achieve their objective, boycotters must not only spend less on consumption, they must "hoard" what they save—preferably in mattresses or safe-deposit boxes. That *would* absorb some of the increase in the quantity of money that is the basic source of inflationary pressure.

But this is fantasy. Boycotters want lower prices in order to be able to buy goods. They are not picketing supermarkets to stuff mattresses.

Where to complain

Housewives have a justifiable complaint. But they should complain to Washington where inflation is produced, not to the supermarket where inflation is delivered. Prices have been going up because the quantity of money increased too much from 1961 to the spring of this year. And the quantity of money increased as much as it did because the monetary authorities—primarily the U.S. Treasury and the Federal Reserve System—planned it that way, or, to be less generous, let it happen (see my column, NEWSWEEK, Oct. 17). The names on the picket signs should be not A&P, but Fowler and Martin.

BURNS AND GUIDELINES
June 15, 1970

Arthur Burns has long been an outspoken, principled and consistent opponent of wage and price guidelines or controls. As a result, he created a sensation when, in a recent speech, he remarked that "an incomes policy, provided it stopped well short of direct price and wage controls and was used merely as a supplement to over-all monetary and fiscal measures, might speed us through this transitional period of cost-push inflation."

Burns's earlier criticisms of wage and price guidelines came during periods of rising excess demand. His support for an incomes policy today comes during a period of declining excess demand. Circumstances do alter cases, yet I remain persuaded that an incomes policy, in any shape or form, is a dangerous expedient.

When excess demand is pulling prices up, wage and price controls work against the basic forces. If firms and unions in some sector of industry are induced or compelled to hold prices or wages down, that is like pinching one corner of a large balloon. The lucky buyers of the goods pay less and have more left to spend elsewhere—driving other prices up still higher and not reducing over-all inflation at all. Jobs in the industry become unattractive, so it will be short of labor. The amount produced will be less than the amount demanded, so buyers will have to be rationed somehow. Distortion of output, black markets, government controls, inefficiency—these are the clearly predictable results. Repressed inflation rolls merrily on, doing far more harm than open inflation. This is the argument that Arthur Burns has always made against wage and price guidelines.

The case for

Suppose, however, that monetary and fiscal policies have altered—as they have in the past year in the U.S.—to reduce excess demand. Wages and prices will still rise for a time because of inertia and inflationary expectations. If monetary and fiscal restraint persists, these higher wages and prices will prove inconsistent with the basic forces. They will mean unemployment and underproduction. Yet, the stickiness of wages and prices will make it hard to get them back down. If persuasion, a little judicious arm twisting, could prevent the initial rise in prices and wages, even the persons whose arms were twisted would be grateful afterward. Incomes policy would have contributed to "speed us through this transitional period of cost-push inflation."

This is the intellectual case for "incomes policy." Why do I reject it?

The case against

Exhortation by high government officials will not persuade businessmen or labor leaders that inflation is on the way out. They have vivid memories of similar exhortations in the past that were belied by subsequent experience. As a result, an incomes policy that did stop "well short of price and wage controls" would have little effect on anything.

If an "incomes policy" is to have an appreciable effect, it must go beyond talk. We know what that means. Threats of political reprisals or of income tax investigations, withholding of government contracts, and similar politically corrupting exercises of extralegal powers. Or the establishment of formal wage and price controls with arrangements for appeals and all the rest of the cumbrous bureaucratic machinery. In either case, the "transitional period" would be over before the machinery was set up. And how then do we get rid of it?

The way to eliminate inflationary expectations is not by talk but by demonstrating that inflation is tapering off and will continue to do so. The right policy is: (a) moderate monetary expansion; (b) moderate fiscal restraint; (c) complete avoidance of price and wage controls. These policies will work and will bring inflation to an end. They will also provide the basis for a sound expansion without inflation. We need patience and persistence, not gimmicks.

Central banks (like the rest of us) have a tendency to try to shift responsibility and blame to others for economic troubles. The favorite tactic of the Fed in earlier days was "moral suasion" in the field of credit—appeals to banks not to make "speculative" or inflationary loans. Today central bankers worldwide blame fiscal policy, on the one hand, and propose the exercise of "moral suasion" on business and labor, on the other.

It is disheartening to observe so tough-minded, so independent, and so knowledgeable a person as Arthur Burns conform to this pattern so soon after becoming chairman of the Fed.

INFLATION AND WAGES
September 28, 1970

I have seldom met a businessman who was not persuaded that inflation is produced by rising wages—and rising wages, in turn, by strong labor unions—and many a nonbusinessman is of the same mind. This belief is false yet entirely understandable. To each businessman separately, inflation comes in the form of higher costs, mostly wages; yet for all businessmen combined, higher prices produce the higher costs. What is involved is a fallacy of composition. Any one person may be able to leave a crowded theater in two minutes without difficulty. Let everyone try to leave in two minutes and there may be utter chaos. What is true for each separately need not be true for all together.

It is easy to show that the widely held union-wage-push theory of inflation is not correct. If A is *the* cause of B, then whenever A occurs, B will also occur, and whenever B occurs, so will A. *Trade unions* (A) were as strong in the U.S. in 1961-64, when there was no *inflation* (B), as in 1965-69, when there was inflation. Prices in the U.S. more than doubled in the Civil War, when unions were almost nonexistent, in World War I, when unions were weak, and in World War II, when unions were strong. Prices in the U.S. rose more than 30 per cent from 1849 to 1857, and again from 1895 to 1914, both periods when unions were extremely weak. Inflation has plagued countries with negligible trade unions and with strong trade unions; and both kinds of countries have had periods of price stability. Communist countries, like capitalist countries, have experienced both inflation and price stability.

Why appearances deceive

In light of these historical examples, why do businessmen believe so firmly in a wage-push theory of inflation? A simple hypothetical example may explain the puzzle.

Suppose that there was a sudden fad in the U.S. for male footwear. Despite a rush of customers, the shoe stores would not immediately raise the prices they charge. They would, with pleasure and profit, sell more shoes, depleting their inventories. Orders would pour in to wholesalers, who similarly would fill them at list prices, depleting their inventories in turn, and sending on larger orders to manufacturers. The manufacturers, delighted with the flood of business, would try to step up production. To produce more shoes requires more leather. But at any time, there is only a limited stock of leather. To get more leather for themselves, the shoe manufacturers will have to offer higher prices at auctions, in order to bid the leather away from other uses. To produce more shoes, they will also have to hire more labor. How? One way is surely by offering higher wages.

At this point, manufacturers discover that their costs have risen—because of rising wages and the higher cost of leather. They reluctantly raise their prices. Wholesalers discover that their costs have risen and reluctantly raise their prices. Retailers discover that their costs have risen and reluctantly raise their prices.

The real culprit

At each step, prices rise because costs rise—yet the whole process was initiated by a rise in demand.

This example describes accurately a period of inflation. An increase in aggregate money demand leads businessmen to try to increase output. Beyond some limited point, when manpower, equipment and other resources are fully occupied, they cannot all do so, but the *attempt* to increase output raises costs and makes it look to each businessman as if he must raise his prices because his costs have risen.

The only exception is for a brief period after the turning of the tide. Let an inflationary increase in demand subside. For a time, wages and other costs will continue to rise, reflecting the unspent impetus from the earlier rise in demand. That is what we have been experiencing this past year. But it is a temporary phase that cannot be sustained.

The common element in inflation is not strong unions but an increase in money demand accompanying a rapid increase in the quantity of money. In 1848-1857, the increased quantity of money was produced by gold discoveries in California; in 1896-1913, by the perfection of the cyanide process for extracting gold from low-grade ore; in the Civil War and the two world wars by the creation of money to finance military expenditures; in 1964-1969 by the Federal Reserve System, partly to help finance large government deficits.

Inflation is always and everywhere a monetary phenomenon.

IMITATING FAILURE
January 11, 1971

The Johnson Administration tried wage-price guidelines. The guidelines failed and were abandoned. The British tried a wage-price board. It failed and has just been abolished. The Canadians tried voluntary wage-price controls. Their Prices and Incomes Commission recently announced the program was unworkable and would be abandoned Jan. 1.

Yet, in the U.S., the Committee for Economic Development, an influential organization of businessmen, issues a report recommending (though with some vigorous dissents) a wage-price board on British lines and voluntary wage-price controls on Canadian lines. Arthur F. Burns, chairman of the Federal Reserve Board, supports the recommendation for a wage-price board. The Council of Economic Advisers' second "inflation alert" uses stronger adjectives than the first to describe price developments. Mr. Nixon, in a speech to the National Association of Manufacturers, tries mild jawboning, calling on labor and business to exercise restraint in the national interest.

Surely, this must mean that the experience of the Johnson Administration, of Britain and of Canada is the exception, that there are other examples of the successful use of incomes policy to slow inflation. Not at all. I do not know a single successful example and the current proponents of an incomes policy do not claim that they do. The refrain is rather, "despite the limited success of these measures elsewhere, they offer promise."

Soft promise

If the promise is not based on direct experience, is it based on economic analysis? Hardly. Economic analysis largely reinforces experience. It suggests that voluntary wage and price controls are likely to be honored in the breach—because those who observe them will suffer at the expense of those who do not—and that compulsory wage and price controls simply repress rather than eliminate inflationary pressure. The only analytical case for wage-price control is to shorten the delayed impact of an inflationary episode after excess demand has been eliminated, not temporarily, but for good (see my NEWSWEEK column, June 15, 1970). That case is indeed cited by proponents of incomes policy, but it is a weak reed, since most of them regard the incomes policy as a *substitute* for demand restraint, not a supplement. The policy is based on neither experience nor analysis but simply on the "For God's sake, let's do something" syndrome.

The talk about incomes policy reflects a general tendency: the belief that there is a sugar-coated pill for every economic and social ill, and that only malice and ill will prevent its use. Time and again, I have had anguished letters from sincere readers to the effect, "Since you acknowledge that there is a real problem, it is irresponsible of you to criticize a proposed solution unless you offer an alternative. What is your solution?"

Suppose an expert on cancer criticized a proposed cure. Would any of my correspondents regard him as irresponsible because he did not offer an alternative cure? Why is economics different? In economics, as in medicine, we have imperfect knowledge. Some ills we cannot cure at all, and some only with undesirable side effects. In economics, as in medicine, our knowledge will improve further but there will always remain unsolved problems of both kinds.

Hard fact

We know very well how to cure inflation: by restricting the growth of money demand through monetary and fiscal policy. At present, we know no other way to do it. We know also that this cure has the unpleasant side effect of a recession and of temporarily higher unemployment. We do not know how to avoid this side effect. There have been many inflations in history. I know of none that has ever been stopped in any other way or that has been stopped without temporary economic difficulties.

In the present episode, monetary and fiscal restraint have been working as they always do. The rate of inflation is slowing down and will continue to do so if restraint is maintained. As always, a side effect has been a recession. So far, it has been mild, milder indeed than past experience gave us any reason to expect. We have been attacking the severest U.S. inflation on record except in time of major war; yet we have experienced one of the mildest recessions in our history.

But standards of performance have been driven so unrealistically high that an extremely successful policy, as judged by past experience, is widely regarded as a major failure. What a triumph of rhetoric over reality.

MORALITY AND CONTROLS*

I (October 28, 1971)

Most discussion of the wage-price freeze and the coming Phase II controls has been strictly economic and operational: were they needed, will they work, how will they operate. I have recorded my own opposition to them in three columns in Newsweek.

There has been essentially no discussion of a much more fundamental issue. The controls are deeply and inherently immoral. By substituting the rule of men for the rule of law and for voluntary cooperation in the market-place, the controls threaten the very foundations of a free society. By encouraging men to spy and report on one another, by making it in the private interest of large numbers of citizens to evade the controls, and by making actions illegal that are in the public interest, the controls undermine individual morality.

One of the proudest achievements of Western civilization was the substitution of the rule of law for the rule of men. The ideal is that government restrictions on our behavior shall take the form of impersonal rules, applicable to all alike, and interpreted and adjudicated by an independent judiciary rather than of specific orders by a government official to named individuals. In principle, under the rule of law, each of us can know what he may or may not do by consulting the law and determining how it applies to his own circumstances.

The rule of law does not guarantee freedom, since general laws as well as personal edicts can be tyrannical. But increasing reliance on the rule of law clearly played a major role in transforming Western society from a world in which the ordinary citizen was literally subject to the arbitrary will of his master to a world in which the ordinary citizen could regard himself as his own master.

The ideal was, of course, never fully attained. More important, we have been eroding the rule of law slowly and steadily for decades, as government has become more and more a participant in economic affairs rather than primarily a rule-maker, referee, and enforcer of private contracts. It was, after all, the development of the private market that made possible the

*The New York Times.

original movement from a world of status to a world of voluntary contract. As government has tried to replace the market in one area after another, it has inevitably been driven to restore a world of status.

The freeze and even more the pay board and price board of the Phase II controls are clearly another massive step away from the rule of law and back toward the rule of men. True, the rule of men will be *under* law but that is a far cry from the rule *of* law—Stalin, Hitler, Mussolini, and now Kosygin, Mao and Franco all rule under law.

The price that you and I may charge for our goods or our labor or that we may pay others for their goods or their labor will now be determined, not by any set of legislated standards applying to all alike, but by specific orders by a small number of men appointed by the President. And if governmental edict is to replace market contract, there is no alternative. There are millions of prices, millions of wage rates arrived at by voluntary agreements among millions of people. The collectivistic countries have been unable in decades to find simple rules enabling prices and wages to be established by any alternative impersonal mechanism. We are not likely to succeed. And we are not trying. Instead, the appeal is to the patriotism, civic responsibility, and judgment of political appointees, most of whom represent vested interests. How do patriotism and judgment determine that the price of a widget may rise 2.8 per cent but the price of a wadget, only 0.3 per cent; the wage of a widgeteer by 2 per cent but of a wadgeteer, by 10 per cent? Clearly they do not. Arbitrary judgment, political power, visibility—these are what will matter.

The tendency for such an approach to violate human freedom is even more clearly exemplified by the present situation with respect to dividends. The President has *requested* firms not to raise dividends—he has no legal power to do more. The request has been accompanied by surveillance, a calling down to Washington and public lambasting of the handful of corporations that did not conform, and a clear implied threat to use extralegal powers. These measures have no legal basis at all. Yet I know of only one small company that has had the courage to refuse to cooperate on grounds of principle.

The full logic of the system will not work itself out this time. Our strong tradition of freedom, the ineffectiveness of the controls, the ingenuity of the people in finding ways around them—these will lead to the collapse of the controls rather than to their hardening into a full-fledged straitjacket. But nonetheless, it is disheartening to see us take this further long step on the road to tyranny so lightheartedly, so utterly unaware that we are doing something fundamentally in conflict with the basic principles on which this country is founded. The first time, we may venture only a small way. But the next time, and the next time?

II (October 29, 1971)

Enforcement of the price and wage controls, as of the freeze, must depend heavily on encouraging ordinary citizens to be informers—to report "violations" to Government officials.

When you and I make a private deal, both of us benefit—otherwise we do not have to make it. We are partners, cooperating voluntarily with one another. The terms, so long as they are mutually agreeable, should be our business. But not any longer. Big Brother is looking over our shoulders. And if the terms do not correspond with what he says is O.K., one of us is encouraged to turn in the other. And to turn him in for doing something few people have ever regarded and do not now regard as in any sense morally wrong; on the contrary, for doing something that each of us regards, when it affects us, as our basic right. Am I not entitled to sell my goods or my labor for what I consider them worth as long as I do not coerce anyone to buy? Is it morally wrong for Chile to expropriate the property of Anaconda Copper—i.e., to force it to sell its copper mines for a price less than its value; but morally right for the U.S. Government to force the worker to sell his labor for less than its value to him and to his employer?

By any standards, the edicts of the pay board and the price board, like the initial freeze, will be full of inequities and will be judged to be by ever increasing numbers of people. You believe that you are entitled to a pay raise, your employer agrees and wishes to give you one, yet the pay board says no. Will there not be a great temptation to find a way around the ruling? By a promotion unaccompanied by any change in duties but to a job title carrying a higher permitted pay. Or by your employer providing you with amenities you formerly paid for. Or by one or another of the innumerable stratagems—legal, quasi-legal, or illegal—that ingenious men devise to protect themselves from snooping bureaucrats.

In general, I have little sympathy with trade unions. They have done immense harm by restricting access to jobs, denying excluded workers the opportunity to make the most of their abilities, and forcing them to take less satisfactory jobs. Yet surely in the present instance they are right that it is inequitable for the Government retroactively to void contracts freely arrived at. The way to reduce the monopoly power of unions is to remove the special legal immunities they are now granted, not to replace one concentrated power by another.

When men do not regard governmental measures as just and right they will find a way around them. The effects extend beyond the original source, generate widespread disrespect for the law, and promote corruption and violence. We found this out to our cost in the 1920's with Prohibition; in World War II with price control and rationing; today with drug laws. We shall experience it yet again with price and wage controls if they are ever more than a paper facade.

One feature of price and wage controls makes their effect on individual morality especially vicious. Because these controls distort the use of resources, the evader benefits not only himself but society. The more rigorously the controls are enforced, the more harm they do. They render behavior which is immoral from one point of view socially beneficial. They thus introduce the kind of fundamental moral conflict that is utterly destructive of social cohesion.

Our markets are far from completely free. Monopoly power of labor and business means that prices and wages are not wholly the product of voluntary contract. Yet these blemishes, real and important though they are, are minor compared to replacing market agreements by government edict, compared to giving arbitrary power to a small number of appointed officials, compared to inculcating in the public contempt for the law.

The excuse for the destruction of liberty is always the plea of necessity—that there is no alternative. If indeed, the economy were in a state of crisis, of a life-and-death emergency, and if controls promised a sure way out, all their evil social and moral effects might be a price that would have to be paid for survival. But not even the gloomiest observer of the economic scene would describe it in any such terms. Prices rising at 4 per cent a year, unemployment at a level of 6 per cent—these are higher than we would like to have or than we need to have, but they are very far indeed from crisis levels. On the contrary, they are rather moderate by historical standards. And there is far from uniform agreement that wage and price controls will improve matters. I happen to believe that they will make matters worse after an initial deceptive period of apparent success. Others disagree. But even their warmest defenders recognize that they impose costs, produce distortions in the use of resources, and may fail to reduce inflation. Under such circumstances, the moral case surely deserves at least some attention.

CONTROLS: AN EXERCISE IN FUTILITY
May 22, 1972

The accompanying fever chart of inflation can be used for a parlor game. Just cover up the dates at the bottom and try to guess when the most momentous change in economic policy in the past quarter century was introduced in order to halt inflation. On the basis of the chart alone, you would surely pick October 1970. In the next six months, the rate of inflation fell more sharply than in any other six-month period since the peak of inflation in early 1970 (from 5.8 per cent to 4.3 per cent, or by 1.5 percentage points). But of course that is the wrong date. The right date is August 1971, when President Nixon froze prices and wages. In the next six months, the rate of inflation fell less than half as much as in the six months after October 1970 (from 4.4 per cent to 3.7 per cent, or by 0.7 percentage point).

This comparison is not entirely fair, since I picked the first six-month period by hindsight, but it does dramatize two important facts: first, despite all the hoopla in the summer of 1971 about the lack of progress against inflation, there clearly had been a systematic and substantial tapering off of inflation since early 1970; second, despite the extravagant claims for the price and wage controls and the political hurricanes that have swirled about them, the statistics give no sign that price and wage controls have had any appreciable effect on the course of inflation. The recent modest tapering off, like the earlier tapering off, reflects the delayed influence of the restrictive monetary policy of 1969 and the subsequent recession of 1970, not the effect of the controls. (Charts for wholesale prices and for wage rates tell much the same story as the chart for consumer prices.)

Potemkin village?

Does this mean that the wage and price controls are nothing but a modern Potemkin village that have no real effects on the economy? Hardly. The controls have had appreciable, and adverse, effects on output and on productivity. Most important of all, the controls have significantly eroded your freedom and mine, significantly extended the power of Big Brother over our lives.

The immediate effect of the new economic policy was to chill the recovery then under way by introducing great uncertainty into the calculations of every businessman. The resulting hesitation in the economy during the final months of 1971 seems by now to have been largely overcome. Though further hesitation cannot be ruled out, the incredibly expansive fiscal and monetary policy of recent months almost surely spells a real boom in the final months of 1972.

The controls affect productivity in three ways: (1) millions of man-hours in government and industry devoted to administering controls constitute pure and unadulterated waste; (2) insofar as any wage rates are prevented from rising, workers have less incentive to do their best and employers are hampered in hiring as many and as high quality workers as they demand; (3) insofar as profit margins approach the permitted ceilings, businesses lose much of their incentive to keep down costs.

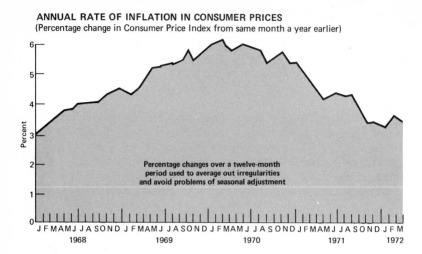

ANNUAL RATE OF INFLATION IN CONSUMER PRICES
(Percentage change in Consumer Price Index from same month a year earlier)

Percentage changes over a twelve-month period used to average out irregularities and avoid problems of seasonal adjustment

All three effects have been minor so far. Distortions develop only gradually, and the controls have so far been working with the economic tide.

The adverse effects on productivity are almost certain to become much more severe in the coming months. Whatever happens to the basic inflationary forces, distortions will accumulate, so that the backward-looking structure of prices, wages and profit margins imposed by the price and pay boards will increasingly depart from market requirements.

Higher inflation ahead

Equally important, it looks from the chart as if the tapering off of inflation has come to an end. For the past six months, the rate of inflation has been roughly constant. And this observation is consistent with what has been happening to monetary and fiscal policies. After being contractionary in 1969 and moderately expansive in 1970—which is what produced the tapering off of inflation that we have had—monetary policy turned highly inflationary in early 1971 and has remained so ever since, except for a notable interruption during the last five months of 1971. Fiscal policy has become increasingly expansionary throughout the past year and a half, which will make it even harder for the Fed to restrain monetary growth. As a result, I believe that we are now poised for a renewed acceleration of inflation. There will be erratic movements from month to month, but from now on the trend of inflation is far more likely to be up than down. The controls will from now on be working against the economic tide, not with it.

In short, the worst is yet to come. But the record in the nine months since the imposition of the freeze is enough to show how fully justified President Nixon was in his long-held and courageously defended opposition to government intervention into the setting of prices and wages. What a shame—for himself and the country—that he finally gave in to the wide-spread, politically motivated pressure to impose controls.

Chapter Three
MONETARY POLICY

My major professional interest for many years has been the role of money in the economy. This fact has led me to write more on money, including international monetary arrangements (Chapter 5), than on any other topic. But it has also made it more difficult for me to write on a level that is accessible to the general reader—or at least so I infer from the many letters I have received complaining that these columns are too "technical." I have tried to mend my ways, but with imperfect success. Perhaps the repetition of some of the same ideas in slightly different form will make the set of columns more accessible than each one separately.

The reader who is not an expert in the field of money may find it helpful to start with the final column "The Case for a Monetary Rule," since that states in general form the basic viewpoint that underlies the discussion of specific episodes in the separate columns.

There is no other area in economics in which professional and lay opinions have changed so greatly in recent years. As of the end of World War II, the revolution in economic thought produced by John Maynard Keynes's *General Theory of Employment, Interest, and Money* led most of the economic profession to dismiss the quantity theory of money—which had held undisputed sway until the 1930s—as an outmoded superstition having about as much relation to "correct" economics as astrology has to astronomy. The Keynesian revolution replaced the emphasis on money with emphasis on investment and government spending. Fiscal policy was the road to high and stable employment.

Experience and scholarly work have produced drastic changes in these views in the past quarter century. The enormous confidence placed in fiscal policy as a precision instrument for controlling the economy was shaken by the political and technical difficulties encountered in trying to use it for that purpose. The confidence was temporarily restored when the 1964 tax cut, sold as a device to stimulate the economy, was followed by economic expansion. But it was then shaken again when the expansion bred inflation and especially when the tax increase of 1968 failed to stem the inflation.

On the monetary front, "cheap money" policies—i.e., low interest rate policies—were adopted in country after country in response to Keynesian theories. In every country, they had to be given up when inflation rather than the widely heralded postwar depression proved to be the order of the day. The result was a revival of interest in monetary policy and the role of money.

In the scholarly world, the most important event was the reinterpretation of the Great Depression. The initial rejection of the quantity theory and acceptance of Keynesian ideas was strongly fostered by the belief that monetary policy had been tried as a means of stemming the Great Depression and had failed. When Anna Schwartz and I came to examine this episode (in our book *A Monetary History of the United States, 1867–1960*), we found that this conventional view was almost precisely the reverse of the truth, that the Great Depression was a tragic testament to the potency of bad monetary policy. From 1929 to 1933, the quantity of money in the United States declined by no less than one-third. More important, the Fed at all times had the power to prevent that decline. The policies required to do so were neither novel nor daring. They were of a kind explicitly contemplated by the founders of the System to meet precisely the kind of banking crisis that developed in late 1930 and persisted thereafter. Had the decline in the quantity of money been prevented, it is almost certain that the Depression, if it had occurred at all, would have been much milder and briefer.

These findings were buttressed by extensive statistical analyses of the relationship between the quantity of money and other variables, and by statistical comparisons between the performance of the quantity theory and the Keynesian theory in predicting movements in income. A professional controversy developed that filled the pages of the journals—and also changed many opinions.

The final clincher was a series of almost controlled experiments that happened to develop in the late 1960s and that are summarized in the column in Chapter 1, "Which Crystal Ball?" (July 5, 1971). These pitted monetary effects against fiscal effects. In each case, monetary effects proved more potent than fiscal effects.

The result is that the area of dispute in the profession has shifted. To begin with, those of us who maintained that the quantity of money mattered at all were a beleaguered minority, viewed with almost amused tolerance by the more advanced members of the profession. Today, this issue has disappeared. Everyone agrees that the quantity of money affects the flow of spending, income, and prices. The issue is now whether the fiscal influences stressed in Keynesian analysis have a major effect independent of what is happening to the quantity of money or exert their influence primarily by affecting the quantity of money.

As this way of putting it makes clear, Chapter 4 on Fiscal Policy is in many ways a mirror image of this chapter on Monetary Policy. They complement and reinforce one another.

The change in the conduct of monetary policy has, I am sorry to say, been less drastic than in professional ideas about the role of money in the economy. Yet even here there has been great change. The views about policy that I express in these columns were regarded as "crackpot" by central bankers and commercial bankers a decade ago. Bankers knew that credit and interest rates mattered, not the quantity of money.

They are largely still of that view, but they have begun to pay far more attention to what happens to the quantity of money. The key actions in the United States were the decision by the Fed in January 1970 to give "monetary aggregates" (quantity of money) pride of place in preference to "credit market conditions" (interest rates); and in January and February 1972, to change the technique of monetary management by adopting bank reserves as an intermediate policy target. These actions are in the direction that I have consistently recommended in the columns reprinted here: of recognizing that the proper function of the Fed is to control the quantity of money and that it should not permit itself to be diverted by what happens to interest rates. We are closer to that outcome today than at any time in the past 56 years—but we are still not there. Until we are, I expect that I shall continue to write columns on monetary policy deploring the wide swings in the rate of monetary growth.

INFLATIONARY RECESSION
October 17, 1966

Our record economic expansion will probably end sometime in the next year. If it does, prices will continue to rise while unemployment mounts. *There will be an inflationary recession.*[1] Many will regard this prediction as a contradiction in terms, since it is widely believed that rising prices always go with expansion and falling prices with recession. Usually they do, but not always. In the great boom of the 1920s, for example, prices of goods and services held stable or fell; in the recession of 1957 and 1958, prices rose.

Since 1961, when the current expansion began, consumer prices have been rising, slowly at first, then more rapidly. Since January, they have been rising at a rate of more than 4 per cent per year.

Why prices have risen

This price rise is a result mainly of rapid growth in the quantity of money—the number of dollars of coin, currency and deposits in commercial banks (demand and time) held by the public. This quantity grew 7½ per cent per year from 1961 to 1965; total output, 5 per cent per year.

Though most money consists of deposits of commercial banks, these banks must hold reserves in currency or deposits at Federal Reserve banks. The Fed can therefore control the quantity of money by such measures as buying and selling government securities. The quantity of money rose as rapidly as it did because the Fed chose to let it do so.

---

[1] There was a sharp slowdown in economic activity in the first half of 1967 that came to be designated a "mini-recession" because it was brief and mild. Prices did continue to rise during the mini-recession, though the rate of rise slowed appreciably.]

At first, monetary growth stimulated production but had little effect on prices. There was much slack in the economy and many prices, particularly wages, had been set in advance in the anticipation that prices would be stable—an anticipation that was fostered by the low level of economic activity from 1958 to 1961.

As rapid monetary growth continued, the pressure of demand raised prices as well as production. Two factors accelerated the price rise. First, people came to expect rising prices and this expectation was embodied in higher wage and price contracts. Second, the Federal Reserve let the quantity of money grow still faster—at the rate of nearly 9 per cent a year from 1965 to April 1966.

At this stage, rising prices stimulated economic activity because they were rising faster than people had anticipated. Hence, selling prices rose more rapidly than costs, which are typically set by advance contracts, so profits rose even faster.

The only way to make an expansion of this kind last is to continue to accelerate monetary growth. However, that would produce still more rapid inflation. To avoid this consequence, the Federal Reserve has already sharply reduced monetary growth—indeed, too sharply—to a rate of about 3 per cent a year since April.

The tapering off of monetary growth, like the initial monetary expansion, will at first affect production more than prices. Prices and wages, now set in the light of anticipations of inflation, will continue to rise. Inflation has a momentum of its own; it cannot be turned off like a water tap. With lower monetary growth, total spending will not be sufficient to support these higher prices at full employment. This will check the rise in prices somewhat and produce some unemployment. Prices will rise less than anticipated, thus discouraging production and employment.

The policy dilemma

The inflationary recession will present a dilemma to the Federal Reserve, the Treasury and the President. Rising prices will tempt them to step hard on the brake by slowing down monetary growth, raising taxes and reducing government spending. Rising unemployment will tempt them to step hard on the accelerator by speeding up monetary growth cutting taxes and increasing spending.[2]

Both policies would be wrong. The right policy—not alone for this episode but as a general rule—is to *let the quantity of money increase at a rate that can be maintained indefinitely without inflation* (about 5 per cent per year) and to keep taxes and spending at levels that will *balance the budget at high employment.*

---

[2] In the event, the rising unemployment proved more potent. The Fed did step sharply on the accelerator.

If this is done, the public will gradually adjust to the new policy. People will stop expecting perpetual inflation. It is probably too late to avoid a mild recession, but this policy will at least prepare the basis for a subsequent noninflationary expansion.

CURRENT MONETARY POLICY
January 9, 1967

I have been watching with increasing apprehension, concern and incredulity the behavior of the quantity of money over the past eight months. The Federal Reserve System clearly does not intend to produce a *serious* recession in 1967. Yet continuation of their present policy will make such an outcome all but inevitable.

The accompanying chart shows the reason for concern. It plots two monetary magnitudes: M_1, the total usually designated "the money supply" by the Fed; and M_2, a broader total that includes also time deposits at commercial banks. The striking feature of the chart is the sharp reversal in both totals in April 1966. Before then, both totals were growing rapidly. Since April, M_1 has actually declined—something it has rarely done except before and during severe recessions—and M_2 has grown at a sharply reduced rate. Since September, both totals have been declining.

This is the sharpest turnaround since the end of the war. Slower monetary growth was badly needed in order to stem inflation—but a good thing was carried too far.

Do changes in the quantity of money matter? There is massive historical evidence that they do. *Every economic recession but one in the U.S. in the past century has been preceded by a decline in the rate of growth of the quantity of money.* And the sharper the decline, the more serious the subsequent recession—though this tendency is far from uniform.

Changes in monetary growth affect the economy only slowly—it may be six or twelve or eighteen months or even more before their effects are manifest. That is a major reason why the connection is easily overlooked.

Recent experience conforms to the historical record. Acceleration of monetary growth in 1962 was followed by economic expansion. The monetary growth rate was too high—but it took until 1965 for its cumulative effects to produce rising prices. The price rise started the Fed *talking* about the need for tighter money, but it *acted* in the opposite direction: monetary growth accelerated still more, intensifying inflationary pressure and producing the rapid price rises of recent months. The sharp braking of monetary growth in April 1966 has in turn only recently been showing up in spreading signs of pending recession.

Why has the Fed permitted the quantity of money to behave so erratically? Primarily, I believe, because it has used misleading criteria of policy—it is inconceivable that the quantity of money as measured by M_1 could

ERRATIC MONETARY GROWTH

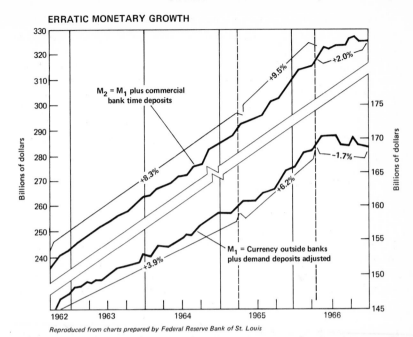

Reproduced from charts prepared by Federal Reserve Bank of St. Louis

decline for eight months if the Fed had been determined to have it grow. It is as if a space vehicle took a fix on the wrong star. No matter how sensitive and sophisticated its guiding apparatus, it would go astray. Similarly, the men who guide the Fed have been going astray because they have been looking at interest rates and other measures of credit conditions rather than at the quantity of money.

Interest rates began rising in 1965 because of the sharp rise in the demand for credit that accompanied the onset of inflation. The Fed slowed the rise by accelerating monetary growth--but the rates continued rising, and the Fed interpreted this as a sign that it had tightened, whereas in fact it had eased.

Similarly, interest rates are currently showing some weakness—because the demand for credit has been declining in response to monetary restriction since April 1966. Yet the Fed interprets the weakness as a sign that it has eased—whereas only the Fed's continued tightness prevents interest rates from falling more rapidly.

The Fed's erratic policy reflects also its failure to allow for the delay between its actions and their effects on the economy. Said Governor Robertson of the board in a recent speech: "Monetary policy will be formulated by the Federal Reserve, day by day, in the light of economic conditions *as they emerge*." This is a formula guaranteed to produce bad policy. If it is followed, the Fed will continue to step too hard on the brake until the recessionary effects are clear and unmistakable, and then will step too hard on the accelerator. Like a good duck hunter, the Fed should lead its target, not shoot where it now is.

What policy should the Fed now adopt? It is almost surely too late to prevent a recession—that damage has already been done. It is not too late to prevent the recession from turning into a severe downturn. To that end, the Fed should at once act to increase the quantity of money at a rate of about 5 per cent per year for M_2. If the Fed adopted and persisted in such a policy, it could moderate the coming recession without paving the way for a new burst of inflation.[1]

CURRENT MONETARY POLICY
October 30, 1967

Last January (NEWSWEEK, Jan. 9), I criticized the Federal Reserve Board for producing the sharpest turnaround in monetary growth since the end of the war—the sharp deceleration in growth beginning in April 1966 that is recorded in the accompanying chart. "Slower monetary growth was badly needed in order to stem inflation," I wrote, "but a good thing was carried too far."

The same month, the Fed reversed its policy. A decline in M_1, the total usually designated "the money supply" by the Fed, was succeeded by an even more rapid rate of growth than in 1965. Slow growth in M_2, a broader total including time deposits at commercial banks, was succeeded by one of the fastest rates of growth on record. The turnaround in January was even sharper than in the prior April, setting a new postwar record.

In my earlier column I wrote, "It is almost surely too late to prevent a recession—that damage has already been done. It is not too late to prevent the recession from turning into a severe downturn. To that end, the Fed should at once act to increase the quantity of money at a rate of about 5 per cent per year for M_2. If the Fed adopted and persisted in such a policy, it could moderate the coming recession without paving the way for a new burst of inflation."

There is much dispute about whether we have in fact experienced the recession that I saw looming, but the dispute is wholly semantic. Total output, which had been rising vigorously, showed no gain at all in the first quarter of 1967 and only a mild gain in the second quarter; industrial production fell absolutely; and so did civilian employment (from January 1967 to May 1967). The percentage of the labor force reported as unemployed rose slightly, despite an almost unprecedented recorded exodus from the labor force. A slowdown in economic activity clearly occurred. But many economic analysts regard it as too mild and too brief to justify calling it a full-fledged recession.

[1] See the next column for the actual outcome.

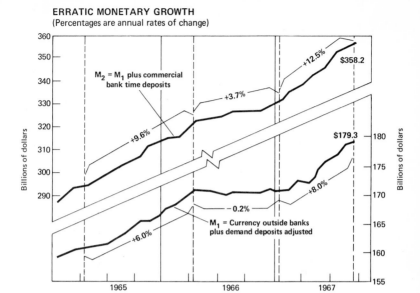

ERRATIC MONETARY GROWTH
(Percentages are annual rates of change)

SOURCE: *Federal Reserve Bulletin*

The Fed reverses too much ...

The slowdown was mild and brief because the Fed did turn around. Unfortunately, the Fed once again carried a good thing too far. Instead of increasing M_2 at 5 per cent per year, it increased it at two-and-a-half times that rate. The result was to moderate the recession (or slowdown, if you prefer), but also to pave the way for a new burst of inflation.

This monetary expansion, not the state of the Federal budget, deplorable as that is on other grounds, has produced the widening signs of inflationary pressure. Just as it took some time—from April 1966 to December 1966—for monetary tightness to slow down the economy, so also it took some time— from January 1967 to June or July 1967—for monetary ease to stimulate the economy. That is why we are only now seeing the effects, and still only the early effects, of the Fed's overreaction in January.

... But passes the buck

The Fed is naturally reluctant to accept responsibility for inflation. Consequently it blames Federal spending and says that only higher taxes will stop inflation. But that is simply passing the buck.

If the Fed lets the quantity of money continue to increase at the pace of recent months—8 per cent per year for M_1 and 12½ per cent for M_2—further acceleration of inflation is a near certainty, whether taxes are increased or not and whether Federal spending is reduced or not.

What happens to taxes is important. It may affect the level of government spending. It may affect the rate of interest that accompanies whatever monetary policy is followed. But it is not decisive for the course of prices.

The Fed's behavior in this episode is part of a general pattern. Throughout the postwar period—and for much of its earlier life as well—the Fed has tended first to delay action and then, when it did act, to go too far. Too late and too much has been the general rule. The reasons for this pattern are complex—partly the economic analysis accepted by the Fed, partly its administrative convenience, partly the political environment in which it operates. But the results are simple. Instead of offsetting other forces making for economic instability, the Fed has itself been a major source of instability.

It is almost surely too late to prevent an appreciable price rise—that damage has already been done. It is not too late to prevent the price rise from turning into a severe inflation. To that end, the Fed should at once act to limit the increase in the quantity of money to a rate of about 5 per cent per year for M_2. If the Fed adopted and persisted in such a policy, it could moderate the coming inflation without paving the way for a new recession.

Any resemblance between this prescription and the one in my January column is not purely coincidental.

MONETARY POLICY
June 3, 1968

In two earlier columns on monetary policy, I was highly critical of the Federal Reserve System for acting too late and then, when it did act, for overreacting. This time, I come to praise, not to criticize. Since November 1967, the Fed has moved not only in the right direction but also by about the right amount.

The recent record is summarized in the accompanying table, which gives the annual rate of growth for two monetary totals, for industrial production, which is a sensitive index of changes in economic activity, and for consumer prices. Because it takes time for monetary changes to exert their influence,

	Rate of Change (per cent per year)				
Period for Money	Money*		Industrial Production	Consumer Prices	Period for Production and Prices
	M_1	M_2			
Apr. '65 to Apr. '66	6.0	9.6	9.9	3.7	Oct. '65 to Oct. '66
Apr. '66 to Jan. '67	−0.2	3.7	−2.3	2.3	Oct. '66 to July '67
Jan. '67 to Nov. '67	7.7	11.9	5.2	3.9	July '67 to Apr. '68
Nov. '67 to Apr. '68	4.7	5.3			

*M_1 = Currency plus adjusted demand deposits. M_2 = M_1 plus time deposits in commercial banks

the rates of growth of production and prices are given for periods that begin six months later than the corresponding periods for money.

As an aid in interpreting these numbers, let me note that a long-term rate of growth in M_2 of about 5 per cent per year would be consistent with roughly stable prices. The 5 per cent would match the growth in output and leave a little over to satisfy the desire of people to hold somewhat more money relative to their income as they become richer.

From April 1965 to April 1966, the Fed permitted the money supply to grow rapidly, despite signs that inflation was accelerating. At long last, in April 1966, it stepped on the brake—abruptly and, as the table shows, too hard. The result was the so-called "money crunch" in the fall of 1966, the slowdown in the economy recorded in the decline in industrial production, and a cut in price inflation from a rate of 3.7 per cent per year to a rate of 2.3 per cent per year.

The sharper response of production than of prices is typical. An inflationary process, once under way, develops an inertia of its own. It takes an economic slowdown to stop the acceleration of prices and, even then, it takes a long time to restore price stability. That is why it is so important to prevent inflation from gaining momentum.

Concerned by the signs of emerging slack in the economy, the Fed reversed policy in January 1967. This time, to its credit, it acted more promptly than usual. But, as usual, it reacted too sharply, not only restoring, but exceeding the earlier excessive rate of monetary growth.

As a result, I wrote last October, "it is almost surely too late to prevent an appreciable price rise—that damage has already been done. It is not too late to prevent the price rise from turning into a severe inflation. To that end, the Fed should at once act to limit the increase in the quantity of money to a rate of about 5 per cent per year for M_2. If the Fed adopted and persisted in such a policy, it could moderate the coming inflation without paving the way for a new recession."

It *was* too late to prevent an appreciable price rise. Prices have recently been rising at nearly 4 per cent per year. But in November 1967, the Fed did reverse its policy, and M_2 has been growing since at only slightly more than 5 per cent per year.

There has not yet been time for this moderate policy to have much effect—as is reflected in the absence of any entries for production and prices in our table matching the final period for money. But if the Fed persists in its present policy, the exuberant expansion in the economy will taper off later this year and so will the rate of price rise—whether or not there is a tax increase. There may also be some rise in unemployment before the price inflation is brought under control, though any rise is likely to be small.

But will the Fed persist? Will it keep its cool? Or will continuing inflation lead it, as in April 1966, to step still harder on the brake in the hope of getting quicker results? Alternatively, will the first signs of reduced expansion and increased unemployment lead it, as in January 1967, to start the printing presses whirring again and set off a new burst of inflation?

The Fed's steadiness in the past six months—despite the gold crisis, high and rising interest rates and the controversy over government expenditures and taxes—is a hopeful augury.[1]

THE INFLATIONARY FED
January 20, 1969

Seldom has promise diverged so widely from performance as it has in recent monetary policy.

Listen to the words that emanate from the Federal Reserve System and you will conclude that the Fed is a bastion of defense against inflation, that it is bending its every effort and using its every power to stem the onrushing inflationary tide.

Look at the Fed's actions, and you will reach precisely the opposite conclusion. The quantity of money (defined as currency plus all commercial bank deposits, demand and time) is rising by more than 11 per cent a year. For the past two years, it has risen at an average rate of nearly 10 per cent a year—or twice as fast as output. Little wonder that prices have been rising faster and faster—currently by roughly 5 per cent a year.

Diagnosis

Is the Fed to blame for the accelerating monetary growth? Or has the rise in the quantity of money been produced by forces outside its control—such as the need to finance government deficits—so that the Fed is the victim rather than the villain of the inflationary surge? The answer is clear. The Fed has ample power to control the quantity of money, whatever the state of the Federal budget, by buying and selling government securities. When it buys securities, it pays for them by creating money that adds to bank reserves. When it sells securities, the proceeds are subtracted from bank reserves. It was able to bring the rate of monetary growth down sharply in 1966—from more than 9 per cent a year before April 1966, to less than 4 per cent a year from April 1966 to January 1967—despite a large and growing government deficit. It has been able to step up sharply the rate of monetary growth in the past six months despite the tax surcharge that has been restraining the government deficit.

The plain fact is that inflation is made in Washington, in that stately and impressive Grecian temple on Constitution Avenue that houses the Board of Governors of the Federal Reserve System. Prices have been rising at faster and faster rates because William McChesney Martin and the other distinguished men who govern the system have decreed that they shall.

[1 Unfortunately, as the next column explains, the augury proved false.]

Why have they so decreed? Do these able and patriotic men want inflation? Obviously not. Why then do they produce inflation? Because they are and have been misguided—and, like the rest of us, find it incredibly difficult to admit that they have been wrong. They have taken the behavior of interest rates rather than of the quantity of money as their guide—and this mistake has led them far astray from their intended path.

For example, the recent rise in the discount rate by one-quarter of 1 per cent was trumpeted as a major step against inflation. It was nothing of the sort. It was simply a belated and timid response by the Fed to the Fed's own inflationary policy—which has been pushing up market interest rates, leaving the pegged—and unimportant—discount rate behind.

The inflation produced by the Fed cannot be stopped overnight. Monetary growth today has little effect on *today's* income and prices. Its major effects are on income and prices three or six or more months from now. The rapid monetary expansion of the past six months assures continued inflation for some months to come.

Prescription

But the Fed can and should start at once to slow down monetary growth. That is the only way to slow down inflation six months from now.

In the past few years, I have consistently recommended that the Fed move directly to the rate of monetary growth of about 5 per cent a year, and keep it there. That would mean roughly stable prices over the long pull. But by now, the Fed has departed so widely from the desirable rate of growth that moving to it in one step may involve too large a wrench for the economy. I therefore now recommend a two-step move—first, to about 7 per cent a year and then to 4 or 5 per cent a year.

I am not optimistic that such a moderate policy will be followed. If the Fed does change its policy—as it is giving some signs of doing—the more likely outcome is that it will swing from one extreme to the other, from too rapid an increase in the quantity of money to too slow an increase—bringing on an unnecessarily sharp reaction in the economy and laying the basis for a further overreaction later on. That is how the Fed has behaved time and again in the past 55 years—and there is no sign that it has changed its spots.[1]

MONEY AND INFLATION
May 26, 1969

Money tightens. Prices soar. So go the headlines. Since December, the rate of monetary growth has been reduced sharply. Yet, the cost of living rose from February to March at the incredible rate of 9.6 per cent per year.

[1 And that is how it behaved again on this occasion, as the next two columns make clear.]

Does this mean that monetary policy is impotent to stem inflation? Or, that the Fed has not tightened enough? No.

The explanation is different. A monetary slowdown affects prices only after a considerable delay. Prices today are still being pushed up by the rapid monetary growth of 1968. Such a pattern is entirely consistent with experience. It was fully anticipated by those of us who have long urged monetary restaint to stem inflation.

As I wrote some months ago (NEWSWEEK, Jan. 20), "The inflation produced by the Fed cannot be stopped overnight. Monetary growth today has little effect on *today's* income and prices. Its major effects are on income and prices three or six or more months from now. The rapid monetary expansion of the past six months assures continued inflation for some months to come.

"But the Fed can and should start at once to slow down monetary growth. That is the only way to slow down inflation six months from now."

Just about the time that column was written, the Fed changed its policy. But six months have not yet elapsed, so there is as yet no reason to expect any significant change in the pace of inflation.

It would be a major blunder for the Fed to step still harder on the monetary brakes. That would risk turning orderly restraint into a severe economic contraction. If anything, the Fed has already gone too far.

A decade of experience

These conclusions are derived from the examination of the monetary experience in many countries for many decades—in the U.S., for more than a century.

Evidence for the past decade for the United States is summarized in the accompanying table, which gives the annual rate of growth for two monetary totals, for industrial production, which is a sensitive index of changes in economic activity, and for consumer prices.

The time periods for money are defined by dates when monetary growth changed its pace significantly, either speeding up or slowing down. The periods for income and prices begin six months later than the corresponding periods for money, to allow for the time that it takes for a changed rate of monetary growth to exert its influence. Of course, this time delay is itself variable: sometimes three months, sometimes nine months, sometimes longer. Six months is about the *average* delay.

To facilitate reading the table, the periods of slow monetary growth are in bold face. With one exception, they alternate with periods of rapid growth. The exception is the shift in April 1965 from an already high rate of growth to a still higher one. That shift ushered in the inflation that has been plaguing us ever since.

There clearly is a close relation between monetary growth and the behavior of output and prices. Every period of slower monetary growth is followed by slower growth in industrial production. Every period of more

Rate of change (per cent per year)

Period for Money	Money*		Industrial Production	Consumer Prices	Period for Production and Prices
	M₁	M₂			
Jan. '58 to May '59	4.3	6.2	7.4	1.0	July '58 to Nov. '59
May '59 to June '60	− 2.0	1.0	0.2	1.3	Nov. '59 to Dec. '60
June '60 to Mar. '62	2.4	6.1	8.6	1.2	Dec. '60 to Sept. '62
Mar. '62 to Sept. '62	− 0.3	3.8	3.6	0.2	Sept. '62 to Mar. '63
Sept. '62 to Apr. '65	3.8	7.1	7.1	1.5	Mar. '63 to Oct. '65
Apr. '65 to Apr. '66	6.0	8.9	9.6	3.7	Oct. '65 to Oct. '66
Apr. '66 to Jan. '67	0.0	4.4	− 2.6	2.4	Oct. '66 to July '67
Jan. '67 to Dec. '68	6.8	9.4	5.3	4.6	July '67 to Mar. '69
Dec. '68 to Apr. '69	4.3	4.0			

*M_1 = Currency plus adjusted demand deposits. M_2 = M_1 plus time deposits in commercial banks other than large Certificates of Deposits. CD's are excluded partly to make the data more homogeneous over the whole period (CD's were negligible before 1961) and partly because their amount is so sensitive to Regulation Q ceilings on interest rates.

rapid monetary growth is followed by more rapid growth in production. For prices, there is one exception—the 1959-60 slowdown. However, even that exception simply reflects the fact that the speed-up in monetary growth that started in June 1960 took rather longer than usual to have an impact on price change: the rate of price change is less from November 1959 to May 1961 than either before or after.

Until 1965, the price rise was modest—at most 1.5 per cent per year. And even these numbers may overstate the true rise in prices because they probably do not allow sufficiently for improvements in quality.

By 1965 we were rapidly approaching full utilization of our resources. The further acceleration of monetary growth that occurred in that year therefore had its impact mainly on prices, which, six months later, started rising at a rate of nearly 4 per cent per year.

The crunch of 1966 produced a tapering off of the price rise. However, the Fed, having overdone the crunch, also overdid the subsequent expansion. As a result, inflation resumed at a still more rapid pace.

Recent policy

The final line records the most recent change in monetary policy. There are no entries for production and prices because six months have not yet elapsed since the change in monetary growth.

Fortunately, the change in monetary growth has been more moderate than in 1966, so it is less likely to produce an overreaction later. Even so, the change is probably somewhat too severe to produce the kind of gradual unwinding of our inflationary binge that will do the least harm. A long-term rate of growth of about 5 per cent per year in M_2 would be consistent with roughly stable prices—this is roughly the average rate of rise in M_2 from 1958 to 1965. It seems most unwise to hold monetary growth below that level for any extended period.

If the Fed continues its present policy of modest growth in the money stock, we should start seeing results in the near future. By summer or early fall, the rise in income should start slackening. The effect will first be on output. However, by fall at the latest, the pace of price rise should start coming down.

Patience, perseverance and moderation—those are the requisites of sensible monetary policy at the present juncture.

MONETARY OVERKILL
August 18, 1969

The Federal Reserve System is at it again. Once more, it is overreacting as it has so often in the past.

To mention only the most recent examples, in 1965 the Fed accelerated monetary growth just as the economy was reaching full capacity. It thereby set off the inflation that has been bedeviling us ever since. In early 1966, the Fed abruptly halted monetary growth for about nine months. This produced the credit crunch in August 1966 and the minirecession in the first half of 1967. The Fed then overreacted again, reviving the inflation that had been showing some signs of tapering off. The Fed continued to raise the money supply at an inordinate rate up to the very end of 1968. The consequences of that mistake are still with us in the form of rapidly rising prices—at a rate of 6 per cent per year so far in 1969.

As these episodes illustrate, it takes about six to nine months for the Fed's actions to affect the economy. That is why we are just now beginning to see the effects of the Fed's belated move to restraint last December.

That move to restraint was moderate at first. Then, around April, the Fed tightened the screw another turn, repeating its classic pattern of overreacting. This new policy threatens to convert a moderate economic slowdown into a severe contraction.

These developments raise three questions:

1 What is the evidence that the Fed is overreacting?
2 Why is the Fed overreacting?
3 What consequences are likely for the economy?

1 THE EVIDENCE From January 1967 to December 1968, the Fed was highly inflationary, and the quantity of money, defined narrowly as currency plus demand deposits, rose at a rate of 7 per cent a year. From December 1968 to April 1969, the Fed was moderately restrictive, and the quantity of money rose at a rate of 4 per cent a year. From April 1969 to the four weeks ending July 23 (the latest four-week period for which figures are available as I write this), money supply has not grown at all. Other monetary magnitudes (broader monetary totals, the monetary base, member bank reserves, unborrowed reserves) all confirm this shift to a highly deflationary policy.[1]

---

[1]Subsequent revisions of the figures did not alter the general pattern of monetary growth but raised appreciably the absolute rates of growth.

The use of April as the turning point may slightly overstate the magnitude of the shift because some April figures are abnormally high. However, reasonable alternative dates show the same general pattern.

2 THE REASON Federal Reserve officials have given no public indication that they have deliberately changed their policy since the move to restraint last December. Yet the figures show that the Fed has drastically restricted monetary growth still further since April. Why? Because the Fed's methods are obsolete and have not been adjusted to our growing understanding of monetary relations.

For most of its history, the Fed has concentrated on interest rates or "money-market conditions" as measures of monetary influence and has paid little attention to the quantity of money. Recently, the board has come increasingly to recognize that interest rates are highly defective measures of monetary influence and has begun to pay more attention to monetary aggregates. But its policy directives are still expressed largely in terms of "money-market conditions," which the New York Federal Reserve Bank, where the directives are actually carried out, interprets as referring primarily to interest rates.

These obsolete procedures automatically produce overreaction. When the rate of monetary growth is reduced, the *initial* effect is to raise interest rates. The Fed reduces monetary growth by selling bonds (or buying a smaller amount), which tends to lower the price of bonds and raise their yield. However, after about six to nine months, the reduced rate of monetary growth starts to affect income and spending, which, in turn, produces a decline in the demand for loans. The *delayed* effect of reduced monetary growth is therefore to lower interest rates. When this effect starts operating, the New York Federal Reserve Bank interprets it as a sign that monetary influence is easing and reduces the rate of monetary growth still more in order to keep interest rates from falling. That is how the present operating procedures of the Federal Reserve automatically produce overreaction.

3 THE CONSEQUENCES The cessation of monetary growth since April has already affected securities markets—which reflect the effect of monetary changes much more promptly than does the economy as a whole. In the stock market, the squeeze on money balances has intensified the recent sharp decline. In the bond market, interest rates have recently shown some tendency to decline—the typical delayed effect of the shift to monetary restraint last December. The shift to additional tightness has kept this incipient decline from materializing.

Economic activity as a whole has so far been little affected by the cessation of monetary growth. Indeed, if the Fed were even now to correct its course and return to a more moderate policy, the effects on economic activity might not be serious. The effects of monetary changes on total spending are spread out over many months. Hence brief perturbations in monetary growth tend to be averaged out. Only persistent movements in money have persistent effects on the economy.

Let the Fed continue on its present course much longer, however, and the economic consequences are sure to be serious. Stable non-inflationary economic growth in the U.S. requires that the quantity of money grow about 4 or 5 per cent per year. If the quantity of money does not grow at all, as it has not since April, total dollar income is very likely, after some delay, to stop growing also or even to decline. We cannot go quickly from nearly 8 per cent a year—the recent rate of growth in total dollar income—to zero per cent without a severe economic contraction. Inflation has an inertia of its own. Many prices and wages are determined long in advance and will continue to rise even after the pull of demand has eased. We shall be doing well if, by early 1970, the price rise is brought down to 4 per cent a year.[2] Under those circumstances, a zero rate of growth of total dollar income would mean that *real* income would *decline* at 4 per cent a year. This is a rate of decline that has not been exceeded for more than an isolated quarter since 1957-58. It is also a rate of decline that would produce a sharp rise in unemployment.

Some retardation in growth and some increase in unemployment is an inevitable, if unwelcome, by-product of stopping inflation. But there is no need—and every reason to avoid—a retardation of the severity that will be produced by a continuation of the Fed's present monetary overkill.

That is why it is so urgent for the Federal Reserve System—which does not wish and does not intend any such outcome—to start the quantity of money growing again. It is equally urgent that they do so without overreacting in an inflationary direction. We need moderation and steadiness, not erratic jerks from one side to the other.

A NEW CHAIRMAN AT THE FED
February 2, 1970

This week Arthur F. Burns takes over as chairman of the Board of Governors of the Federal Reserve System, replacing William McChesney Martin, who is retiring after nineteen years as chairman—the longest period anyone has held that post.

The chairman of the board has only one vote out of seven on the board itself and only one vote out of twelve on the all-important Open Market Committee. Yet this greatly understates the influence that the chairman can exert—especially when he is a man with the extraordinary intellectual qualities and personal force of the incoming chairman. My close friend and former teacher Arthur Burns is not just another chairman. He is the right man in the right place at the right time.

[2Unfortunately, this did not occur. Prices were still rising at 6 per cent per year in early 1970.]

The right man . . .

Arthur Burns is the first person ever named chairman of the board who has the right qualifications for that post. Prior chairmen have been able, public-spirited men with high standards of integrity and service. But none has had any training or special competence in the problems of the economy as a whole. All have come with a background of experience in individual business or financial institutions.

This distinction is crucial. It so happens that in the monetary area—as in many other parts of economics—the whole is very different from the sum of its parts. An individual bank does not "create" money—as it sees matters. It simply borrows from some and lends to others. It is a financial intermediary operating in the market for credit. In contrast, the banking system as a whole plays a minor role in the market for credit but is the primary creator of money.

The difference between the individual bank and the banking system is a basic source of the erroneous philosophy that has guided the Fed these many years. Generalizing from the individual financial institution, the men who run the Fed have regarded monetary policy as concerned primarily with *credit*.

This preoccupation, which has been strongly reinforced by the Fed's special concern with the Federal debt, is reflected in the use of interest rates as a guide and criterion of policy. It is reflected also in the importance the Fed attaches to limiting interest rates on deposits and margins on stock purchases, and to regulating the lending and investing activities of banks.

For the economy as a whole, this is all a sideshow. The key function of the Fed, the function that it and it alone can perform, is to control the quantity of *money*. Yet the Fed's concentration on credit conditions has led it to pay little attention to the effect of its actions on the quantity of money. The result has been highly erratic movements in the quantity of money that have produced economic instability and price inflation.

Arthur Burns will not make this mistake.[1] His training, experience and special competence are precisely in the relation between the individual enterprise and the economy as a whole—as a college professor; as one of the world's leading scholars in the analysis of business cycles; as chairman of the Council of Economic Advisers; and most recently, as Counselor to the President. He understands the *monetary system* and its relation to the economy at a depth and subtlety that has not been equaled by any past chairman of the board.

. . . At the right place . . .

Arthur Burns is at the right place because of the extraordinarily important influence that monetary actions exert on the economy as a whole—and also

[1For the first year after his appointment, monetary growth was relatively stable. Contrary to my expectations, however, monetary growth was highly unstable in 1971. It has again been relatively stable in the first half of 1972.]

because the Fed is the pre-eminent financial institution in the world. In the heat of debate, critics have attributed to those of us who have stressed the importance of money the view that "money is all that matters." This is an absurd position—certainly if one does not say matters for what—and it is one that we have never held. But even the critics now concede that money matters and matters very much.

In particular, inflation is always and everywhere a monetary phenomenon. And inflation is today our major economic problem.

. . . At the right time

The time is ripe for a change in the Fed's basic philosophy. Even as recently as three or four years ago, the erroneous credit view was so firmly entrenched that the alternative monetary view was simply ridiculed. But the past few years have forced an "agonizing reappraisal." It has become painfully obvious that the use of interest rates as a guide to policy produces wide swings in monetary growth and that these swings can be a major source of economic instability.

The shift in view is far from complete. More important, the shift has as yet had a negligible effect on the operating procedures at the open-market desk of the New York Federal Reserve Bank. Those procedures are well adapted to smoothing short-term movements in interest rates. They are poorly adapted to controlling smoothly the quantity of money.[1]

This is also a critical time in a more immediate, if less fundamental, sense. Burns takes office as the economy is not only slowing down but seems on the verge of sliding into a full-fledged and fairly severe recession—thanks to an unduly restrictive monetary policy.

The real test

The Fed can no longer prevent this outcome. The damage, if damage it be, is already done. Because of the delay between monetary actions and their effects, *what happens to the economy during most of 1970—insofar as that is affected by monetary policy—is already determined.*

What the Fed can do is shift promptly to a less restrictive policy and thereby build now a base for a healthy recovery from the recession.

The real test will come during the next six months or so, if and when the recession becomes a clear and pressing reality and shows every sign of deepening still further. The temptation will then be strong for the Fed to overreact as it has so often in the past, to go from too slow a rate of monetary growth to too high a rate. If it acts in that way, it will simply set off another round of inflation.

Let us hope that the Fed will this time have the foresight, the patience and the courage to hold to a steady and moderate course, to keep the quantity of money expanding at a rate high enough to encourage recovery from the recession but low enough to avoid renewed inflation.

[1]In January and February 1972, the Fed altered these operating procedures in the direction urged in this and later columns.]

If, under Burns's leadership, the Fed can meet this immediate challenge and also modernize its philosophy and its operating procedures, the nation will, for the first time in its history, have a monetary framework for stable economic growth. Such an achievement would be a worthy capstone to Arthur Burns's distinguished career.

MONETARY OVERHEATING?
July 6, 1970

This column is the counterpoint to a column I wrote nearly a year ago entitled "Monetary Overkill" (Newsweek, Aug. 18, 1969). In December 1968, the Fed had shifted from rapid monetary expansion—which produced the inflationary surge we are still trying to contain—to a more moderate rate of monetary growth. In midyear, it went farther and halted monetary growth completely. In commenting on this, I wrote, "Let the Fed continue on its present course much longer . . . and the economic consequences are sure to be serious."

Unfortunately, the Fed continued on its course throughout the rest of 1969. Finally, in December 1969—too late to prevent a recession but soon enough to keep it brief—the Fed did change course. The critical question about monetary policy is not whether the Fed has moved too far. In recent months, the quantity of money has been rising at a rate of about 8 per cent a year. That is a rate of growth which, if long continued, would be certain to produce a sharp acceleration of inflation.

In my earlier column, I attributed the overkill in 1969 partly to the Fed's use of interest rates rather than the quantity of money as the primary criterion of policy. In January, the Fed revised its policy directive to give much greater weight to monetary aggregates. In addition, Fed officials, including chairman Arthur F. Burns, have publicly stated that the system is aiming for a moderate expansion in the quantity of money.

Can the Fed control the quantity of money?

In the light of this background, the recent rapid rate of monetary growth has led many observers to question whether the Fed can control the money supply. The answer is clearly yes—not to the final dollar at every instant of time but within very narrow limits over periods of a few weeks.

However, until very recently, the Fed had no great interest in the quantity of money. As a result, even the data on monetary aggregates are inaccurate. More important, the operating procedures whereby the Federal Reserve Bank of New York translates the policy decisions of the Open Market Committee into day-to-day actions were developed to affect "money market conditions" and are highly inefficient for controlling the quantity of money.

These defective data and these obsolete procedures do not prevent the Fed from controlling the quantity of money, but they do introduce error and delay.

Why the recent rapid growth?

The deficiencies in data and procedures are partly to blame but two other factors may play a larger role. First, the recent rapid growth may be an attempt to correct a lower-than-desired rate of growth in the early months of the year. From December 1969 to June 1970, as a whole, the rate of growth averages about 6 per cent per year.

Second, the Fed has not completely given up its concern about "money-market conditions" or Treasury financing. Recent monetary growth partly reflects the Fed's reaction to the stock-market crisis in May and to a Federal debt issue that happened to come out just when the President announced the Cambodian operations.

What consequences will the rapid monetary growth have?

That depends entirely on what happens from here on out. As I wrote in my earlier column, "The effects of monetary changes on total spending are spread out over many months. Hence brief perturbations in monetary growth tend to be averaged out. Only persistent movements in money have persistent effects on the economy."

Suppose, however, that the recent spurt in monetary growth were to continue. Then, as the economy begins turning up sometime in the last half of this year, the rapid monetary growth would begin to take effect. In early or middle 1971, it would start showing up in the behavior of prices. The tapering off of inflation would cease. We would be off on another inflationary binge.

Where do we go from here?

It is essential for the Fed to see to it that the recent spurt is a temporary perturbation—but without going too far in the other direction. An average rate of growth in the quantity of money of about 4 or 5 per cent per year for 1970 and 1971 is a requisite for the simultaneous achievement of real growth, lower unemployment, and less inflation.

For the longer run, it is no less essential for the Fed to improve its statistics and its operating procedures and for the Treasury to modernize its management of the debt in order to keep Treasury financing from being a serious handicap to monetary policy.

I closed my column last August with a plea to the Fed "to start the quantity of money growing again," and then added, "It is equally urgent that they do so without overreacting in an inflationary direction. We need moderation and steadiness, not erratic jerks from one side to the other." The passage of time has only added to the urgency.

MONEY—TIGHT OR EASY?
March 1, 1971

The increasing importance assigned to monetary policy in recent years has brought to the fore the problem of how to assess what the stance of monetary policy is—let alone what it should be.

Recent experience highlights the problem:

> Short-term interest rates have declined sharply since August—the rate on three-month Treasury bills, for example, has fallen from 6.5 per cent to less than 4 per cent. By this measure, money has "eased" substantially in recent months.

> The money supply defined as currency plus demand deposits (M_1) has grown since August at a rate of 3.5 per cent a year, less than half as fast as from February 1970 to August 1970 (table). By this measure, money has "tightened" substantially in recent months.

> The money supply defined to include also time deposits of commercial banks other than large negotiable certificates of deposit (M_2) has grown since August at a rate of more than 10 per cent per year—a higher rate than from February 1970 to August 1970, and, indeed, a higher rate than preceded the acceleration of inflation. By this measure, money has been easy since February 1970 and has eased still further since August.

Which measure is the relevant one?

INTEREST RATES VERSUS MONETARY AGGREGATES Interest rates are the price of "credit" not of "money." Interest rates may be low because the Fed has been increasing the quantity of money and thereby indirectly the quantity of credit or because the demand for credit is low. For example, short-term interest rates fell in the U.S. from 1929 to 1933, yet the quantity of money *declined* by one-third. Similarly, interest rates may rise sharply as they did in 1967 and 1968, even though the quantity of money is rising rapidly.

Clearly, interest rates are an exceedingly unreliable measure of the stance of monetary policy.

M_1 VERSUS M_2 Wide divergence between the growth rates of M_1 and M_2 is a new phenomenon, reflecting the effect of Regulation Q, which specifies the maximum rates of interest that commercial banks may pay on deposits (zero on demand deposits, and specified higher rates on various categories of time deposits). True, legal maxima have been in force ever since the mid-1930s. However, most of the time the legal maxima were higher than market rates, and hence were largely irrelevant. The rapid rise in market interest rates in 1968 and 1969, and the reluctance of the Fed to raise the legal maxima, changed the situation drastically.

As market rates rose above the maxima, time deposits became less attractive than market instruments. Holders of such deposits tried to shift into Treasury bills, commercial paper and the like. But this involved a loss of liquidity, so part of the shift out of time deposits took the form of an increased demand for demand deposits. As a result, during 1969, M_1 rose more rapidly than M_2. Money was tighter than indicated by M_1, less tight than indicated by M_2.

As interest rates declined in 1970, especially after August, the process was reversed. M_2 rose more rapidly than M_1. Money was "easier" than indicated by M_1 but "tighter" than indicated by M_2.

So long as Regulation Q operates in this intermittent fashion, it will distort the behavior of these aggregates. There is every reason on other grounds to get rid of Regulation Q. It involves compulsory government price fixing of precisely the kind that President Nixon and Federal Reserve Board chairman Arthur Burns have repeatedly objected to in other connections. Abolition of Regulation Q would make *either* M_1 or M_2 a satisfactory measure of the ease or tightness of money and *both* would tell the same story.

Until this occurs, the observer of monetary policy must monitor both M_1 and M_2 and allow as best he can for the distorting effect of Regulation Q. On this basis, money cannot be said to have become either appreciably tighter or appreciably easier since August. Monetary policy has been highly expansive ever since February 1970—not as expansive as it was in 1967 and 1968 yet more expansive than can long be maintained without reigniting inflation.

Statistical accuracy

In late 1969, and again in late 1970, the Fed revised its prior estimates of the monetary aggregates, raising them substantially both times. For example, the unrevised figure for M_1 in October 1970 was $206 billion, the revised figure $213—a difference of 3.4 per cent. The unrevised figures showed M_1 growing at the annual rate of 5.1 per cent from February 1970 to October

Monetary Growth Rates

Period	Rate of Change (Per cent per year)	
	M_1	M_2
January 1967 to January 1969	7.6	9.8
January 1969 to July 1969	5.1	3.9
July 1969 to February 1970	1.2	0.1
February 1970 to August 1970	7.3	9.8
August 1970 to January 1971	3.5	10.4

M_1 = Currency plus adjusted demand deposits
M_2 = M_1 plus time deposits in commercial banks other than large negotiable certificates of deposit
Source: Federal Reserve Bank of St. Louis

1970; the revised figures, at the rate of 6.3 per cent! Money was in fact appreciably easier than the Fed intended it to be.

Statistical errors of this magnitude are, to put it bluntly, inexcusable. Imagine what would happen in a well-run private enterprise if the chief accountant reported that for many months he had been underestimating total costs substantially. Heads would roll. So should they at the Fed.

The explanation of the major errors of the past two years is highly technical and cannot be spelled out here. I can only report my judgment that the errors would not have been anything like so large, and might not have occurred at all, if, years ago, the Fed had devoted to improving its measures of the money supply anything like the attention and research effort it has lavished on its index of industrial production, let alone on its surveys of liquid assets.

The Fed neglected monetary statistics for years because it took interest rates rather than monetary aggregates as its criterion of policy. It has corrected the mistake in policy. But it has not corrected the mistake in statistics. As a result, its present estimates of monetary aggregates are still defective.

By removing Regulation Q and improving its monetary statistics, the Fed could assure itself far more reliable measures of its actual policy than it now has. By modernizing its operating procedures in New York, it could make its actual policy conform more closely to its intended policy—but that is grist for another column.

MONEY EXPLODES
May 3, 1971

The quantity of money has been exploding in recent months:

> Money narrowly defined (M_1), to include currency and demand deposits alone, grew at the rate of 13 per cent a year in the two months from January to March.

> Money more broadly defined (M_2), to include also commercial bank deposits, other than large CD's, grew at the rate of 22 per cent.

These rates of growth have not been exceeded in any other two-month period in the past quarter century!

Despite this explosion, the news columns are still filled with complaints that the Federal Reserve System is exercising undue restraint.

Why the explosion?

The explosion is the result partly of a deliberate decision by the Fed, partly of a mistake.

In the last quarter of 1970, M_1 grew at the annual rate of 3.4 per cent, well below the Fed's target of 5 to 6 per cent. Smarting under a barrage of criticism, the Federal Open Market Committee decided in January to aim for something like 7½ per cent in the first quarter of 1971—in order to achieve about 5½ per cent for the two quarters combined.

For reasons stated earlier (Newsweek, March 1), I believe that the Fed was mistaken in looking primarily at M_1. In the last quarter of 1970, M_2 grew at a rate of more than 9 per cent. If anything, monetary policy was already too easy.

Be that as it may, the Fed decided to speed up monetary growth. But when it moved late in January to do so, it overdid it.

This mistake—as well as the mistake in the last quarter of 1970 and repeated earlier mistakes—arose from the obsolete procedures used by the New York Fed, which carries out the policies decided in Washington.

The New York Fed tries to control monetary aggregates by operating indirectly through interest rates and money-market conditions rather than directly through bank reserves—a heritage of an earlier period when money-market conditions were the primary criterion of Fed policy. As a result, whenever the demand for credit is declining—as it was in the fall quarter because of the GM strike—New York tends to "lean against" the downward pressure on interest rates and to produce a smaller increase in monetary aggregates than it intends. Whenever the demand for credit is rising—as it has been recently because of economic expansion—New York tends to "lean against" the upward pressure on interest rates and to produce a more rapid increase in monetary aggregates than it intends. Hence the mistakes in the past two quarters.

The likely consequences

The explosion adds to the danger that inflation, which has been tapering off, will again accelerate. The danger is not immediate, because monetary changes take many months to have their full effects. More important, two months do not make a trend.

If the Fed corrects its mistake, stops the explosion, and brings monetary growth down sharply—to not more than 5 per cent in M_1—no lasting harm will have been done. But even then, the erratic changes in monetary growth will have subjected the financial and economic system to completely unnecessary instability. *It is entirely feasible for the Fed to keep the growth in monetary aggregates stable if it will modernize its operating procedures.* It is long past time that it did so.

On the other hand, if the Fed were to continue monetary growth at anything like the present rate, rapid acceleration of inflation by late 1971 or early 1972 is all but inevitable.

What now?

The Fed is surely as concerned as I am about the recent monetary explosion. Chairman Burns and other Fed officials have stated time and again that they do not intend to repeat the Fed's mistake in 1967 and 1968 of overreacting to recession, that they do not intend to start a new acceleration of inflation. The Fed must therefore be planning to reduce the rate of monetary growth. But will it succeed in reducing it sufficiently and soon enough—and without going too far in the other direction? I honor its intentions, but I am disturbed by its tardiness in developing effective machinery to convert intentions into performance.[1]

Economic expansion is under way. The danger is not that it will proceed too slowly but that it will proceed too rapidly. We can achieve both less inflation and less unemployment—but only if we do not push too hard.

IRRESPONSIBLE MONETARY POLICY
January 10, 1972

Monetary growth was more erratic in 1971 than in any year for the past two decades and more. From January to July, M_1 (currency plus demand deposits) rose at a rate of nearly 12 per cent per year, M_2 (currency plus demand deposits plus commercial-bank time deposits other than CD's) at a rate of nearly 15 per cent per year. These are truly explosive rates. Then the Federal Reserve Board slammed on the brakes. From July through the latest four weeks for which data are available as I write this (four weeks ending December 15, 1971), M_1 was essentially unchanged, and M_2 rose at the annual rate of 5 per cent.

True, the *average* rate for the year as a whole, though on the high side, is not too bad, but that is like assuring the nonswimmer that he can safely walk across a river because its *average* depth is only 4 feet.

Why does it matter?

Why should we be concerned about these gyrations in monetary growth? Because they exert an important influence on the future course of the economy. Erratic monetary growth almost always produces erratic economic growth. The monetary explosion is only now beginning to show up in the pace of economic recovery—several months behind schedule because of the chilling effect of the new economic policy on business activity. The monetary freeze has not yet had a significant impact (except perhaps in the stock market) but, unless we are extremely lucky, it will produce a decidedly slower pace of economic recovery in the first half of 1972 than is now envisioned by the much publicized and highly optimistic "consensus" forecast.

The chart illustrates the kind of evidence that underlies these statements. For each month of the past five years, the solid line shows the rate of growth

[1]As the next column documents, it took until July before the Fed ended the explosion; for the rest of 1971 it did go too far in the other direction, and in early 1972 it set off on another explosion.]

MONEY IN THE POCKET

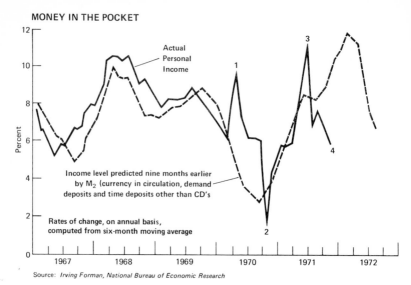

Source: *Irving Forman, National Bureau of Economic Research*

over the preceding six months of personal income (that is, the total received income of all the persons in the U.S.). A six-month period is used to average out the highly erratic month-to-month changes. The dashed line shows the corresponding rate of growth of M_2 nine months earlier, adjusted in scale to correspond to personal income—which is why it is designated "predicted." (The adjustment is based on a correlation computed for the period 1954 to 1970.)

Clearly, the actual rate of change of personal income mirrors with remarkable fidelity the rate of change of M_2 nine months earlier.

There are only four significant discrepancies, which I have numbered on the chart. Each has a readily identified special explanation.

1 The upward spike in early 1970 reflects a retroactive Federal pay increase that was statistically reported in two months.

2 The downward spike in late 1970 is the result of the General Motors strike.

3 The upward spike and subsequent downward spike in mid-1971 are the result of stockpiling for the steel strike that never occurred and the subsequent running down of stockpiles.

4 The downward movement in September, October and November 1971 is the result of the new economic policy. By spreading uncertainty and confusion domestically and internationally, the new policy nipped a healthy recovery in the bud, at least temporarily. The outcome has been the opposite of the intention.

The November figure is the latest available for personal income. But we can follow the path presaged by earlier monetary growth for a further nine months. It rises sharply to a peak in early February—reflecting the monetary explosion—then declines sharply to August—reflecting the monetary freeze.

What now?

The tough question is how the discrepancy introduced by the new economic policy will work itself out. Will personal income return to the predicted path before the monetary freeze starts taking effect? Will dissipation of uncertainty by the actual operation of phase two and by the international monetary agreement counter some of the effects of the monetary freeze just as the creation of the uncertainty countered some of the effects of the monetary explosion? We shall be very fortunate indeed if this occurs. But the Fed will be pushing our luck beyond reason if it continues the monetary freeze. That can be counted on to kill and not merely slow down the economic revival under way.

Responsible policy calls for staying in the middle of the road, not lurching from side to side. And the Fed can produce a steady rate of monetary growth if it only overcomes the infatuation with interest rates that has sapped its will.

THE CASE FOR A MONETARY RULE
February 7, 1972

I and most other monetarists have long favored a policy of a steady and moderate rate of growth of the quantity of money. We have strongly opposed the Fed's trying to fine-tune the economy.

Recent policy conformed to our prescription only in 1970.

Critics ask why we are so modest. Why not use the powerful instrument of monetary policy to offset other forces pushing the economy toward inflation or recession? Why tie the hands of the Fed? Why not trust their discretion in adapting to changing circumstances?

We favor the rule of steady monetary growth for several reasons.

1 THE PAST PERFORMANCE OF THE FED Throughout its history, the Fed has proclaimed that it was using its powers to promote economic stability. But the record does not support the claim. On the contrary, the Fed has been a major source of instability.

The Fed was responsible for converting what would have been a serious recession after 1929 into a major catastrophe by permitting the quantity of money to decline by one-third from 1929 to 1933, even though it had ample power to prevent the decline.

In recent years, the Fed set off the accelerating inflation that Mr. Nixon inherited by expanding the money supply too rapidly in 1967 and 1968, then stepped too hard on the brake in 1969, and too hard on the accelerator in the first seven months of 1971. Federal Reserve officials have often admitted their errors after the fact—as chairman Burns did in July 1971, in testimony before the Joint Economic Committee—and have promised better performance in the future. But then the same forces have produced a repetition of the same errors.

We conclude that the urgent need is to prevent the Fed from being a source of economic disturbance.

2 THE LIMITATIONS OF OUR KNOWLEDGE Economic research has established two propositions: (1) there is a close, regular and predictable relation between the quantity of money, national income and prices over any any considerable period of years; (2) the same relation is much looser from month to month, quarter to quarter, or even year to year. In particular, monetary changes take time to affect the economy, and the time delay is itself highly variable.

The first proposition means that a steady price level over the long pull requires that the quantity of money grow at a fairly steady rate roughly equal to the average rate of growth of output.

The second proposition means that any attempt to use monetary policy for fine-tuning is likely simply to introduce additional instability. And this is indeed what has happened.

3 THE PROMOTION OF CONFIDENCE An announced, and adhered to, policy of steady monetary growth would provide the business community with a firm basis for confidence in monetary stability that no discretionary policy could provide even if it happened to produce roughly steady monetary growth.

4 NEUTRALIZATION OF THE FED An independent Fed may at times be too insulated from political pressures—as it was in the early '30s—and yet at other times unduly affected by political pressures. If we really knew enough to use monetary policy for fine-tuning, we would probably experience a four-year cycle, with unemployment reaching its trough in years divisible by four and inflation reaching its peak in the succeeding year.

A monetary rule would insulate monetary policy both from the arbitrary power of a small group of men not subject to control by the electorate and from the short-run pressures of partisan politics.

Is the rule that we have proposed technically feasible? Can the Fed control the quantity of money? No serious student of money—whatever his policy views—denies that the Fed can, if it wishes, control the quantity of money. It cannot, of course, achieve a precise rate of growth from day to day or week to week. But it can come very close from month to month and quarter to quarter.

As I wrote some five years ago, if the monetary rule were followed, "other forces would still affect the economy, require change and adjustment, and distort the even tenor of our ways. But steady monetary growth would provide a monetary climate favorable to the effective operation of those basic forces of enterprise, ingenuity, invention, hard work and thrift that are the true springs of economic growth. That is the most that we can ask from monetary policy at our present stage of knowledge. But that much—and it is a great deal—is clearly within our reach."

Chapter Four
FISCAL POLICY AND TAXATION

The columns in this chapter stress three main themes. (1) the limitations of fiscal policy as a means of countering inflation or recession; (2) the relation between taxes and the scope of government and (3) the defects of the individual income tax.

The first theme, as noted in the introduction to Chapter 3, is the mirror image of the emphasis in that chapter on the importance of monetary policy. As I say in the first column in this chapter, questioning whether higher taxes would necessarily be contractionary was, in the light of the economic orthodoxy of the day, "like questioning whether 2 plus 2 equals 4." The failure of the 1968 surtax to stem inflation shook that orthodoxy, so the situation today is somewhat less extreme. Yet the stress in late 1971 and early 1972 on "expansive fiscal policy"—i.e. big deficits—to stimulate the economy—both by the administration and its leading Democratic opponents—reveals that the belief in the potency of fiscal policy is still alive and well. It is kept alive primarily, I believe, by two factors stressed in these columns: first, the tendency to look only at the direct effects of government spending and taxes and to neglect the indirect effects; second, the failure to keep fiscal effects separate from monetary effects. Insofar as government deficits are financed via the printing press (whether literally in the form of currency or figuratively in the form of Federal Reserve creation of deposits to purchase government securities), the resulting monetary growth will stimulate spending, and it is easy to attribute this effect to the deficits per se rather than to the method of financing them.

My view seems to be supported by the bulk of the empirical evidence on this question. Yet I should warn the reader that even more than on the issue of monetary policy, that view is a minority view in the economic profession.

The second theme—the relation between taxes and the scope of government—reflects a political judgment rather than an economic judgment. As a matter of technical economics, the decision about how much to spend and the decision about how to finance the spending can be regarded as largely independent if related decisions. As a political matter, I believe that in the long run the level of taxes comes closer to determining the level of spending than the other way around. Occasionally, as in World War II, a special emergency produces a willingness to raise taxes and spending is the moving force. But once the new level of taxes is in place, it tends to become permanent or nearly so, and thereafter spending is determined in large part by how much the revenue structure will raise.

Explicit increases in tax rates are one source of increased revenue and spending. But in the postwar period an even more important source has been the automatic and unlegislated increase in the burden of taxes as a result of economic growth and inflation. Both tend to raise not only the amount of tax revenue but, even more important, the *fraction* of total income going to the tax collector. They have this effect by pushing individuals into higher tax brackets of our graduated income tax.

In this way, the second theme is related both to the first (how to control inflation) and to the third (the defects of the individual income tax). My own favorite device for reforming the tax is to substitute a flat rate tax on income above personal exemptions for the present graduated rates and at the same time to eliminate all deductions other than strictly defined business and occupational expenses. In addition, I would provide for an automatic increase in the personal exemption and in the base for computing capital gains to allow for inflation (an escalator clause).

HIGHER TAXES? NO
January 23, 1967

Like many other economists, I oppose the increase in taxes recommended by President Johnson—but for different reasons than most.

I oppose a tax increase because I believe that the Federal government is already absorbing too much of the community's resources. We need lower taxes, not higher taxes.

Taxes and federal spending

My fellow economists will tell me that I am confusing taxes and spending. Government *spending* measures the absorption of resources. The level of *taxes* determines "only" how much of the spending is financed by taxes and how much by borrowing.

This is true as an accounting matter—but not politically. The postwar period has demonstrated time and again that Congress will spend whatever the tax system will raise—plus a little more. Raise taxes and the main effect is likely to be higher spending. The President has asked for a *temporary* increase in taxes to finance a *temporary* increase in war spending. But temporary increases have a way of becoming permanent. The way to meet extra needs is to cut nonwar spending, not to increase taxes.

My fellow economists will tell me also that the major issue is not the level of government spending but whether the economy is overheated and needs higher taxes to restrain it, or, alternatively, is headed into a recession that higher taxes will deepen.

Taxes and the economy

I believe that we are headed for a recession, albeit an inflationary one—but this plays no part in my opposition to a tax increase. Though these days it is like questioning whether 2 plus 2 make 4, I do not share the widespread view that a tax increase which is not matched by higher government spending will necessarily have a strong braking effect on the economy.

True, higher taxes would leave taxpayers with less to spend. But this is only part of the story. If government spending were unchanged, more of it would now be financed by the higher taxes, and the government would have to borrow less. *The individuals, banks, corporations or other lenders from whom the government would have borrowed now have more left to spend or to lend to others—and this extra amount is precisely equal to the reduction in the amount available to them and others as taxpayers.* If they spend it themselves, this directly offsets any reduction in spending by taxpayers. If they lend it to business enterprises or private individuals—as they can by accepting a lower interest rate for the loans—the resulting increase in business investment, expenditures on residential building and so on indirectly offsets any reduction in spending by taxpayers.

To find any *net* effect on private spending, one must look farther beneath the surface. Lower interest rates make it less expensive for people to hold cash. Hence, some of the funds not borrowed by the Federal government may be added to idle cash balances rather than spent or loaned. In addition, it takes time for borrowers and lenders to adjust to reduced government borrowing. However, any net increase in spending from these sources is certain to be temporary and likely to be minor.

Taxes and monetary policy

To have a significant impact on the economy, a tax increase must somehow affect monetary policy—the quantity of money and its rate of growth. It clearly need not have any such effect. The Federal Reserve can increase the quantity of money by precisely the same amount with or without a tax rise. However, a tax rise may embolden the Fed politically to hold down the quantity of money, because such a policy would then be more consistent with lower interest rates than if taxes were kept unchanged.

The tax reduction of 1964 had this effect—in the opposite direction. It encouraged the Fed to follow a more expansionary policy. This monetary expansion explains the long-continued economic expansion. And it is the turnabout in monetary policy since April 1966 that explains the growing signs of recession.

The level of taxes is important—because it affects how much of our resources we use through government and how much we use as individuals. It is not important as a sensitive and powerful device to control the short-run course of income and prices.

FISCAL RESPONSIBILITY
August 7, 1967

For the twelve months ending June 30, 1967, the Federal government ran a deficit of about $10 billion. And this may be only a mild foretaste of things to come. On present projections, the current year's deficit is likely to be two or three times as large. What does fiscal responsibility call for in the face of these staggering deficits?

At first glance, the answer seems straightforward: restraint in spending and higher taxes. That is why there is a "Rising Consensus for a Tax Hike" (NEWSWEEK, July 24).

In my opinion, this is a shortsighted answer. The deficit in the Federal budget is only a symptom of a more deep-seated malady: the size of government spending.

When the Administration urges higher taxes, it points to Vietnam as the source of the deficit. That is a half-truth. Of course, if military spending were lower—and other spending the same—the deficit would be smaller. But civilian spending too has been rising rapidly—as the Administration proudly proclaims when it seeks to calm the liberal critics of its Vietnam policy. And this rise has been reinforced by growing spending by state and local governments.

All in all, we work from Jan. 1 to nearly the end of April to furnish the wherewithal for government spending; only then can we turn to providing for our private needs.

Taxes and spending

This situation would be dangerous to our liberty even if we were getting our money's worth from present government spending. But there is scarce a man so rash as to say that we are. Most of us regard high military spending as a necessary evil. But even many proponents of big government are having second thoughts about numerous civilian programs—from the agricultural subsidies of the New Deal to the zooming welfare measures of the Great Society. Time and again, extravagant promises have been made that this or that expensive program will solve this or that social problem. And time and again, the result is that both costs and problems multiply.

But what relevance does this have to taxes? If we adopt such programs, does not fiscal responsibility at least call for imposing taxes to pay for them? The answer is that postwar experience has demonstrated two things. First, that Congress will spend whatever the tax system will raise—plus a little (and recently, a lot) more. Second, that, surprising as it seems, it has proved difficult to get taxes down once they are raised. The special interests created by government spending have proved more potent than the general interest in tax reduction.

If taxes are raised in order to keep down the deficit, the result is likely to be a higher norm for government spending. Deficits will again mount and the process will be repeated.

If government spending can be restrained, growth in the economy will, at present tax rates, add enough to revenues in a few years to eliminate the deficit and even to permit tax reduction. This is a big if. But let taxes be raised and there is no if about it at all. The deficits can be temporary; higher taxes are almost certain to be permanent.

Deficits and inflation

If we do not cut spending and do not raise taxes, will not the large interim deficits produce severe inflation?

Deficits have often been connected with inflation, but they need not be. Deficits were large in 1931 and 1932 when prices were falling drastically. There was a surplus in 1919-20 when prices were rising rapidly. Whether deficits produce inflation depends on how they are financed. If, as so often happens, they are financed by creating money, they unquestionably do produce inflationary pressure. If they are financed by borrowing from the public, at whatever interest rates are necessary, they may still exert some minor inflationary pressure. However, their major effect will be to make interest rates higher than they would otherwise be. A short spell of high interest rates is vastly to be preferred to a long spell of high taxes.

Those of us who believe that government has reached a size at which it threatens to become our master rather than our servant should therefore (1) oppose any tax increase; (2) press for expenditure cuts; (3) accept large deficits as the lesser of evils; (4) favor the financing of these deficits by borrowing from the public rather than by undue creation of money; and (5) urge the elimination of artificial ceilings on the rate of interest at which the government may borrow in order to foster this objective.

In the long view, that is the course of true fiscal responsibility.

FISCAL TRICKERY
August 28, 1967

The 10 per cent surcharge on individual income taxes that President Johnson has proposed is disarmingly simple. It sounds as if it would impose the same extra burden on people at all levels of income, as if it would be neutral and leave unchanged the degree of graduation in the tax rates. Yet, in fact, it imposes very different burdens on people at different levels of income and increases the steepness of the graduation of tax rates, thereby undoing some of the reforms achieved in the 1964 tax reduction.

I oppose any increase in Federal taxes, for reasons stated in this column three weeks ago. But the purpose of this week's column is neither to oppose nor to support the proposed surcharge. Its purpose is to unveil it, to make clear what its actual effect would be, so that we can all judge its desirability with open eyes.

The proposed extra tax is stated as 10 per cent of present taxes. But you cannot pay any extra tax out of the part of your income that is already mortgaged to pay existing taxes. The extra tax must come out of the rest of your income. The burden it imposes on you is therefore seen most clearly by expressing the extra tax as a percentage of your income after present taxes rather than as a percentage of either your total income or of the taxes you now pay.

The tax burden

A few numerical examples will show the importance of this distinction (chart). A single taxpayer with an income under $500 after exemptions and deductions is now taxed at the rate of 14 per cent. This leaves him 86 cents out of every dollar of taxable income to spend as he wishes (and to pay other taxes). The 10 per cent surcharge would raise his tax rate by 1.4 percentage points. The additional tax works out to 1.6 per cent of the 86 cents he has left after present taxes. This is a measure of the *additional* tax burden on him.

Suppose his taxable income is between $6,000 and $8,000. The additional tax on each dollar in that income bracket works out to 3.3 per cent of the 75 cents he has left after present taxes. The *additional* burden is twice as high as it is in the under-$500 tax bracket.

For the taxable-income bracket of $22,000-$26,000, the additional tax burden is 10 per cent of income after tax; for the bracket with the highest rate (more than $100,000), it is 23.3 per cent.

This is a very steeply graduated set of rates. It is very far indeed from an equal burden on all income levels.

Effect of Proposed 10 Per Cent Surcharge on Single Taxpayer

Present Law

Selected Taxable Income Brackets (Line 11d of Tax Form)*	Marginal Tax Rate	Percentage of Income Left	Marginal Tax Rate With Surcharge	Surcharge as Percentage of Income After Tax
Less than $500**	14%	86%	15.4%	1.6%
$ 6,000-$ 8,000	25%	75%	27.5%	3.3%
$22,000-$26,000	50%	50%	55.0%	10.0%
More than $100,000	70%	30%	77.0%	23.3%

*For married taxpayers filing joint returns, the numbers in the first column should be doubled.
**Neglects exceptions proposed by President Johnson for low incomes.

Average vs. marginal

The chart shows the rates on income in each bracket—in tax jargon, the marginal rates. The *average* rate is of course different for everyone above the first bracket. To illustrate, a single taxpayer who has a taxable income of $8,000 now pays $1,630 in taxes and has $6,370 left. He would have to pay an extra $163 or 2.6 per cent of his income after present taxes.

A single taxpayer who has a taxable income of $26,000 now pays $9,030 in taxes and has $16,970 left. He would have to pay an extra $903 or 5.3 per cent of his income after present taxes.

A single taxpayer who has a taxable income of $150,000 now pays $90,490 in taxes and has $59,510 left. He would have to pay an extra $9,049 or 15.2 per cent of his income after present taxes.

You may favor or, as I do, oppose increasing the steepness of graduation of income-tax rates. In either case, you should know that that is what President Johnson is proposing.

TAXES: THE HARD SELL
May 13, 1968

Madison Avenue puffing of commercial products sounds like British understatement compared with the current campaign for a tax increase.

Does the economy have an ill? A tax increase is just the pill. Are prices rising too fast? Just raise taxes. Is the construction industry being hurt by high interest rates? Just raise taxes. Are foreign payments out of balance? Just raise taxes. Are restrictions on foreign investment too burdensome? Just raise taxes. And, goes the advertising pitch, "virtually all experts agree."

What is the miracle drug that will solve all these problems? Has it been tested sufficiently to win certification from Pure Food and Drugs? Does it have any side effects? Just who are the experts who speak in a single voice? Are they, by any chance, the same ones who told us in 1963 that the way to solve the balance-of-payments deficit was to *cut* taxes?

The proposed 10 per cent surcharge would yield about $10 billion per year when fully effective—from an $800 billion economy. Prices are now rising at a rate of more than 4 per cent per year. Just to eliminate the inflationary pressure requires cutting attempted spending by more than $30 billion a year, without counting the additional reduction required to release resources for construction, exports and foreign investment.

Effects on spending

How can a $10 billion tax increase produce such prodigies?

Some $3 billion would come from corporations. This might induce them to cut somewhat their spending for new investment. But the effect would be small. Corporations invest for the long pull, and would borrow to finance promising investment—especially if the tax increase lowered the interest rate at which they could borrow.

The remaining $7 billion would come from individuals. Here the effect on spending might be larger per dollar of taxes, though, if the claim that the tax increase will be temporary were taken seriously, most of the effect might be on saving, not on consumer spending.

Any initial cuts in spending would reduce the incomes of others, who in turn might cut their spending, and so on *ad infinitum*, so the total effect on this score would be larger than the initial effect.

However, these effects on corporations and consumers are only one side of the account. If the government collects more in taxes, it needs to borrow less. Every dollar less that is left in the hands of taxpayers means a dollar more that is left in the hands of whoever would have purchased the government securities to finance the deficit. That dollar is available to pay the surcharge, or to spend, or to lend to someone else to spend.

Where is the evidence?

That is why a tax increase, with unchanged government spending, would tend to reduce interest rates—which would encourage additional spending on construction, business investment, and the like. This additional spending would offset, at least in part, any reduction in spending by taxpayers.

There is still likely to be a net effect on spending because the lower interest rates may induce some people to hold more cash than they otherwise would.

Ten billion dollars is a lot of money. If not matched by extra government spending (a big *if*), it would have a sizable effect on the deficit. But by itself, it would not even come close to offsetting present inflationary forces.

Perhaps I am wrong. Perhaps a tax increase is such potent medicine that every tax dollar will reduce spending by $4 or $5. In that case, there should be evidence from past experience. After all, we have had tax increases and decreases before.

Where is the evidence? Have well-documented studies of past experience revealed a close, dependable and multiplied effect of changes in government taxes and expenditures on total spending? Not so far as I know. On the contrary, the attempts I know of to find such a relation have failed and tend rather to confirm the view that the relation is uncertain and erratic.

Personally, I oppose a tax increase for reasons that I have spelled out in earlier columns. But whether you favor or oppose a tax increase you should know that no convincing evidence—from economic analysis or from historical experience—has yet been presented to support the extravagant claims that have been made for a tax increase.

Is it too much to ask that we apply the same standards of evidence to alleged cures for inflation as to alleged cures for cancer?

REGRESSIVE INCOME TAX
April 22, 1968

In the boom year 1929, more than 4,000 persons reported a taxable income of more than $250,000. Since then, our population has risen by more than 60 per cent and average income has quadrupled—half real, half as a result of a doubling of prices. Hence, today's counterpart would be about 6,500 persons reporting a taxable income of more than $1 million. The actual number of million-dollar taxable incomes reported in 1966 was 626.

Does this dramatic fall in the number of high incomes reported on personal tax returns reflect a major reduction in the inequality of income? The success of a social policy directed at eliminating the extremes of wealth and poverty? Nothing of the sort. It is simply evidence of how successful high-income people have been in getting more and more loopholes introduced into the income-tax law and in taking advantage of them to avoid paying taxes. In 1929, the highest tax rate was 25 per cent. It hardly paid then to engage in complicated and expensive transactions to avoid paying taxes. Today, the highest tax rate is 70 per cent. It clearly pays to adopt very expensive devices.

The personal income tax professes to adjust the tax to "ability to pay," to tax the rich more heavily and the poor less heavily and to allow for each individual's special circumstances. This is an elaborate façade.

Equity on paper

The tax rates are steeply graduated on paper, rising from 14 to 70 per cent. But the law is riddled with so many loopholes, so many special provisions that the high rates are almost pure window dressing. In 1966, total personal income taxes paid amounted to less than 20 per cent of total reported taxable income. In other words, all the rates above the very lowest, the 14 per cent rate that applies to the first $1,000 of the taxable income of a married couple, accounted for less than 30 per cent of total taxes collected. Moreover, had there been a low flat rate, it would not have paid taxpayers to go to the lengths they now do to avoid high marginal rates. They would have reported more income and less deductions. Hence a flat rate well below 20 per cent would have yielded as much as the actual steeply graduated rates.

Suppose we classified people by what you and I would regard as their actual income rather than by the taxable incomes they report. Suppose we then expressed the tax they actually pay as a percentage of their actual income. We would find that this percentage is much smaller for persons in very high income classes (and, incidentally, because of exemptions, also in very low income classes) than for persons with incomes of middle size. And within each income class, we would find enormous variation. Two men with the same income may pay vastly different taxes—because one's income is wages and the other's interest on tax-exempt securities or capital gains.

So long as the rates are steeply graduated, it is politically impossible to eliminate the present loopholes and deductions, as is demonstrated by repeated failures to do so. But even if politically possible, it would be undesirable. The present high rates applied to all income would have disastrous effects on incentives. We would lose more in output than we would gain in fairness. Rate reform must accompany other tax reforms.

Equity in fact

The personal income tax would come far closer to achieving its professed objectives if we substituted a flat rate on income above personal exemptions for the present graduated rates and, simultaneously, eliminated the present loopholes and deductions that enable so many persons to avoid paying their fair share of the taxes and that require so many more to take tax considerations into account in their every economic decision.

If every deduction were eliminated except occupational expenses strictly interpreted, and if income of all kinds in excess of personal exemptions were subject to a single low flat rate, we could double our present personal exemptions—which are disgracefully low—and still raise as much revenue. That would be more equitable, vastly simpler, and far more efficient.

It would also release all of us from the unpaid bookkeeping we are forced to engage in to satisfy the Internal Revenue Service and make available for productive use the highly skilled accountants and lawyers who now devote their great talents to advising their clients how to avoid taxes under present law, to creating new and ever more complex tax shelters, and to litigating cases in court.

SPEND, TAX, ELECT
July 15, 1968

Harry Hopkins, an intimate of FDR, is reputed to have remarked in the late 1930s, "We shall spend and spend, tax and tax, elect and elect." Whether Hopkins actually said it or not, this formula has proved extraordinarily effective. It has kept the White House firmly in Democratic hands, except only for the eight Eisenhower years.

I doubt that even Hopkins foresaw just how the formula would work—with the Democrats doing the spending and electing and the Republicans doing the taxing. Yet that has proved the division of labor.

The latest example is the 10 per cent surcharge recently passed by Congress. Republican votes provided the margin of victory—and not just the votes of a few Democrats in Republican clothing. On the contrary, the Republican leadership in both Senate and House backed the tax increase. It could not have passed without their support.

The largest single source of Federal revenue is an individual income tax that automatically imposes heavier taxes as incomes rise—whether the rise be in output or in prices. As a taxpayer's income rises, so does the tax *rate* levied on that income, because the fixed dollar exemption becomes a smaller percentage of income and he moves into higher tax brackets. In order to keep the effective rate constant, nominal tax rates must be lowered. The absence of legislation lowering rates automatically means higher taxes. This is the "fiscal drag" that was made so much of during the Kennedy Administration.

The tax escalator

In 1940, before our entry into World War II, individual income taxes amounted to less than 2 per cent of total personal income. At their wartime height in 1945, they were just under 10 per cent. Postwar tax reductions were followed by rises during the Korean War that carried the effective rate to over 10 per cent in 1953. The Eisenhower tax reduction in 1954 brought the rate down to 9 per cent—but then economic expansion pushed it up to an all-time high in 1963, well over 10 per cent. The Kennedy tax reduction in 1964 again carried the rate back to 9 per cent—but the subsequent expansion pushed it back up to around 10 per cent. *Even before the surcharge, the effective individual income tax rate was as high as it was at its peak in World War II.* The surcharge will carry it to a new all-time high.

The standard scenario has been that the Democrats—in the name of the New Deal, the Fair Deal, or the Great Society—push through large spending programs, with the assistance of a few Republicans but generally against the opposition of the Republican leadership. The spending programs not only absorb the increased tax yield generated by "fiscal drag," they go farther and produce deficits. The Democrats then appeal to the Republicans' sense of fiscal responsibility to refrain from cutting tax rates or, as in this case, to raise them. The Republicans cooperate, thereby establishing a new higher revenue base for further spending. The Democrats get the "credit" for the spending; the Republicans, the "blame" for the taxes; and you and I pay the bill.

Guns and butter

The current tax increase, like the increase during the Korean War, was sold as a temporary war measure. That is an excuse, not a reason. Only half of the $53 billion increase in Federal spending from 1965 to 1968 went for the military. Not the Vietnam war but the policy of spend and spend produces the need to tax and tax.

The Republicans point to the $6 billion legislated cut in spending to justify their support of the tax increase. That is wishful voting. The tax increase is for real. The spending cut is a hope for the future. And at that, it is window dressing. Even if the full $6 billion cut in the President's proposed budget were achieved, actual spending would go up by $4 billion. And it requires no crystal ball to predict that the full $6 billion will not be achieved.

I honor the Republicans for putting what they regard as the national interest ahead of partisan considerations. But I believe that they have been shortsighted in judging the national interest. True fiscal responsibility requires making the legislators who vote for high spending also vote for the high taxes required to finance it—not bailing them out. True fiscal responsibility requires resisting every tax increase and promoting tax decreases at every opportunity. That is the only way to put an effective ceiling on Federal spending.

END THE SURTAX
February 10, 1969

"Once wrong, twice right" is apparently the motto of the many politicians, economists, businessmen, and journalists who have joined former President Johnson and his Council of Economic Advisers in urging continuation of the surtax.

The surtax was sold to a reluctant Congress as the only effective way to halt inflation. It has now been in effect for over six months. Inflation has not only continued; it has even accelerated. Yet we are now being told that the surtax must be retained. Why? To fight inflation!

True, proponents grant, the surtax did not even dent inflation. But now, they say, it is taking hold—look at the sharp slowdown in consumption spending in the fourth quarter of 1968.

This slowdown provides no evidence that the surtax is affecting the pace of inflation. Those few of us who opposed the surtax granted all along that taxpayers would very likely restrain their spending in response to the surtax. But, we said, that is only half the story. The persons from whom the government would otherwise have had to borrow to finance its expenditures will have more to spend or to lend to others. They will make funds available for additional spending by business enterprises or individuals. Why should *total* spending be much affected by the surtax?

Inflation: a smoke screen

That is precisely what has happened. The slowdown in the growth of consumer spending has been matched by an acceleration in spending for new investment, construction, inventories and the like.

Once again, as so often in the past, what happened to the quantity of money was far more critical *for inflation* than what happened to the level of Federal taxes and spending. The inflationary Fed (NEWSWEEK, Jan. 20) rather than the deflationary surtax dominated the scene.

LBJ has much company in stressing inflationary dangers as a justification for continuing the surtax. But this argument must have been strongly buttressed for him by another: recommending a continuation of the surtax enabled him to recommend a sharp further rise in government spending for nonmilitary purposes and at the same time clothe himself in the mantle of fiscal responsibility.

The recommendation to continue the surtax is deceptive. It looks like a recommendation to postpone tax reduction. In fact, it is a recommendation to raise taxes. For individuals, the surtax applied only to part of 1968. Continuing it for all of 1969 raises the effective rate of the surtax from 7½ per cent on 1968 taxes to 10 per cent on 1969 taxes. In addition, inflation and real growth push taxpayers into higher and higher brackets, subject to higher and higher marginal tax rates. And the surtax is a percentage of *tax*, not of *income*.

Spending: the real issue

The real issue for the surtax is not inflation. That is a smoke screen. Inflation must be dealt with by monetary policy. *The real issue for the surtax is the level of Federal spending.* Congress will continue in the future as it has in the past to spend whatever the tax system will raise—plus a little (and lately a lot) more. A vote to continue the surtax is therefore a vote to continue to increase the fraction of our resources that is used by the Federal government.

Is this a road that we want to follow? Are we getting our money's worth now for the roughly one dollar in four of our income that is going to Washington? I believe not. Nonmilitary spending has risen explosively in the past eight years—and so have the problems that the spending was supposed to solve. And there is much evidence that these problems have gotten worse largely because of rather than in spite of the spending.

Taxes and spending are now too high, not too low. The urgent need is to cut both. That will not be easy. The Johnson Administration left a heritage of entering wedges. programs that were started small but with large increases in spending already legislated for the future. Unless the Nixon Administration can at least slow down the rate of rise of spending, it will be unable to achieve its other objectives and it will disappoint many of the voters who elected it.

The first step toward true fiscal responsibility is to let the surtax expire on June 30, 1969, and to cut the cost of Federal spending to the revenues that other taxes will yield. That step taken, it will be easier to take the next—and equally urgent—step: to start a program of moderate but steady reduction in the level of Federal taxes.

NO TAXATION WITHOUT REPRESENTATION
March 3, 1969

Congress has not legislated a reduction in the personal exemption under the income tax since 1942. Yet the exemption today is only about half of what is was then. How come? In dollars, the exemption was reduced to $500 per person in 1942. It is now $600. But a dollar is not a dollar is not a dollar. Today, a dollar will buy less than half as much as a dollar would buy in 1942. Rising prices have cut nearly in half the real value of the income-tax exemption.

Inflation is not ordinarily considered to be a tax. And yet that is what it is. It is a tax twice over. It is, first, a tax on income because it lowers the real value of personal exemptions, and raises the rate applied to our incomes by pushing us into higher tax brackets. As a result, taxes go up faster than prices, which means that the government collects more in real terms.

Second, inflation is a tax on cash balances. When prices rise, all of us must add to the number of dollars we hold in order to keep the purchasing power of our cash balances constant. To get these extra dollars, we must give up some real resources, in the form of labor or of the goods we could have purchased instead—just as we must in order to get the dollars that we pay in explicit taxes. To whom do we give up the real resources? To the government from whom we get the extra dollars it prints or makes available indirectly through deposits at the Federal Reserve System; and to the banks that create book entries labeled "deposits" over and above the amount they hold as currency or as deposits at the Federal Reserve. The total of these extra dollars is the revenue from the tax on cash balances, a revenue that, under our system, is shared between government and the banks.

Why inflation?

The special feature of inflation as a tax is that it is the only tax that can be levied without specific Congressional authorization. It can be and is levied by the U.S. Treasury and the Federal Reserve System on their own say-so, without announcement and without public hearings. That is what has made inflation such a tempting recourse to governments in need of funds. That is why countries that have had their ability to levy and collect explicit taxes destroyed or seriously impaired by defeat in war or by domestic disruption—and only such countries—have experienced hyperinflation that essentially wiped out the value of their money.

What can we do to end such taxation without representation?

We can end taxation of cash balances without representation by adopting a Congressional rule to limit the power of the monetary authorities. That is one reason why I have long favored a Congressional rule specifying that the money supply should be increased by a fixed percentage year in and year out. However, the main reason I favor this rule is different—to promote economic stability.

A simple reform

We can end the taxation of income without representation by legislating in advance that the exemptions, the maximum standard deductions, and the tax brackets under the personal income tax shall be adjusted each year for the change in the price level.

For example, start with the 1968 dollar exemptions, maximum deductions and tax brackets. As a measure of price change, use the BLS cost-of-living index number. Suppose that, by this index, prices turn out to average 4 per cent higher in 1969 than in 1968. The personal exemption for 1969 would then be 104 per cent of the personal exemption for 1968 or $624 per person instead of $600. The maximum standard deduction for a single person would be $312 instead of $300. The first bracket rate of 14 per cent would apply to the first $520 for a single person instead of to the first $500, and so on down the line.

This simple and thoroughly practicable reform will not begin to solve all the defects of the income tax. But it will prevent a creeping and automatic increase in the rate of taxation as a result of inflation. It will not prevent Congress from raising or lowering income-tax rates but it will require Congress to do so openly and by explicit action.

The hearings on tax reform that are now being held will be lengthy, complex, and to judge from experience, unproductive. Here is a simple reform that requires no lengthy hearings, no extensive consideration of technical tax provisions, no attack on long-established vested interests.

Will anyone who can find any objection to enacting it at once please step forth?

TAX FOLLIES OF 1970
April 27, 1970

These past few weeks some 75 million Americans have been struggling with their tax returns and their consciences—or hiring others to do so for them. If we suppose that the taxpayer or his tax service spent four hours on the average on each return, the total time amounted to the horrendous total of 300 million man hours, or the equivalent of 150,000 men working 40 hours a week for 50 weeks a year—and this does not include the time spent by employees of business enterprises in withholding taxes and preparing W-2s, or by high-priced lawyers and accountants advising clients on tax matters, or by the governmental employees on the other side of the Internal Revenue desk.

As I struggled with my own income-tax return, visions kept going through my head of all the useful things that this hypothetical army could accomplish—the rows on rows of new houses, schools, churches, factories, autos, that they might be producing instead of rows on rows of numbers and of uneasy consciences.

We have grown accustomed to this exaction of forced labor and to the prying into personal affairs that accompanies it. Yet, from time to time, we need to look at it afresh and ask ourselves to what purpose we impose these exactions on ourselves. To promote equity? To produce revenue?

Equity?

The claim that the incredible complexities of our income tax promote equity will bring a horselaugh from knowledgeable students of taxes.

The complexities reflect a vicious cycle. To "soak the rich" in the name of equity, tax rates were enacted that range up to 70 per cent without the surtax. To soften the blow, special provisions were then introduced, also in the name of equity, to enable certain categories of income to escape the high rates. Ingenious lawyers and accountants discovered ways to shelter still more income, prompting still more complications to "close loopholes" while of course not disturbing "equitable tax relief."

The result: tax provisions that no ordinary mortal can comprehend and that no rational tax legislator starting from scratch could or would devise. Persons with the same income, as you and I conceive income, pay vastly different taxes depending on their success in finding ways to reduce their taxable income by converting ordinary income into long-term capital gains, or by investing in oil, real estate, or other tax shelters.

As between different levels of income, every study has shown that middle-income groups pay a higher fraction of their income in taxes than higher income groups—because so much more of their income comes from salaries, which it is difficult to shelter.

Despite the fanfare, this situation was remedied only slightly by the Accountants' and Lawyers' Relief Act of 1969 (more euphemistically known as the Tax Reform Act of 1969).

Revenue?

The counterpart to the successful development of tax shelters and loopholes is that the high rates yield little revenue.

For 1967, the latest year for which figures are available, the substitution of a tax rate of 25 per cent for all higher rates would have reduced revenue by 8 per cent—if every taxpayer had nonetheless reported precisely the same net taxable income that he actually did. In fact, the revenue loss would have been much less. If the maximum rate had been 25 per cent, many taxpayers would have found it cheaper to pay the tax than to resort to the expensive devices they used to avoid tax.

Indeed, paradoxical though it sounds, simply replacing all rates higher than 25 per cent by 25 per cent might even have produced more revenue as a result of the larger amount of taxable income that would have been reported. In that case, the only losers would have been tax accountants, tax lawyers, and persons specializing in providing tax shelters.

At most, the high rates yield an amount of revenue that is roughly of the same order of magnitude as the value of the forced labor imposed on taxpayers.

It is long past time that we made the income tax honest by drastically reducing the higher rates and simplifying the base. We should remove all special treatment of particular kinds of income and eliminate all deductions except personal exemptions and strict occupational expenses.

The individual income tax as it now stands is surely an exercise in mass masochism that has few parallels in the annals of mankind.

PURCHASING-POWER BONDS
April 12, 1971

High-quality bonds—corporate or governmental—were long regarded as just the thing for pension funds and university endowments, as well as the cautious individual setting aside a nest egg to cushion his retirement. The past few years have shaken that image.

Suppose our cautious individual had purchased in August 1966 a $1,000 newly issued U.S. Treasury Note yielding 5¼ per cent, maturing in May 1971. In the nearly five years since, he received $250 in interest and he will shortly cash in his note for $1,000. How has he done? Since he bought the note, consumer prices have risen about 23 per cent, so it now takes about $1,250 to buy as much as $1,000 bought five years ago. The investor is back where he started from—except for interest on the interest and that would be more than balanced by income taxes on the "interest" he received. In truth, the investor had to pay for the privilege of lending money to the U.S.

That is why long-term interest rates rose so sharply in the past few years as inflation accelerated and why they have been so stubborn in coming down as inflation has been tapering off. Barnum had a point.[1]

If government does not . . .

The government, and the government alone, is responsible for inflation. By inflation, it has expropriated the capital of persons who bought government securities—often at the urging of high officials who eloquently proclaimed that patriotism and self-interest went hand in hand.

The right way to avoid this disgraceful shell game is for the government to borrow in the form of purchasing-power securities. Let the Treasury

[1 I had intended this to refer to the saying: "You can fool all of the people some of the time, and some of the people all of the time, but you can't fool all of the people all of the time."]

promise to pay not $1,000 but a sum that will have the same purchasing power as $1,000 had when the security was issued. Let it pay as interest each year not a fixed number of dollars but that number adjusted for any rise in prices. This would be the precise counterpart of the escalator clauses that have become so popular in wage contracts.

Unfortunately, the Treasury has shown little interest in issuing purchasing-power securities, and Congress has brought no pressure on it to do so.

Another way to achieve the same result would be for private enterprises to issue such securities. Investors would then have an effective hedge against inflation. Government could sell its securities only if it made them equally attractive.

Such securities have been issued by private enterprises in other countries but, so far as I know, not in the U.S.[2] It is too bad we have departed from a pattern of relative price stability (major wars aside) that made such devices unnecessary. But now that we seem to have done so, market forces here too will lead private enterprises to issue purchasing-power bonds.

. . .Why not private business

Consider a major enterprise selling a wide range of goods. If today it were to issue a twenty-year bond of the traditional kind, it would have to pay something between 7 and 8 per cent, even if its credit rating is high. By committing itself to such a rate, it is gambling on the pace of inflation. If prices in general rise rapidly, so will the prices of the goods it sells. In that case, even 8 per cent will raise no problem. However, if prices in general rise slowly or not at all, its income will also rise slowly, and even 7 per cent will prove a heavy burden.

Suppose instead it were to offer a purchasing-power bond. Given the present uncertainty about inflation, such a bond would be in great demand. Very likely, the corporation could sell the bond at a 3 per cent *real* rate (i.e., for a promise to pay $3 per $100 adjusted for the rate of inflation) instead of a 7 to 8 per cent *nominal* rate.

Both the corporation and the investor would be hedged against inflation. If prices rise rapidly, the corporation will indeed have to pay back a higher dollar total when the bonds mature—but it will be able to do so because its sales and its capital value will also be higher in dollar terms. If prices rise slowly, it will have lower dollar sales and capital value—but also a smaller debt to repay.

Corporations that issued such securities would benefit themselves—by borrowing at a lower average rate and by eliminating uncertainty. Purchasers of the securities would benefit—they would be protected against unanticipated inflation or deflation. We could all benefit—the reduced uncertainty about interest costs would encourage a steadier stream of capital expenditures by business, thereby contributing to a stabler economy.

[2 I have since learned that one was issued in the U.S. in the 1920s by a corporation founded by the great American economist Irving Fisher.]

CAN BUSINESS PAY TAXES?
November 29, 1971

President Nixon's proposals for reductions in taxes have been widely criticized as a "help-the-rich" program "heavily weighted in favor of business at the expense of the individual taxpayer."

Demagoguery

This criticism is sheer demagoguery. The elementary fact is that "business" does not and cannot pay taxes. Only people can pay taxes. Corporate officials may sign the check, but the money that they forward to Internal Revenue comes from the corporation's employees, customers or stockholders. A corporation is a pure intermediary through which its employees, customers and stockholders cooperate for their mutual benefit. A corporation may be large and control large amounts of capital. Yet it does not follow that a reduction in the check it sends to Internal Revenue benefits wealthy individuals.

Consider, for example, the proposed repeal of the excise tax on automobiles. At first glance, the main beneficiaries are the upper-income people who buy the new cars. But this is too simple. Many cars are purchased for business purposes, and the beneficiaries are the customers, employees, proprietors and stockholders of the firms buying the cars. More important, increased production of cars will lower prices of secondhand cars, benefiting their purchasers, who are mostly in lower-income classes. The greater sales of new cars will also benefit employees, proprietors and stockholders of firms producing and selling cars. However, it will harm employees, proprietors and stockholders of firms producing items for which the demand is now lower because spending has been diverted to new cars.

Or consider the proposed investment-tax credit. Surely, you will say, that benefits corporate stockholders, and we know that they are generally wealthy. True, but misleading. The firms that qualify for the credit will have an incentive to expand. But this adds to the demand for loans, which will tend to raise interest rates, spreading some of the benefits to savers and imposing costs on other users of capital. It will also add to the supply of goods that the firms getting the credit produce, benefiting their customers by lowering prices and their employees by providing better employment opportunities. Stockholders or proprietors of these companies will of course also benefit, but stockholders, proprietors, customers and employees of firms that do not qualify for the credit will be hurt.

And even this is only part of the story. The rest depends on how the government replaces the revenue, whether by imposing taxes, by borrowing or by reducing spending, and who is thereby benefited or harmed.

Indirect effects make it difficult to know who "really" pays any tax. But this difficulty is greatest for taxes levied on business. *That fact is at one and the same time the chief political appeal of the corporation income tax, and its chief political defect.* The politician can levy taxes, as it appears, on no one, yet obtain revenue. The result is political irresponsibility. Levying most taxes directly on individuals would make it far clearer who pays for government programs.

Repeal the corporate tax

Under our present tax system, stockholders pay no individual income tax on income that a corporation earns but does not pay out as dividends. Reinvestment of such undistributed income tends to raise the value of the corporation's stock. When and if the stockholder sells his stock, he receives the benefit in the form of a capital gain that is taxed at lower rates than his current dividends. The corporation income tax is defended as a way to prevent such undistributed income from being undertaxed.

A far better way to achieve this objective is to require corporations to attribute undistributed income to their stockholders and to require stockholders to include the undistributed income in their individual income. That is, the XYZ corporation would accompany its dividend check to stockholders with a notice, saying, "In addition to the $1 per share we are now paying you as dividends, we have earned $1.25 per share that we are reinvesting on your behalf." The stockholder would then report $2.25 per share as his income from the stock and pay individual income tax on that amount (and raise his capital gains base by $1.25 per share).

This reform would promote both equity and also greater competition in the capital market. Until it is enacted, and the corporation income tax as such is repealed, the demagogues will continue to have a field day.

A FAMILY MATTER
April 10, 1972

How would you like to get a letter from your married daughter suggesting that you and your wife of more than 30 years' standing get a divorce? That is what happened to us recently. Wrote our daughter (who, I should add, is a lawyer).

Dear Mom and Dad:

Just a quick note to suggest that you call your tax lawyer about my latest theory for saving income taxes—getting a divorce. (Don't gulp too hard, Mom—how much is it worth to you to be married? Not to live together and have the same name—just to be married?) Under 1971 tax rates, a married couple pays more tax than two single people each with half the income. Since alimony is deductible to the husband and taxable to the wife, if you get a divorce and Dad pays you reasonably high alimony, you can save taxes by making sure you split your total income roughly equally. The saving is pretty sizable.

Love, Jan

My daughter did not know that she was bringing coals to Newcastle. Some 30 years ago, as an employee of the U.S. Treasury Department, I helped devise the tax-splitting provisions that prevailed until the Reform Act of 1969—more accurately described as the Lawyers' and Accountants' Relief Act of 1969.

Those provisions were designed precisely to prevent living in sin from being a tax shelter. Under those provisions, a single person was taxed at the same rates as a married person but each rate applied to half the income, i.e., each rate bracket was half as wide. As a result, if two single persons who had equal incomes married, and continued to have the same incomes after marriage, their tax as a family was precisely the sum of their separate taxes.

This provision also meant, however, that if a man married a woman who had no income, the tax for the family was less than the tax that the single man had paid before. The reason this occurred was because of graduated rates. A single man who has an income of $20,000 pays more in tax than the sum of the taxes paid by two single men each with $10,000 income. His higher income puts him into a higher tax bracket. Similarly, under the earlier rules, a married couple was treated as equivalent to two persons each having half the family income. Hence, it was taxed at a lower rate than that applicable to a single person who had an income equal to the total family income.

Personally, I favor substituting a flat rate on income above a personal exemption for the present graduated rates and at the same time eliminating all deductions other than strictly defined business and occupational expenses. But that is not existing policy. Graduated tax rates were introduced and are defended as a device for equalizing income. There is no more effective means of equalizing income than for Prince Charming to marry Cinderella.

To put this point differently, consider a single man who has an income of $20,000 from, let us say, stocks and bonds. He has a niece who is unable to work and has no income. He gives her half of his stocks and bonds so he retains an income of $10,000 and she has an income of $10,000. The sum of their taxes will be less than the tax he paid before his benefaction. If that reduction in taxes is regarded as equitable, is it not also equitable that the same tax consequences should follow from his marrying his niece?

However, the single persons didn't see it that way. And they persuaded the Congress to revise the law by reducing the tax rates applicable to single persons below those applicable to married persons.

As my daughter said, the resulting tax shelter is by no means negligible.

Here are the tax savings from splitting income evenly at various family-income levels.

Here's to April 15 and living in sin!

| | **Tax* on basis of** | | |
Family Income	Joint Return	Two Unmarried Persons	Saving from Living in Sin
$10,000	$ 1,257	$ 1,114	$ 143
15,000	2,298	2,136	162
20,000	3,582	3,192	390
25,000	5,068	4,356	710
30,000	6,794	5,738	1,056
40,000	10,858	8,902	1,956
50,000	15,635	12,640	$2,995

*Assumes standard deduction throughout.

PERSONAL INCOME TAX REFORM
June 12, 1972

As readers of this column know, I have long favored a drastic reform of the Federal personal income tax that would substitute a flat rate on income above a personal exemption for the present graduated rates and at the same time eliminate all deductions other than strictly defined business and occupational expenditures. With such a broadened base, a flat rate of about 16 per cent would yield roughly the same amount of revenue as the present graduated rates running from 14 to 70 per cent. The higher rates are today mostly window dressing. They yield little revenue.

I therefore welcome enthusiastically the dramatic proposal by Representative Mills and Senator Mansfield to terminate all present tax preferences over a two-year period beginning Jan. 1, 1974, and, in the interim, re-examine them systematically.

However, if this proposal is to be more successful than earlier promising ventures at tax reform, two conditions must be met: (1) the elimination of tax preferences must be linked to a reduction in tax rates; (2) the demagoguery that has characterized much of the recent hullabaloo over tax reform must be avoided.

Loopholes

The demagoguery arises from failure to acknowledge (1) that most of the so-called loopholes were enacted by reasonable men for reasonable objectives and are not simply nefarious schemes to line the pockets of the rich, and (2) that the cost of loopholes to the government grossly overstates the gain to taxpayers.

Both points are illustrated by the deductibility of interest. Because the rent you pay for housing is not deductible but the interest that you pay on a mortgage is deductible (along of course with taxes), there is a tax advantage in owning rather than renting your dwelling. This provision was partly motivated by a desire to stimulate widened home ownership and it clearly has had that effect. Along with FHA, it largely explains the rapid growth of the suburbs at the expense of the central city in the past two decades. Personally, I do not favor subsidizing home ownership but the desire to do so can hardly be regarded as an unconscionable submission to vested interests.

The tax incentive increases the demand for home ownership and for mortgage finance. It thereby raises the cost of land and the interest rate on mortgages. Thus, the *net* saving to the taxpayer is very much less than the gross cost to Internal Revenue.

Another excellent example is the exemption from tax of interest on securities issued by states and municipalities. Constitutional questions aside, this exemption has been supported as a way to ease the financial problems of local governments by enabling them to borrow at lower rates than they otherwise could. The taxpayer lends money at, say, 5 per cent tax-free to a municipality instead of receiving, say, 8 per cent subject to tax from a corporate bond. In effect, he pays a tax of ⅜ or 37½ per cent to the municipality issuing the security rather than to the Federal Government. The taxpayer gains by paying a tax of 37½ per cent rather than, say, of 60 or 70 per cent, but clearly he doesn't get away scot-free.

Loss and gain

Precisely the same analysis applies to all sorts of tax shelters—whether in oil, real estate, capital gains or whatnot. In every case, there is a reasonable public aim and the tax shelter costs the taxpayer a substantial fraction of his tax saving.

Unfortunately, most estimates of the loss to the government from tax preferences implicitly treat that loss as if it were dollar for dollar a gain to the taxpayer. Clearly, it is not. The gain to the taxpayer is far less than the loss to the Treasury.

This difference between the loss to the Treasury and the gain to taxpayers is at one and the same time the major justification for tax reform and the major reason why tax reform may be politically feasible. The $50 billion or so difference is pure deadweight loss. No one gains from it except, to a small extent, producers of tax shelters. From a national point of view, it is mostly sheer waste. But also, it is a melon available to be split through tax reform. It is the reason why a tax reform that combines broadening of the base with a lowering of rates can simultaneously yield more tax revenue yet lower the burden of taxes (including the cost of tax shelters) to almost all taxpayers.

And what a rejoicing there would be over ending the bookkeeping nightmare and invasion of privacy that the income tax has become.

Chapter Five
INTERNATIONAL ECONOMIC POLICY

The columns in this chapter present a series of reports on a sequence of events that has been unfolding with all the inevitability of a Greek tragedy. These events had two key origins: (1) President Franklin D. Roosevelt's action on March 6, 1933 ending the internal convertibility of dollars into gold (see the first column in this chapter); (2) the World War II Bretton Woods agreement which established after the war a system of fixed exchange rates that were to be changed only by official action.

Once the United States government terminated its commitment to its own citizens to exchange gold for currency and currency for gold at a fixed rate, it was inevitable that—whether for good or ill—gold would lose its role as an effective determinant of the quantity of money and as an effective element in United States economic policy. The only question was when and by precisely what route. As things turned out, it took a little over 38 years, from March 6, 1933 to August 15, 1971, and there are still vestigial remains of the earlier reign of gold in the international sphere.

Similarly, from the time Bretton Woods became effective, it was inevitable that it would break down. The Bretton Woods system gave the dollar a unique role—the United States and the United States alone had no obligation to support the price of its currency in terms of foreign currencies; the United States and the United States alone was committed to convert its currency into gold at a fixed price on demand of foreign central banks or other official agencies.[1] Other countries committed themselves to keep the exchange rates of their currencies in terms of the dollar within a specified band (plus or minus 1 per cent of the officially stated parity), though they were free to change the parity by up to 10 per cent on their own volition and by larger amounts with the approval of the International Monetary Fund.

This arrangement was designed to solve a simple, yet fundamental and little understood, problem in foreign exchange—the so-called n-country problem. Given n currencies, there are only $n-1$ independent exchange rates. To take the simplest case, let there be just two currencies, say the dollar and the pound. Then there is only one exchange rate—the price of the pound in terms of the dollar or of the dollar in terms of the pound. There is no way in which *both* Britain and the United States can be free to determine that rate, no way in which Britain can make the price of the pound $2.40 and the United States can simultaneously make the price of the dollar 5 shillings, i.e., the price of the pound $4. The two countries either have to agree on a single price or agree to let the single price be determined on the free market

---

[1] Technically, the rules were symmetrical. Any country was free to adopt the same role but only the United States did so, and it was intended and expected that this would be the case.

or agree that one country will be passive and let the other country fix the price at its volition. In effect, the Bretton Woods agreement solved the problem by making the United States the passive country, letting other countries set their prices but requiring them to support the prices they set. Other countries accepted this because the United States agreed to convert its currency into gold.[1]

This system was bound to break down because it tried to achieve incompatible objectives: freedom of countries to pursue an independent internal monetary policy; fixed exchange rates; and relatively free international movement of goods and capital. The incompatibility of these objectives was brilliantly demonstrated by John Maynard Keynes in one of his earliest and, in my minority opinion, best books, *A Tract on Monetary Reform* (1923). As one of the architects of Bretton Woods, Keynes tried to resolve the incompatibility by providing for flexibility of exchange rates through what he intended to be frequent and fairly easily achieved changes in official parities. In practice, this hope was doomed because maintaining the announced parity became a matter of prestige and political controversy, countries therefore held on to a parity as long as they could, in the process letting minor problems grow into major crises and then making large changes. In practice, the system was a system of rigid parities rather than of rates fixed at any point in time but subject to frequent change.

The only countries that were able for a long period to maintain the fixed exchange rate were those, such as Japan and Germany, which were willing to let internal policy be dominated by the needs of the balance of payments.

This system in effect broke down in March, 1968 when the two-tier system for gold was adopted [see column 8 (September 8, 1969) in this chapter]; but the formal announcement of its death was delayed until August 15, 1971, when President Nixon officially suspended the United States commitment to buy and sell gold at a fixed price from and to foreign official agencies. Since then, the international financial system is in flux. The countries are unwilling to accept a system of freely floating exchange rates of the kind that I have supported for over two decades; yet in practice that is the direction in which they are moving. The floating of the British pound on June 23, 1972 is the latest straw.

The sequence of developments is a beautiful example of how much more potent are basic economic forces than the prejudices of central bankers and government officials. That this is not simply hindsight can be readily demonstrated. In my book *Capitalism and Freedom*, published in 1962, I specified in detail the measures that I believed the United States should take to promote a truly free market in both gold and foreign exchange.

"1 The U.S. should announce that it no longer commits itself to buy or sell gold at any fixed price.

---

[1] One way of looking at this is that gold constituted an additional currency.

"2 Present laws making it illegal for individuals to own gold or to buy or
    sell gold should be repealed. . . .

"3 The present law specifying that the Reserve System must hold gold
    certificates equal to 25 per cent of its liabilities should be repealed.

"4 A major problem in getting rid completely of the gold price-support
    program . . . is the transitional one of what to do with accumulated
    government stocks. . . . [M]y own view is that the government
    should immediately restore a free market by instituting steps 1 and 2,
    and should ultimately dispose of all of its stocks. . . . Hence, I propose
    that the government auction off its gold stocks on the free market over
    a five-year period. . . .

"5 The U.S. should announce also that it will not proclaim any official
    exchange rates between the dollar and other currencies and in addi-
    tion that it will not engage in any speculative or other actions aimed
    at influencing exchange rates. . . .

"6 These measures would conflict with our formal obligation as a
    member of the International Monetary Fund. . . . However, the Fund
    found it possible to reconcile Canada's failure to specify a parity with
    its Articles and to give its approval to a floating rate for Canada.
    There is no reason why it cannot do the same for the U.S.

"7 Other nations might choose to peg their currencies to the dollar. That
    is their business and there is no reason for us to object so long as we
    undertake no obligations to buy or sell their currency at a fixed
    price. . . . " (pp. 69–70)

A decade later, five and one-half of these seven points have been realized,
and one more will almost surely be realized soon.

Points 1 and 5 were realized on August 15, 1971, when President Nixon
closed the gold window. Unfortunately, however, the Fed backslid in July
1972 by selling some German marks.

Points 6 and 7 were realized subsequently.

Point 3 was realized in a series of legislative enactments, the final one in
1968.

Point 4 was half realized when the United States gold stock declined from
roughly $20 billion in 1959 to less than $10 billion today, though this
occurred at a fixed price rather than at an auction price and over 12 years
instead of 5 years.

Point 2 is the only one so far not achieved at all, and I predict that it will
be within the next year or so.

This record does not bespeak my powers of persuasion. Far from it. It
bespeaks rather the strength of the basic economic forces that were embed-
ded both in the measures I specified and in the actual sequence of events.

A DOLLAR IS A DOLLAR
May 15, 1967

A dollar is a dollar is a dollar. But why should it also be exactly 7 English shillings, 1 penny, and 3 farthings; 4 French francs and 94 centimes, and 4 German marks?

The explanation is very different today than it was in an earlier era. In 1913, for example, anyone could take $20.67 to the U.S. Treasury and exchange it for one fine ounce of gold. He could take the ounce of gold to London, go to the Bank of England, and exchange it for 4 pounds, 4 shillings, 11 pence, and 1 farthing; or he could take it to Paris, go to the Bank of France, and exchange it for 107 francs and 10 centimes. As a result, the price of the pound could not vary much from its then official parity of $4.8665 or the franc from its then official parity of $0.1930.

A real gold standard

If the pound became appreciably more expensive than $4.8665, alert U.S. financiers would get pounds, not by buying them on the market, but by exchanging dollars at the U.S. Treasury for gold, shipping the gold to London, and converting it into pounds at the Bank of England. If the pound became appreciably cheaper than $4.8665 (i.e. the dollar became more expensive) alert British financiers would get dollars by reversing the process. In this way, the cost of shipping gold set narrow limits—termed the "gold points"—on the price of the pound sterling.

That was a real gold standard. Gold circulated in the form of coin and gold certificates. Britain and the U.S. in effect had a common currency differing only in the names attached to an ounce of gold. Individuals were free to buy or sell dollars for pounds or pounds for dollars at any price. The price of the one currency in terms of the other stayed within narrow limits for the same reason and in the same way that the price of sugar in New York never deviates much from the price of sugar in Chicago—because if it did deviate, it would pay private traders to ship sugar.

The situation today is very different. The dollar and the pound are no longer names for different amounts of gold. They are names for separate national currencies. There still are official prices of gold. But these official prices serve primarily as a means to calculate the official price of the pound in terms of dollars ($2.80). Holders of paper money cannot automatically exchange it for gold at the official prices—indeed, since 1934, when the official U.S. price was raised to $35 an ounce, it has been illegal for U.S. residents to hold gold, except for numismatic or industrial purposes. Gold is now a commodity whose price is supported by governmental action—like butter. Gold no longer determines the quantity of money.

Pegged exchange rates

The price of the pound sterling is kept at $2.80, not by market forces, but by the British and U.S. governments who peg it at that level by buying and selling dollars and pounds at the official price. They can succeed only by controlling the amount people offer to buy and sell. In Britain, it is illegal for residents to trade pounds for dollars except with the permission of a government official. The U.S. still does not have explicit exchange control, but we have extensive informal controls—ask the businessman who seeks to invest abroad or the banker who seeks to lend abroad.

The pegging of exchange rates is the basic reason for our balance-of-payments problem—just as the pegging of rents is the basic reason for the housing "shortage" in New York City; the pegging of the price of silver for the rapid depletion of our silver reserves; the pegging of the price of butter for the accumulation of stocks of butter.

We should set the dollar free and let its price in terms of other currencies be determined by private dealings. Such a system of floating exchange rates would eliminate the balance-of-payments problem, thereby enabling us to abolish the income equalization tax and informal exhange controls, and to move unilaterally toward freer trade.

Paradoxically, most leaders of the financial community are against this free-market solution. They confuse the present use of gold as window dressing with a real gold standard. Staunch opponents of government price-fixing in other areas, they support it in this one. They need to examine their clichés.

THE KENNEDY ROUND
July 17, 1967

The sweeping reductions in tariffs achieved in the Kennedy round deserve the hearty applause of all those who favor freer trade among nations. But they need more than applause if they are to be effective, and not simply a publicity stunt. They need a reduction in nontariff barriers to trade. The mushroom growth of these barriers in recent years has by now made them a far more serious obstacle than tariffs. They could readily nullify the effect of tariff reductions.

The clearest example of a nontariff barrier is an import quota: a limit on the physical amount of a product that may be imported. We now have outright quotas on items ranging from peanuts to meat. In addition, some foreign countries have put "voluntary" quotas on some goods they export to us. So great has been our fear of competition from tiny Hong Kong, for example, that we have twisted their arm to impose "voluntary" quotas on exports of textile products.

The import quota on crude oil, discussed in this column three weeks ago, is a flagrant example. The domestic price of oil is about $3 a barrel at the wellhead. If oil could be freely imported without a tariff, the domestic price would have to be the same as the world price, after allowing for the cost of shipment. The limitation on imports breaks this link and makes the domestic price higher than the world price—by something like$1 to $1.50 a barrel.

Hidden subsidies

The import quota has the same effect on the domestic price of oil and on the amount of oil imported as a tariff of roughly $1.25 a barrel, or 50 per cent to 100 per cent of the world wholesale price. The actual tariff on crude oil is only 10½ cents a barrel (incidentally, unchanged in the Kennedy round). We have few outright tariffs on any product anything like as steep as the implicit tariff on oil.

An outright tariff of $1.25 a barrel on oil would leave the price to the consumer unchanged, but the government would get the excess over the present tariff. That sum now goes to companies fortunate enough to be granted oil-import permits—and amounts in total to a subsidy of about $400 million a year.

I have seen no compilation of the total subsidy hidden in our collection of quotas and their equivalent. However, the total surely amounts to many times the $400 million subsidy to oil importers.

Quotas are but the leading example of a long list. Minor nuisances include labeling and packaging requirements, standards on food allegedly imposed for health reasons, methods of quoting prices in calculating tariffs, and so on in an infinite variety that no nonspecialist like myself even knows anything about.

Major obstacles include: "Buy America" acts which give a nontariff preference to U.S. bidders on contracts; instructions to the military to buy in the U.S. even at a substantially higher cost; requirements that U.S. for-eign-aid funds be spent in the U.S.; the interest-equalization tax; the so-called voluntary" programs limiting foreign loans by U.S. banks and foreign investments by U.S. enterprises.

In short, we preach free trade and practice restriction.

Tariffs vs. quotas

We and the world would flourish best under complete free trade. However, tariffs are a lesser evil than quotas. At least, the government gets some revenue, and foreign producers have some incentive to offer U.S. consumers better terms. If they can cut their price, they can gain a larger share of the U.S. market. Under a quota, a lower foreign price means simply a wider difference between the domestic and the world price and a larger subsidy to importers. Politically, also, a quota is more difficult to eliminate than a tariff. Both importers and domestic producers lobby in favor of a quota—whereas importers oppose a tariff.

Consumers will derive no benefit from tariff cuts under the Kennedy round that affect products subject to quotas. Such cuts will serve only to raise the hidden subsidy to importers.

The national interest may occasionally justify subsidies to particular industries. When it does, the subsidies should be open and aboveboard, explicitly legislated, and subject to periodic review. Political responsibility is undermined when subsidies are granted in hidden form, and when they are distributed by administrative officials who are not directly responsible to the electorate. That is not the way of a free society, or even of a welfare state. It is the way of the special-interest state.

THE PRICE OF GOLD
January 1, 1968

The gold rush of 1967 has subsided. But the lull is temporary. The hard fact is that the price of gold will not be held at $35 an ounce for many more years. The price of gold will be raised or permitted to rise. The only questions are when and how.

A higher dollar price of gold need not mean a change in exchange rates. If the price of gold in terms of other currencies rose by the same percentage, all exchange rates would remain the same. What will or should happen to the dollar price of gold is a different question from what will or should happen to the price of the dollar in terms of other currencies. This column deals with the first question; a later column will deal with the second.

Gold is cheap

The price of gold was last changed on January 31, 1934, when President Roosevelt set it at $35 an ounce. At the time, that was a very high price, and it attracted a flood of gold to the United States. However, other prices have nearly tripled since then. The same price is therefore now low, and our gold stocks are melting away.

At the present price, private purchase of gold exceeds world production. The price is held down to $35 an ounce only by supplementing current production from existing monetary stocks of gold, notably, of course, the U.S. stock. The situation is precisely what it was for silver before June 1967. The U.S. Treasury was then pegging the price of silver at $1.29 an ounce. Declining silver stocks forced the Treasury to free the price. It is now around $2 an ounce.

[1] For details, see Herbert Woolley, "New Patterns, New Outlook for World Gold," Engineering and Mining Journal, October 1967.

Only two things could prevent a similar outcome for gold: (1) a fall in other prices in the U.S.; (2) a fall in the world demand for gold.

The price of gold was constant at $20.67 an ounce from 1879 to 1933 because the U.S. was then willing to let other prices adjust to the fixed price of gold. We no longer are. We have let other prices get far out of line. No Administration and no Federal Reserve Board will tolerate a major deflation to bring other prices back in line with the price of gold. And they need not do so. We no longer have a real gold standard in which the amount of gold determines the amount of money. Gold has been demoted to a commodity whose price is pegged.

In 1933, Congress made it illegal for U.S. citizens to hold gold. This misguided measure reduced domestic demand. If we could do the same thing internationally, and enforce it, the price of gold might well fall rather than rise. But Congress's writ does not run abroad. A further reduction in the demand for gold requires that either private people or central banks be induced to hold less gold.

Only long years of experience with stable money will wean private individuals from the attachment to gold produced by centuries of experience with monetary instability.

Central banks have in recent years held some paper dollars instead of real gold—but only under great pressure from us. That is why our government is striving to get them to accept a new international money—paper gold instead of real gold. But this effort will not succeed. Despite the widely publicized agreement in principle at Rio, conflicts of interest between countries on details will, in my opinion, prevent the creation of more than a token amount of paper gold.[2]

The likely outcome is that we shall experience a series of successive crises like the 1967 gold rush. If we wish, we can surmount one or several more. But sooner or later, we shall have to throw in the sponge.

Free the price of gold

When that occurs, we could raise the price of gold to a new level, say, $50 an ounce, and try to hold it there. That would be a serious mistake. It would be far better simply to stop buying and selling gold at a fixed price, as we did with silver.

But why wait? We should at once stop pegging the price of gold.[3] We should today as we should have yesterday and a year ago and ten years ago and in 1934—announce that the U.S. will no longer buy or sell gold at any

[2Paper gold in the form of SDR's (see column of September 8, 1969) were subsequently created. As of mid-1972, roughly $10 billion had been created, a sum to be compared with $120 billion in total international reserves. Even this overstates the effective amount of SDR's since the terms of issue in effect immobilize a sizeable fraction of the amount created. Moreover, opposition to further issues has grown so that further creation is highly likely to be at a much slower pace than the initial creation.]

[3This was done in March 1968 when a two-tier system was adopted for the price of gold—an official bookkeeping price and an unofficial free market price. See columns of April 1, 1968 and September 8, 1969 below.]

fixed price[4] (except perhaps for a final sale to meet commitments to foreign central banks). We should simultaneously remove all legal restrictions on transactions by U.S. citizens in gold.[5] We should let the price of gold be a free market price, not a pegged price. That would have no adverse economic effects—domestically or internationally. And it would take back the loaded guns we have handed to foreign holders of dollars—notably to General de Gaulle.

THE PRICE OF THE DOLLAR
January 29, 1968

How low we have fallen! The United States, the land of the free, prohibits its businessmen from investing abroad and requests its citizens not to show their faces or open their pocketbooks in foreign ports. The United States, the wealthiest nation in the world, announces that its foreign policy will no longer be determined by its national interest and its international commitments but by the need to reduce government spending abroad by $500 million.[1]

And for what? Are we so poor that we must forgo profitable opportunities to invest capital abroad? The same President who imposes curbs on foreign investment boasts that our income is at an all-time high. Foreign investment in 1967 was less than 5 per cent of total investment and less than 1 per cent of total income.

Are we wasting so much of our substance on foreign travel that we must be cajoled by our betters to stay home? Total spending on foreign travel in 1967 was less than 1 per cent of total consumer spending.

Are government coffers so empty that reducing expenditures abroad by $500 million justifies shaping our whole foreign policy to that end? The President has not hesitated to recommend total Federal expenditures approaching $200 billion.

An oft-told tale

Why then have we imposed such far-reaching restrictions on our citizenry? To put it bluntly, because a small number of public officials—in the U.S. and abroad—cannot as yet bring themselves to admit their impotence to fix the price of the dollar in terms of other currencies. Like modern King Canutes, they have been commanding the tide not to rise—and apparently are determined to continue until we are engulfed by it.

This is an old story. Let the government seek to peg a price—be it of

[4President Nixon did this on August 15, 1971.]
[5This has not yet occurred though a bill has been introduced into Congress to remove these restrictions.]

[1This paragraph refers to a series of measures announced by President Johnson on New Year's day, 1969, designed to reduce the balance of payments deficit.]

wheat or housing or silver or gold or pounds sterling—and it will be driven, as if by an invisible hand, to impose restrictions on producers and consumers in order to contain a surplus or to ration a shortage. It can do so for a time, but only for a time. The tide is too strong.

"In the meantime," as I testified to Congress nearly five years ago, "we adopt one expedient after another, borrowing here, making swap arrangements there, changing the form of loans to make the figures look good. Entirely aside from the ineffectiveness of most of these measures, they are politically degrading and demeaning. We are a great and wealthy nation. We should be directing our own course, setting an example to the world, living up to our destiny. Instead, we send our officials hat in hand to make the rounds of foreign governments and central banks; we put foreign central banks in a position . . . to exert great influence on our policies; we are driven to niggling negotiations with Hong Kong and with Japan and, for all I know, Monaco, to get them to limit voluntarily their exports. Is this posture suitable for the leader of the free world?"

Set the dollar free

We should instead say to the people of the world: a dollar is a dollar. You may borrow dollars in the U.S. or abroad from anyone who is willing to lend. You may lend dollars in the U.S. or abroad to anyone who is willing to borrow. You may buy dollars from or sell dollars to anyone you wish at any price that is mutually agreeable. The U.S. Government will not interefere in any way. On the contrary, it will dismantle immediately its present restrictions: repeal the interest-equalization tax; dissolve the cartel agreement among banks to restrict foreign lending; remove quotas, "voluntary" or otherwise, on imports; stop resorting to World War I emergency legislation to threaten with prison terms businessmen who invest abroad; refrain from interfering with the right of its citizens to travel when and where they will.

If a foreign country wishes to peg the price of its currency in terms of the dollar, we should not interfere. It can succeed only by voluntarily holding dollars, or adjusting its internal monetary policy to ours or engaging in exchange control. In no case can it force us to impose restrictions on the use of dollars.

If we set the dollar free, and at the same time followed responsible fiscal and monetary policies, many another country would be well advised to link its currency with ours. That would promote not only our domestic objectives but also a healthy development of international trade. That is the right way to make the dollar a truly international currency—not behaving like a banana republic.

THE GOLD REQUIREMENT
February 19, 1968

Present law limits the dollar amount of Federal Reserve Notes that may be outstanding to four times the value of the gold in the Treasury. A bill to repeal this requirement, requested by President Johnson, has been favorably reported by committees in both the House and the Senate and will no doubt be enacted soon.

President Johnson gave two reasons for repeal: first, that making the entire gold stock available to meet foreign demands would enhance our ability to keep the price of gold at $35 an ounce and, second, that, by increasing confidence in the dollar, it would also contribute to reducing the balance-of-payments deficit.

These are bad reasons for a good measure.

Removing the gold requirement will not enable us to keep the price of gold at $35 an ounce. At most, it will encourage us to prolong the misery and to sell a larger fraction of our gold stock at a low price before we give up the futile attempt.

Removing the gold requirement will not contribute to reducing the balance-of-payments deficit. At most, it will encourage us to meet a larger fraction of the deficit by shipping gold and to delay effective measures.

Repealing the gold requirement is desirable for a very different reason: to make the law correspond to present reality.

An anachronistic survival

The gold requirement is an anachronistic survival of an earlier era. From 1879 to 1933, gold circulated as coin, and paper money was redeemable in gold. This made for a close link between money and gold. During those 54 years, the amount of money was never more than twelve times that of gold, never less than five times.

Withdrawal of gold from circulation and prohibition of the private ownership of gold in 1933 combined with developments in the rest of the world to convert gold from the kingpin of the monetary system into a commodity whose price is pegged. After President Roosevelt raised the official price of gold from $20.67 to $35 an ounce in 1934, our gold stocks grew explosively until the amount of money equaled only two and a half times the amount of gold. Then, as other prices rose, $35 an ounce became cheap and our gold stocks declined. However, the quantity of money continued to rise until it is now 30 times the amount of gold.

The link between gold and the quantity of money has become a rubber band. A real gold standard has become a pseudo gold standard.

Whether desirable or not, it is impossible to restore now the close link that prevailed before 1933. The legal requirement for a gold cover is therefore a snare and a delusion. It professes to restrain the monetary authority. It does not do so. It serves rather to conceal the true situation.

Removal of the gold requirement will make it crystal clear that there is no effective restraint on the powers of the men in charge of our monetary system. These men are and have been able and disinterested public servants. Yet it is undesirable in a democracy that they should have enormous power, with only the vaguest mandate about how to use that power, and with no effective legislative control over the exercise of the power.

An effective restraint

Removal of the gold requirement offers an occasion for Congress to impose an effective restraint to replace the present ineffective gold cover. Congress could best do so by instructing the Fed to produce a steady rate of growth in a specified monetary total—say, between 3 and 5 per cent a year in a total defined as currency plus all adjusted deposits of commercial banks, time and demand.

If the present gold crisis leads Congress to enact such a rule, it will have proved a blessing in disguise. Monetary policy is not a panacea for all our ills. But steady and moderate monetary growth would make a major contribution to economic stability and to the avoidance of both inflation and deflation. It would provide a monetary climate favorable to the effective operation of those basic forces of enterprise, ingenuity, invention, hard work and thrift that are the true springs of economic growth.

A legislated rule would also restore power to Congress where it belongs. It would eliminate the present grant of large, unspecified, uncontrollable power to men not responsible to the electorate. However able, however public-interested are the men who hold such power, their possession of it is abhorrent to the fundamental values of a democratic society whose ideal is rule by law, not by men.

GOLDEN CLICHÉS
April 1, 1968

Like the rest of you, I have been reading reams of newspaper stories on gold. Unlike most of you, I specialize professionally in money and I have been impressed—and depressed—by the appeal to ritual incantations to conceal the emptiness of thought. Let me cite some examples.

1 *"Why does the U.S. keep losing gold?"*
The U.S. hasn't lost gold. Extremely careful track is kept of the gold at Fort Knox and in the sub-basement of the New York Federal Reserve Bank. I doubt that a single ounce of gold has been lost. Stolen, perhaps. But lost, no. What the U.S. did was to sell gold. We have sold a lot of it. We may have sold it at too low a price but that means giving part of it away, not losing it.

2 *"The $35 price of gold is the keystone of international finance."*
Now just what does that mean? That international finance would come
tumbling down if the price were $50 or $20.67 (as it was for 54 years from
1879 to 1933)? The $35 price lasted only 34 years. International finance
has been around for thousands of years. This is the kind of phrase which
enables those who have nothing to say to say nothing—impressively.

3 *"The gold-buying spree threatens the very existence of the international
money system."*
What would a world look like in which no international money system
existed? Would all international trade be barter? The American tourist
swapping bourbon he toted from home for a ticket to the Folies-Bergère?
The only thing that was ever threatened by the gold-buying spree was a loss
of face by those governmental officials who proclaimed that they could keep
the price of gold fixed while letting all other prices rise.

4 Removal of the gold-cover requirement *"freed the nation's entire gold
stock of $11.4 billion to back the dollar overseas."*
Nonsense. Removing the gold-cover requirement simply made it legal to sell
more gold abroad in an attempt, that sooner or later had to prove vain, to
keep the price of gold abroad pegged at $35 an ounce. For the purpose of
"backing the dollar overseas," in the sense of enabling people who wish to
dispose of dollars to do so, selling them copper or silver or the Congressional
Record would do just as well.

5 *"The dollar is in danger."*
Of what? My dollar is in danger of being spent before I know it. What about
yours? Were the dollars owned by foreigners in some other kind of danger?
The answer presumably is that they were in danger of not continuing to be
able to command 1/35th of an ounce of gold. Why should that have been of
great concern to us—except as we made rash promises that came home to
roost? Why should it produce frantic moves by high government officials?
International conferences of central bankers?

6 *"The dollar is weak."*
A minor variant of the preceding, generally used when the reference is to the
price of the dollar in terms of a foreign currency. Again, why is it vital to us
whether the price of the dollar is 4 marks even or 3 marks and 90 pfennigs?
As for gold, only because we have been so unwise as to commit ourselves to
pegging exchange rates.

7 But, says the pundit, *"fixed exchange rates are the cornerstone of the
postwar liberalization of multilateral trade on a nondiscriminatory basis."*
Say that again. Our interest-equalization tax, oil-import quotas, voluntary
credit restraint, restriction of foreign investment are signs of "liberalization"? On a "nondiscriminatory basis"? Congress is now considering tourist
taxes, a tax on imports, and a subsidy to exports in order to shore up the fixed

exchange-rate system—to promote liberalization of trade? I've heard that before. "It was necessary to destroy the city to save it."

The gold rush was a blessing. It forced us to do what we should have done of our own volition long since: let the price of gold be set in the free market. Hopefully, the continuation of an "official" market at $35 an ounce is a pure face-saving gesture that will involve few or no transactions. The plain fact is that few things are currently less important to the ordinary citizen of the U.S. than whether the price of gold is $20 an ounce, $35 an ounce or $70 an ounce.

But a free market in gold alone will not resolve our balance-of-payments problem. For that, it is necessary to free also the market for foreign exchange. The U.S. should renounce any commitment to peg exchange rates. We could then eliminate at once the growing restraints that are being imposed on what U.S. citizens can do with their dollars. Why should you be free to make any deal you want with a used-car salesman—but not with a Frenchman offering francs?

EXCHANGE CONTROLS
March 24, 1969

In the course of their attempt to stem the outflow of gold, Presidents Kennedy and Johnson imposed numerous controls on foreign payments. The three key items were:

1 The interest-equalization tax on the purchase of foreign securities by U.S. residents. Enacted in 1964 at a rate of 15 per cent as a "temporary" measure, this tax has been renewed several times and the rate is now 18¾ per cent.

2 "Voluntary" restriction of foreign loans by banks begun in 1965 and administered by the Federal Reserve System. It took a special act of Congress to exempt the agreement among banks from the antitrust laws.

3 Restriction of foreign investment by U.S. corporations. This "voluntary" program, also begun in 1965, was made compulsory by President Johnson on January 1, 1968. It is administered by the Department of Commerce.

Candidate Nixon strongly criticized these controls as inconsistent with a free society and promised to end them as soon as possible.

Recent Congressional testimony indicates that the Administration plans to honor this campaign promise by relaxing the controls gradually over a period of years. Commerce Secretary Stans spoke of "the first step toward some type of relaxation" of the control over business investment in "the next 30 to 60 days." Abolition, he said, should be discussed "in terms of years."

Treasury Under Secretary Volcker said that the Treasury would "like" to reduce, "if possible," the interest-equalization tax.

Abolition, not relaxation

So timid a policy is a serious mistake. These controls should be ended at one fell swoop. And they should be ended at once. We are not likely to have a better opportunity.

Tapering the controls off gradually is like cutting a dog's tail off by inches. Each time a relaxation is suggested, civil servants administering the controls will find reason to caution delay, or a milder relaxation. Abolition rather than relaxation of the controls would end such bureaucratic obstruction. It would also end the ever-present temptation to turn to controls when difficulties arise rather than to adopt more fundamental remedies.

Experience teaches that the longer controls stay in effect, the stronger are the vested interests that develop to keep them. The banks that have large loan quotas will, if they do not already, recognize that the credit restriction is a cartel device that enables them to keep this profitable business to themselves. Corporations that have large allocations of investment, or that have found ways to get around the controls, will come to look at the investment controls as highly desirable.

Now, not later

The time to end the controls is now because we are in an extraordinarily favorable position to do so. Capital is currently flowing into, not out of, the country. Commercial banks are borrowing abroad, not expanding their foreign loans. Their foreign loans are well under the ceiling permitted by current controls. The boom in the U.S. plus difficulties abroad have reduced the attractiveness of foreign investment. As a result, it is doubtful that any of the three controls has a real bite at the present time. Eliminating them now would simply get rid of unnecessary nuisances.

Compulsory restriction of foreign investment has in any event almost surely hurt rather than helped our balance of payments—certainly for the long run and possibly even for the short run. Its imposition must have spurred every corporation with extensive interests abroad to accumulate extra foreign balances in order to be prepared for a further tightening of the control screws. Abolition would reverse this tendency; relaxation would not. More fundamentally, foreign investment is accompanied by exports and produces a return stream of income later.

Finally, and most important of all, the U.S. dollar is in a very strong position. A run on our gold by private sources is impossible, thanks to the decision last March to let the London price of gold be a free-market price. A run on our gold by foreign central banks is technically possible but politically almost inconceivable. The strong flow of capital into the United States has at least temporarily eliminated the balance-of-payments deficit. If the Administration succeeds in slowing down inflation, the trade balance should improve rapidly to offset any future slackening in the capital inflow.

Here is also one bold campaign promise that can and should be honored by bold action.

THE OBSOLETE SDR'S
September 8, 1969

At its meeting this month, the International Monetary Fund is expected to approve the creation of $9.5 billion of Special Drawing Rights—so-called "paper gold"—over an initial three-year period. This is the sum that the ten principal member countries agreed this summer to sponsor. This agreement has been hailed in the press as a "major diplomatic success" for the U.S. Perhaps it is, but if so, the fewer such successes the better. Whatever it may be diplomatically, the agreement is an economic mistake for the world as a whole and the U.S. in particular.

Circumstances alter cases

There was a case for the SDR's when they were first proposed. But in the years of negotiation that preceded the recent agreement, conditions have changed. Today they will, I believe, do more harm than good. They have become obsolete even before the first ones are issued. Yet they will nonetheless be issued. The cumbrous process of international diplomacy is not to be diverted by the mere fact that it is going in the wrong direction!

The key change is the collapse of the "gold pool" in March 1968 and the adoption of the "two-tier" system. Under this system, the price of gold is free to find its own level in private markets (this is one tier) but is fixed at $35 an ounce for transactions among central banks (this is the second tier). In addition, the central banks have agreed not to buy or sell gold in the free market.

Before this agreement, the members of the "gold pool" had been pegging the price in private markets at $35 an ounce by standing ready to buy at that price any amount offered and by furnishing gold from their own reserves in agreed proportions whenever the net private demand exceeded the supply available from current gold production. Given the enormous stocks of gold held by central banks (about half of the world's estimated stock of gold), they could have maintained the market price at $35 an ounce for many years if they had been willing to replace the gold in their reserves by dollars or other currencies.

However, they were not willing to do so (which is why the gold pool ultimately collapsed). That was the origin of the idea of creating a new asset, which was to be preferable to any one nation's currency because it was to be the obligation of several nations jointly. It was hoped that the central banks would be willing to substitute this new asset for gold. Hence the designation "paper gold."

The great hopes placed in the SDR's might have been disappointed in any event. But there was at least some possibility that central banks would hold SDR's *instead of gold*. This possibility disappeared as soon as the two-tier system was established. Central banks now furnish no gold to the market. They simply exchange gold among themselves—and, indeed, they are doing very little even of that.

It follows that SDR's will now be held by central banks not instead of gold but instead of other reserve assets. What are these other reserve assets? Mainly dollars. Though no one likes to say so, the fact is that the world is on a dollar standard, the second tier serving only as a cloak to keep this politically unpalatable fact from being patently obvious.

Diplomatic masochism

The SDR's will therefore now be held by central banks *instead of dollars*. Much has been made of the fact that for every billion dollars' worth of SDR's issued, the U.S. will receive roughly a quarter of a billion. That is true. But it is also true that for every billion dollars issued, central banks in other countries will want to hold $750 million fewer dollars. The U.S. has been persuading other countries to create a substitute for the dollar as a reserve currency: diplomatic masochism is a generous description.

But what of the world as a whole? May not our foolishness benefit other countries? Not at all. What the international financial system needs is not a greater capacity to postpone adjustment—which is the most that SDR's or other reserves can provide—but a better adjustment mechanism. In today's conditions, that mechanism can only be greater flexibility of exchange rates. Such flexibility would make additional reserves unnecessary. In its absence, the creation of SDR's will only make for still larger financial crises.

I apologize to the reader for presenting my opinions so dogmatically. Unfortunately, these are highly complex matters that require volumes not columns for a full analysis. Yet it seems desirable for you to know that uniformity of press reports conceals diversity of expert opinion.

FREE TRADE
August 17, 1970

We have heard much these past few years about using the government to protect the consumer. A far more urgent problem is to protect the consumer from the government.

The immediate occasion for these remarks is the bill that is being considered by the House Ways and Means Committee to impose import quotas on textiles, shoes and other products. Such a bill will, like present tariffs, raise prices to customers and waste our resources. Unlike present tariffs, it will not even yield any revenue to the government. The higher prices will all go to the producers—mostly simply to pay for higher costs. The consumer will be forced to spend several extra dollars to subsidize the producers by one dollar. A straight handout would be far cheaper.

Tit for tat

The proponents of quotas say, "Free trade is fine in theory but it must be reciprocal. We cannot open our markets to foreign products if foreigners close their markets to us." Japan, they argue, to use their favorite whipping boy, "keeps her vast internal market for the private domain of Japanese industry but then pushes her products into the U.S. market and complains when we try to prevent this unfair tactic."

The argument sounds reasonable. It is, in fact, utter nonsense. Exports are the cost of trade, imports the return from trade, not the other way around.

Suppose Japan were incredibly successful in her alleged attempt to restrict imports into Japan, managing to dispense with them entirely. Suppose that Japan were incredibly successful in her alleged attempts to push exports to the U.S., managing to sell us large quantities of assorted goods. What would Japan do with the dollars she received for her exports? Take crisp greenbacks back to Tokyo to stash in the vaults of the Bank of Japan? Let deposits at U.S. banks pile up? Jolly for us. Can you think of a better deal than our getting fine textiles, shiny cars and sophisticated TV sets for a bale of green printed paper? Or for some entries on the books of banks? If the Japanese would only be willing to keep on doing that, we can provide all the green paper they will take.

The Japanese might accumulate, as they have been doing, a moderate sum in greenbacks or dollar deposits or dollar securities as a reserve for possible future needs. But they are too smart to do so indefinitely. Very soon Japan would take steps either to reduce exports or to use the dollars to buy imports (by changes in trade restrictions, or in the internal price level, or in the exchange rate between the yen and the dollar). We would again be under the unfortunate necessity of having to pay in real goods for real goods.

But, you may say, what if the Japanese asked for gold? Like greenbacks, gold would be useful to them only as a reserve for future purchases. They would derive no current services from the gold any more than we do from the gold buried at Fort Knox. I for one would rather have the useful goods than the idle gold. But if the U.S. authorities thought differently, they could readily refuse to sell the gold for the dollars at a fixed price of $35 an ounce. In that case, Japan would again have only the alternatives of greenbacks, deposits, dollar securities—or buying U.S.-produced goods.

Hurt for hurt

Japan does impose numerous restrictions on trade—though in recent years she has been reducing them. Those trade restrictions hurt Japan and they hurt us—by denying them and us mutually profitable trade. In Japan no less than in the U.S., concentrated producers exert a greater influence on government than widely diffused consumers and are able to persuade the government to fleece the consumer for the benefit of the producers.

However, we only increase the hurt to us—and also to them—by imposing additional restrictions in our turn. The wise course for us is precisely the opposite—to move unilaterally toward free trade. If they still choose to impose restrictions, that is too bad but at least we have not added insult to injury.

This is clearly the right course of action on economic grounds. But it is also the only course of action that is in keeping with our political position in the world. We are a great nation, the leader of the free world. Yet we squander our political power to appease the textile industry in the Carolinas! We should instead be setting a standard for the world by practicing the freedom of competition, of trade and of enterprise that we preach.

SET THE DOLLAR FREE
October 19, 1970

In his latest column in this space, on "International Finance" (NEWS-WEEK, October 5), Paul Samuelson recommended that we "should stop following uneconomic policies . . . whose only rationalization is to defend a parity of the dollar that is indefensible, and which is in any case not worth defending." I heartily agree.

An overvalued dollar?

Professor Samuelson believes that the dollar is overvalued, but that the overvaluation is concealed by the various expedients that we have adopted to improve our balance of payments. He may be right. However, the major effect of the expedients has been to induce ingenious operators in international finance to find ways to get around the governmental controls. Such evasions, however effective, are generally costly. As a result, the expedients may well be counterproductive. That is why I am not persuaded that the dollar is overvalued.

But any disagreement on this score is of no importance because we both agree that the right way to determine whether the dollar is overvalued is by the test of the market. We would have such a test if, in Professor Samuelson's words, "we (1) stopped tying foreign aid and let those funds be spent anywhere, (2) eliminated mandatory capital controls on corporations and banks, (3) let the interest equalization tax lapse, (4) revalidated the military dollar by discontinuing the practice of buying goods at home even when they cost 50 per cent more than abroad"; and then "let supply and demand determine the parity of the dollar relative to other currencies."

These restrictive measures were mostly introduced during the Kennedy and Johnson Administrations. They were entirely consistent with the propensity of those administrations to enlarge the role of the government, and to interfere more and more with the freedom of individuals to use their resources at home and abroad in accordance with their own values.

The present Administration professes a very different philosophy. It is dedicated to reducing the power of the state, to giving the individual greater control over his own destiny. It has made a start toward dismantling the interferences with international payments that it inherited. President Nixon has recommended elimination of the tying of foreign aid. Capital controls on corporations and on banks and the interest equalization tax have all been reduced. Yet it is a sign of the extraordinary force of inertia, of the tyranny of the status quo, that these interferences with individual freedom— interferences that go against the whole of the American tradition as well as the philosophy proclaimed by the Republican Party—have not been completely swept away. It is past time that they were.

As I wrote in this space more than two and a half years ago, in commenting on President Johnson's imposition of mandatory controls on foreign investment (NEWSWEEK, January 29, 1968), "How low we have fallen. The United States, the land of the free, prohibits its businessmen from investing abroad and requests its citizens not to show their faces or open their pocketbooks in foreign ports . . . We should instead say to the people of the world. a dollar is a dollar. You may borrow dollars in the U.S. or abroad from anyone who is willing to lend. You may lend dollars in the U.S. or abroad to anyone who is willing to borrow. You may buy dollars from or sell dollars to anyone you wish at any price that is mutually agreeable. The U.S. Government will not interfere in any way. On the contrary, it will dismantle immediately its present restrictions."

Now is the time to act

Nothing has happened in the past two and half years to change my opinion. On the contrary. The gold crisis that led to the adoption of the two-tier system in early 1968, the crises that preceded the devaluation of the franc and the pound sterling and the appreciation of the German mark, have all underlined the defectiveness of an international monetary system that rests on rigid exchange rates subject to change from time to time and buttressed by open or concealed exchange controls. At the moment, there is no crisis. Now, when it is not raining, is the time to fix the roof.

The first step is to end our exchange controls and set the dollar free. Whether that would also mean a free market exchange rate between the dollar and other currencies would be up to other countries. If they chose to continue to peg their currencies to the dollar, they could do so. But nothing they do can force *us* to impose restrictions on what anyone may do with his dollars.

THE MARK CRISIS
May 24, 1971

Few things are so puzzling to the ordinary person as an international currency crisis. Herewith a hypothetical dialogue between an innocent reader **(R)** and myself **(F)**.

R Why was there a dollar crisis?

F There wasn't a dollar crisis. There was a mark crisis. A widespread belief developed that the price of the mark was likely to rise from the 27.3 cents at which the West German Government had been pegging it. Hence, many people wanted to buy marks. Since the dollar is the international currency, marks were purchased with dollars, just as a widespread belief that the price of silver was going to rise would lead people to buy silver with dollars.

R Isn't this a quibble? A distinction without a difference?

F Not at all. A dollar crisis would mean a widespread desire by holders of dollars to reduce their dollar balances. That would lead to purchases of all currencies—not just the mark and currencies closely linked to the mark. In fact, there was no great rush into French francs, British pounds, Canadian dollars, or even Japanese yen, despite the fact that the yen, like the mark, is widely regarded as undervalued at existing exchange rates. The selective character of the money flows confirms that this episode was a mark, not a dollar, crisis.

R Why was it widely believed that the mark would rise in price?

F Because West Germany had been selling or borrowing abroad more than it was buying and investing abroad. Hence, it was accumulating dollars.

R But why should Germany object to accumulating dollars? Isn't that a good position to be in?

F Not at all. It means that Germany is shipping abroad more than it is receiving from abroad. It means that people are earning incomes without having goods to buy. That part of their incomes must be immobilized—by taxes, by government borrowing, or by inflation.

R How would a higher price for the German mark affect the situation?

F If a mark costs 30 cents, say, rather than 27.3 cents, then German goods, priced in marks, would be more expensive in terms of dollars, which would reduce exports from Germany. Foreign goods, priced in dollars, would be cheaper to Germans because they could get more dollars for a given number of marks. Germany would export less and import more.

R Why then was there opposition in Germany to a higher price of the mark?

F Because the Germans, like most of us, would like to have their cake and eat it too. Exporters object to anything that would reduce exports; domestic producers object to competition from imports; the consumers who would benefit are, as in most countries, not aware of their stake. Put differently, some Germans would like to export more, other Germans would like to import less, yet both groups would like to avoid the accumulation of dollars. But Germany cannot suspend the laws of arithmetic.

R How does all this explain the sudden massive flood of funds? It is reported that purchases of marks totaled over $2 billion in just two days.

F The system under which Germany was operating, of exchange rates that are temporarily pegged by the government but are subject to change from time to time, is a wide-open invitation to massive speculation whenever a change in the exchange rate seems likely. There never was any doubt that, if the price of the German mark changed at all, it would rise. Yet, until the German central bank stopped selling them, marks were for sale at a fixed price. That gave speculators a free ride. At worst, if the mark was not revalued, they lost commissions on the purchase and sale of marks. At best, they made a handsome profit.

R Was the German central bank forced to suspend the sale of marks?

F No. As a technical matter, it could have sold an indefinite amount since it prints them.

R But wouldn't it have been inviting open inflation if it had printed all the marks that the speculators wanted to buy?

F Not at all. The speculators wanted marks to hold for future resale, not to spend in Germany. That is the key difference between the speculative flow of dollars and the accumulation of dollars in the ordinary course of trade.

R Why then did the German central bank suspend the sale of marks?

F The only answer that makes sense is that the German authorities were in fact contemplating a rise in the price of the mark, and they did not want to have to buy back the marks they printed at a price higher than the price at which they sold them.

R Is there an alternative that would avoid massive speculative swings?

F A free-market exchange rate—the system Canada returned to in 1970. Under such a system, if there is a belief that the price will rise, and speculators start buying Canadian dollars, the price rises at once, which discourages speculation because there is no longer a one-way option.

When the German central bank stopped selling marks, that did not mean that you could not buy marks, but only that you could no longer buy them from the central bank *at a fixed price*. On Monday, May 10, Germany explicitly adopted a floating exchange rate.

R Is that bad?

F I believe that it is good. It provides an effective automatic mechanism that will eliminate crises—provided the German central bank doesn't try to manipulate the rate. I have myself been in favor of floating exchange rates for more than twenty years. Incidentally, an article that I wrote at that time stating the case for floating rates was a by-product of a study of the problems facing Germany and other continental countries under the so-called Coal and Steel Community—a precursor to the Common Market.

R If the price of the mark rises, isn't that equivalent to a devaluation of the U.S. dollar?

F Vis-à-vis the mark, yes. At the same time, the dollar was not devalued vis-à-vis the French franc, British pound, etc. With floating exchange rates, the U.S. dollar would appreciate every day vis-à-vis some currencies, depreciate vis-à-vis other currencies.

R What should the U.S. have done to avert or ease the crisis?

F Nothing. For domestic reasons we should continue a monetary policy directed at slowing down inflation while at the same time encouraging moderate expansion. That is also the best policy for the world. The dollar has become *the* international currency. The world, like the U.S., will be served best by a currency that remains stable in value.

R In sum, has the crisis seriously impaired the world monetary system?

F On the contrary, it has strengthened it. A system of fixed exchange rates subject to change from time to time is not a viable system. The sooner it is replaced by floating exchange rates, the better.

R Can I now consider myself a fully qualified expert on international monetary arrangements?

F Afraid not. No area in economics is so complex and full of pitfalls. Despite the length of this column, I have not even mentioned interest arbitrage, futures markets, official price of gold, special drawing rights, IMF, exchange controls or Eurodollars.

GOLD
August 16, 1971

The West Coast Commodity Exchange recently initiated public trading in gold futures. The Exchange thought it had found a loophole in the Treasury Regulations issued under the Gold Reserve Act of 1934, which prohibits U.S. residents from owning, buying or selling gold except for industrial and numismatic purposes. The Treasury objected and after a few days the Exchange suspended trading. The matter will now be decided in the courts.

There never was, and there is not now, any valid reason to prohibit individuals from owning, buying or selling gold. Individuals should have the same right to trade in gold as they have to trade in silver, copper, aluminum or other commodities.

Misguided legislation

It is widely believed that the prohibition had a valid monetary justification when it was first imposed. That is false. When President Roosevelt severed the link between the dollar and gold on March 6, 1933, the U.S. gold stock was higher relative to the total quantity of money than at any time since the Federal Reserve System was established in 1914. There was no major run on gold in 1933, separate from the run on banks which led holders of deposits to try to convert them into currency, including gold coin and gold certificates. FDR severed the link between the dollar and gold and then deliberately raised the price of gold—first in 1933 by manipulating the market and then in early 1934 by fixing the price at $35 an ounce under the Gold Reserve Act of 1934—in order to devalue the dollar relative to other currencies, and thereby raise the dollar prices of farm products and other internationally traded goods. He did not raise the price to protect a dwindling official stock of gold or in order to permit monetary expansion. The rise in the price of gold produced a flood of gold into the U.S. The U.S. gold stock more than tripled from 1934 to 1940.

Why then did President Roosevelt forbid the private ownership of gold and require all holders of gold to deliver their holdings to the government? This "nationalization" of gold was for one purpose and one purpose only: to keep private individuals from profiting by the rise in the dollar price of gold that the government deliberately engineered. Private holders of gold were required to turn their gold over to the U.S. Treasury at $20.67 an ounce when the market price was well above this sum.

This was an act of expropriation of private property in no way different in principle from Castro's nationalization of U.S.-owned factories and other properties without compensation or from Allende's nationalization of U.S.-owned copper mines in Chile at a price well below market value. As a nation, we do not have a leg to stand on when we object to these acts of expropriation. We did precisely the same thing to residents of the U.S.

Of course, holders of gold resisted the expropriation. Those who held gold certificates were helpless, since the Treasury would no longer honor them. But those who held coin were in a different position. Of the gold coin estimated to be held by the public in February 1933 ($571 million), only half was ever turned in—and much of this was probably turned in by commercial banks whose holdings were a matter of official record.[1]

---

[1]To maintain the fiction that the law had been obeyed, the official statistics were "revised" to exclude the $287 million not turned in, on the ground that this amount must have been lost, destroyed, exported without record or held in numismatic collections. In its official statistics, the Federal Reserve System went so far as to subtract this amount from its estimates of the quantity of money all the way back to 1914. This revision cannot be justified. It can be demonstrated conclusively that the maximum error on this score was trivial. Accordingly, in estimates of the U.S. money stock made by Anna J. Schwartz and myself, we have eliminated the spurious revision.

End the prohibition

Whatever arguments there might once have been for prohibiting the private ownership of gold, there are none today. The reduction in the monetary role of gold that President Roosevelt began has now been completed. Gold-reserve requirements for Federal Reserve notes and deposits have been abolished. The attempt to maintain the world market price of gold at $35 an ounce has been abandoned. There is a free market in London on which the price is currently more than $40 an ounce. The official price is wholly symbolic, and so is the monetary role of gold.

Congressman Philip Crane has introduced a bill repealing the prohibition on the ownership, purchase, or sale of gold by private individuals. That bill should be passed promptly. Let us end once and for all an utterly unnecessary and shameful, if niggling, restriction on individual freedom.

KEEP THE DOLLAR FREE
December 20, 1971

Rumor hath it that the U.S. is on the verge of agreeing to a rise in the official dollar price of gold (or of SDR's) as part of an international agreement to establish a new structure of fixed exchange rates. If this rumor proves correct, we shall have squandered a great opportunity.[1] The actions of August 15 set the dollar free—from gold and from other currencies. We should keep the dollar free—from gold and from other currencies.

The price of gold

So long as the U.S. neither buys nor sells gold, a change in the official price of gold (or SDR's) is a purely bookkeeping change that need have no technical effects whatsoever. What conceivable difference can it make to the U.S., or to other countries, if we don't sell gold to foreign governments at $35 an ounce or if we don't sell gold to them at $38 an ounce? Yet other countries want us to take this step. It looks as if we can make them happy at no cost to us. As the Morgan Guaranty Survey recently put it: "One can perhaps marvel that other countries would place so much importance on what is really a token action on the part of the U.S. but the fact is that they do. And if that's what it takes to break the international stalemate . . . it seems extremely questionable for the U.S. to hold back."

The fallacy in this argument is that it treats foreign central bankers as utter fools, which they clearly are not. If raising the official price of gold is simply "a token action," why do they "place so much importance" on it? The

[1] It did prove correct. The United States rounded the official price to $38 an ounce in legislation enacted early in 1972.

answer, I submit, is that *in a longer-run context,* it is very far indeed from a token act.

Over the past decade, other countries—France and Germany in particular—have exerted an influence on us out of all proportion to their true political and economic strength because of our unwise commitment to convert dollars into gold at $35 an ounce. By undervaluing the franc, de Gaulle accumulated dollars that he could threaten to present to us for gold; by undervaluing the mark, Germany did the same thing, though without the public gestures that de Gaulle gloried in. The demeaning result, as I put it in Congressional testimony as early as 1963, was that we "send our officials hat in hand to make the rounds of foreign governments and central banks; we put central banks in a position to determine whether or not we can meet our obligations and thus enable them to exert a great influence on our policies."

Foreign central banks and governments naturally regret our ending a commitment that gave them so much power. They are desperately anxious to induce us to undertake a new commitment—be it to convert dollars into gold or into SDR's or into some other international asset. They recognize that they cannot do so at once. But if they get us to take the first step—to proclaim publicly that the dollar does have a fixed relation to gold that is only temporarily suspended—they will be well on the road to persuading us once again to fasten a rope around our neck. That—and not stupidity, or ignorance, or irrationality—is why they set such a high value on our changing the official price of gold.

Fixed exchange rates

What do they have to offer us in return? Not a single thing in the monetary area. The President's dramatic actions of August 15 broke an ice jam and jarred exchange rates loose. It is not in our interest—or in the world's interest—to have them fixed again. That will simply once again set the stage for monetary instability, balance-of-payments crises, and exchange controls. We cannot, on our own, establish a flexible exchange rate between the dollar and any other currency. It takes two to make that bargain. But so long as we do not commit ourselves to converting the dollar into any other currency or asset at a fixed rate, we have done our part. If other countries wish to avoid surpluses, they can let the market set exchange rates that will balance payments. In that case, we shall not have a deficit. If other countries choose to peg their currencies to the dollar, they must bear the consequences.

Public pressure at home and abroad to re-establish a system of fixed exchange rates largely reflects the fear that flexible exchange rates will mean unstable exchange rates that will hamper foreign trade. These fears are not justified. The postwar period demonstrated that supposedly fixed exchange rates are unstable exchange rates. When they change, they change by a lot. Flexible exchange rates change frequently but by much less. Gradual changes produce gradual adjustments that prevent big problems from arising. In practice, flexible exchange rates are more stable, and more favorable to the healthy and vigorous expansion of foreign trade and investment, than temporarily rigid rates subject to large changes from time to time. The past three months is too short a time to demonstrate the full effects of a system of flexible rates but surely it is long enough to discredit the prophets of doom.

Trade policy

Monetary neutrality would liberate trade policy from balance-of-payments problems. Trade policy could and should be directed at promoting the freer movement of goods, services and capital. The current emphasis on stimulating exports is misguided. The *imports* we get from other countries are the gain to us from foreign trade. Exports are the price we pay. The less we must export to acquire imports the better off we are. Producing exports simply to give them away is a make-work project strictly on a par with hiring people to dig holes.

The 10 per cent surtax succeeded beyond expectation in shaking exchange rates loose. Once it did that, it should have been abolished promptly. Its continuation has been fostering the new wave of mercantilism that is sweeping the U.S. and the rest of the world. What does it profit us to hurt ourselves simply in order to hurt other countries as well? We are a great nation and should act like one. We should move on our own to eliminate exchange controls and barriers to the movement of goods and capital. A bold and farsighted U.S. example is likely to produce a healthier response from other countries than threats of retaliation.

At home, the dollar is a dollar is a dollar. The U.S. Government makes no commitments to its own citizen to exchange dollars for anything else at a fixed rate. He cannot turn them in for SDR's or any other funny money, let alone for gold or silver. President Nixon's action on August 15 put citizens and governments of other countries precisely on a par with U.S. citizens. That is as it should be. However, if the rumored agreement becomes fact, our government will once again be making commitments to foreign countries that it is unwilling to make to its own citizens. Secretary Connally and President Nixon will have snatched defeat from the jaws of victory.

Chapter Six
A VOLUNTEER ARMY

It would be nice to record that this chapter has only historical interest, that the move from conscription to an all-volunteer armed force, currently scheduled to be completed on June 30, 1973, can be regarded as a *fait accompli*. Unfortunately, that would be premature. I believe that the draft will end on June 30, 1973, both because President Nixon and Secretary Laird have committed themselves to that outcome and also because Congress will be unwilling to enact a further continuation of conscription. But sad experience has taught me that there is many a slip between predictions and their realization. The clear departure from the will of both houses of Congress described in the final column in this chapter ("The Draft Uncompromise") was not prevented, despite the valiant efforts of Senator Allott and some of his colleagues. The success of the armed forces operating through the Armed Services Committees in seriously weakening the effectiveness of the pay rise as a step toward an all-volunteer force is evidence both of their legislative power and of their reservations about the desirability of ending conscription.

Despite these doubts, the record does give real ground for optimism. We have come a long way from the period when the draft was routinely and with hardly a murmur of opposition renewed for four years at a clip (always in odd-numbered years when there were neither congressional nor presidential elections). There is widespread, informed, and vigorous opposition to the draft, and despite all their hesitancy, the armed forces are making a determined and intelligent effort to implement a volunteer force.

Though this issue is outside my major field of professional interest, it happens to be one in which I have been passionately involved for many years—indeed, it is the only issue on which I have engaged in any extensive personal lobbying with members of the House and Senate (as contrasted with testifying before relevant congressional committees on subjects in my fields of competence).

My interest has been on two grounds. First, and most obvious, because conscription is such a blatant and serious restriction on individual freedom, the most extreme form of compulsory servitude now practiced in the United States. Second, because public acceptance of a strong armed force seems to me essential to maintain the freedom of the United States. Conscription undermined that acceptance and has played a major role in bringing the military into the low public estate to which it has fallen.

In the course of my involvement in this issue, I have come into contact with many other persons concerned with the draft—both in favor of it and opposed to it. I have observed many persons initially in favor of the draft change their opinions as they have looked into the arguments and studied the evidence; I have never observed anyone who was initially in favor of a volunteer force reverse his position on the basis of further study. This greatly enhances my confidence in the validity of the position I have taken.

For the reader who is interested in a comprehensive summary of the arguments pro and con, I recommend *The Report of the President's Commission on an All-Volunteer Armed Force* (Macmillan Company, 1970). This commission was headed by Thomas Gates, and I was a member of it, so this is not an unbiased recommendation even though I think the report is unbiased.

A VOLUNTEER ARMY
December 19, 1966

A military draft is undesirable and unnecessary. We can and should man our armed forces with volunteers—as the United States has traditionally done except in major wars.

Only a minority of young men now enter the armed forces. Hence, some method of "selective service"—of deciding which young man should serve and which two or three should not—is inevitable. But our present method is inequitable, wasteful and inconsistent with a free society.

On this point there is wide agreement. John K. Galbraith and Barry Goldwater, the New Left and the Republican Ripon Society have all urged that conscription be abolished. Even most supporters of the draft regard it as at best a necessary evil.

The draft is inequitable because irrelevant considerations play so large a role in determining who serves. It is wasteful because deferment of students, fathers and married men jams colleges, raises the birth rate and fuels divorce courts. It is inconsistent with a free society because it exacts compulsory service from some and limits the freedom of others to travel abroad, emigrate or even to talk and act freely. *So long as compulsion is retained, these defects are inevitable.* A lottery would only make the arbitrary element overt. Universal national service would compound the evil—regimenting all youth to camouflage the regimentation of some.

The pay is low

Two principal objections are made to a volunteer force:

1 That a "professional" army endangers political freedom. There *is* a real danger, but it arises from a strong armed force not from the method of recruiting enlisted men. Napoleon and Franco both rose to power at the head of a conscript army. However we recruit, the essential need is to maintain close links between the officer corps and the body politic.

2 That a volunteer army is not feasible because, at present terms, too few men volunteer. Little wonder: the starting pay, including cost of keep, is about $45 a week! We could readily attract more volunteers simply by paying market wages. Estimates of how much total military pay would have to go up vary from $4 billion to $20 billion a year.

Whatever the extra amount, we are now paying a larger sum in concealed form. Conscription is a tax in kind—forced labor exacted from the men who serve involuntarily. The amount of the tax is the difference between the sum for which they would voluntarily serve and the sum we now pay them—if Joe Namath were drafted, his tax might well run into hundreds of thousands of dollars. The real cost of manning the armed forces now, *including this concealed tax*, is greater than the cost of manning a volunteer force of the same size because the volunteers would be the men who find military service the most attractive alternative.

The cost is high

Moreover, a volunteer force would need fewer recruits. We now waste manpower by high turnover, unnecessary training and retraining and the use of underpaid servicemen for menial tasks.

Adding to cost, low pay for men in service encourages extravagant veterans' bonuses—currently more than $6 billion a year (over 40 per cent as much as total military pay). Young men seeking shelter from the draft impose unnecessary costs on colleges and universities. Other young men fritter away their time in stopgap jobs awaiting conscription, while industry seeks men to train.

The monetary savings that would come from abolishing conscription are dwarfed by even greater nonmonetary advantages: young men could arrange their schooling, careers, marriages and families in accordance with their own long-run interests; draft boards could be freed from the appalling task of choosing which men should serve, deciding claims for conscientious objection, ruling whether young men may leave the country; colleges and universities could be free to pursue their proper educational function; industry and government could hire young men on their merits not their deferments.

One of the greatest advances in human freedom was the commutation of taxes in kind to taxes in money. We have reverted to a barbarous custom. It is past time that we regain our heritage.

THE DRAFT
March 11, 1968

The arbitrariness and deficiencies of our present method of manning the armed forces are highlighted by the recent directive ending automatic exemption for hitherto protected occupations and automatic deferments for most graduate students (the exceptions are students already in their second year or beyond, and students going into medicine, dentistry and related fields or into the ministry).

Academic administrators are expressing great concern that graduate-student enrollments will decline sharply and that teaching assistants will be scarce. This concern would be fully justified if all the young men who would have been deferred or exempted under earlier rules will in fact now be drafted—except of course for those who do not meet physical or mental standards or are granted status as conscientious objectors.

Only college graduates?

But arithmetic plus the needs of the military assure that this will not occur. The number of young men added to the eligible rolls is at least double the number who will be drafted. Supposedly, the oldest are to be drafted first. If that were done, all of the new draftees would be in their middle 20s, and most would be college graduates. Not one of the roughly 2 million young men turning 18 would be taken. Would the military be satisfied with this outcome? If there be conscription, it is certainly inequitable to give special treatment to young men who go to college. But, on the other hand, is soldiering one of the occupations for which college graduation should be a prerequisite? Is that a reasonable use of our manpower?

What is likely to happen is that, by one expedient or another, most college graduates and persons now exempt on occupational grounds will continue to be deferred. Public pronouncements will be one thing, practice another. But that does not mean that the pronouncements do no harm. On the contrary, hundreds of thousands of young men will be subjected to needless uncertainty and distress. They will find it more difficult to get employment because of the risk that they will be drafted. Employers will be induced to get along with less satisfactory employees. Thousands of colleges will take measures that will prove unnecessary or harmful. We shall have another striking example of the defect of compulsion as a method of deciding which young man shall serve in the armed forces and which two or three or four shall not.

Over a year ago, I wrote in this column that "a military draft is undesirable and unnecessary. We can and should man our armed forces with volunteers—as the United States has traditionally done except in major wars" (NEWSWEEK, Dec. 19, 1966).

Why not volunteers?

In the interim, Congress has passed a bill extending conscription for another four years, yet there has also been increasing recognition of the defects of conscription. The case for a voluntary system has been presented in testimony before Congressional committees. Several bills have been introduced in both the Senate and the House providing for the early transition to a fully voluntary system of manning the armed forces.

Three books on the subject have recently appeared: "The Draft," which summarizes a conference held at the University of Chicago in December 1966 and presents evidence on all the alternatives (edited by Sol Tax, University of Chicago Press); "How to End the Draft," by five congressmen (edited by Douglas Bailey and Steve Herbits, National Press, Inc.); and "Why the Draft?" by seven young men connected with the University of Virginia (edited by James C. Miller III, with an introduction by Senator Brooke, Penguin Books). These books demonstrate that conscription is neither necessary nor desirable, that it is entirely feasible to man our armed forces by voluntary means provided the military stop underpaying new recruits and take effective steps to make a career in the services more attractive. These books consider and meet every objection that has been raised to a voluntary army.

Draft or no draft, this country would be now engaged in a searching debate over Vietnam. But the virulence and the divisiveness of the debate have been greatly increased by the draft, with its threat to civil liberties and with its closing of all alternatives except open revolt to young men who disagree strongly with our policy. Must we continue to add to the strain on our society by using a method of manning our armed forces that is inequitable, wasteful and basically inconsistent with a free society?

NO DRAFTEES TO VIETNAM
December 30, 1968

President-elect Nixon is committed to ending military conscription and establishing an all-volunteer armed force as soon as manpower needs in Vietnam decline substantially. That is a consummation devoutly to be desired. But, in the interim, the new Administration could reduce enormously the bitterness, dissension and division arising from the Vietnam conflict by taking a major first step toward an all-volunteer army. sending no more draftees to Vietnam.

This proposal raises two basic questions. Is it desirable? Is it feasible?

The first question hardly needs discussion. Men who agree on little else about Vietnam would agree on the desirability of not using conscripts to fight the war.

The key question is, therefore, whether it is feasible to man the Vietnam war with volunteers. I believe the answer is, Yes. Will it be easy to do so? The answer is clearly, No. But that is hardly decisive. The aim of national policy should not be to make life easy for government officials, whether civilian or military.

The facts

Here are the basic facts. Currently, about 540,000 men are in Vietnam. 360,000 in the Army, the remaining 180,000 in the Marine Corps, Air Force and Navy. The Air Force and the Navy use no conscripts; the Marines, a negligible number. Hence, only the Army raises a problem.

The strength of the Army worldwide is about 1.5 million. Only about 600,000 are conscripts; the other 900,000 are volunteers.

On a purely arithmetic basis, it seems clearly feasible to provide 360,000 men in Vietnam out of the 900,000 volunteers plus any conscripts who might waive their exemption. But this is misleading. The problem is harder than these numbers suggest.

1 The adoption of the new policy, *if nothing else were done*, might well reduce the number of "reluctant volunteers"—those who volunteer mostly under the threat of conscription. To offset this reduction, it would be highly desirable to raise substantially the pay of men who serve in Vietnam—a step that is called for in any event on grounds of equity.

Even substantial increases in combat pay are clearly feasible on budgetary grounds. A rise of $1,000 a year for all men in Vietnam would cost around a half billion dollars. Yet this rise, even if flat and across the board, would raise the pay of enlisted men by something like 40 per cent. And the rise should not be across the board. It should be concentrated on the positions for which volunteers are fewest.

2 Currently, the term of service of enlisted men in Vietnam is limited to twelve months. Disregard officers, and suppose that all of the nearly 900,000 volunteers in the Army enlisted for a single term of three years. Then each could spend only one-third of his service in Vietnam, so that a maximum of 300,000 men could on the average be in service in Vietnam.

The policy of limiting the term of service in Vietnam to twelve months has been strongly criticized on strictly military grounds as highly unsatisfactory and inefficient. It takes several months for men to learn their jobs; their last several months are homeward-looking; at most, six out of the twelve months are useful service. In addition, the perpetual rotation makes it impossible to establish those informal lines of communication that are at least as important in every large administrative structure as the formal channels. Lengthening the normal term of service would cut sharply the number of men needed in Vietnam and thus doubly facilitate a policy of no draftees to Vietnam.

3 A third possible difficulty is that the Army needs units rather than individual men in Vietnam and it is undesirable to segregate all Army recruits from the outset into conscript and non-conscript units. However, this difficulty is not relevant. Initially, units as a whole were sent to Vietnam but currently men rather than units as a whole are sent as replacements.

The challenge

The difficulties are real. But they are far from insuperable. They offer a challenge to the men who run the armed forces, not a reason for rejecting a policy that offers so many advantages. President Nixon and Secretary of Defense Laird should set a definite and near date after which no more draftees will be assigned to Vietnam—unless they volunteer for that duty. There is no other measure that they can take that will do more to unify the country and at the same time increase the effectiveness of our military forces in Vietnam.[1]

THE DRAFT LOTTERY
July 7, 1969

President Nixon's proposal of a draft lottery as an interim step to an allvolunteer military force has received generally favorable notices in the public press. These notices have stressed the reduction in uncertainty for men aged 18 to 26. Under the proposed plan, a young man would know by age 19 how large a chance he ran of being drafted, and this chance would not be affected significantly by his future behavior. He could then plan for the future in light of this knowledge. He would not, as now, have to keep a weather eye out year after year for how his current behavior will affect the likelihood that he will be drafted.

This is certainly a significant advantage. But there are also disadvantages of the lottery, less obvious to the naked eye, that have been overlooked. When account is taken of these disadvantages, it is by no means clear that the lottery would be a major improvement. What is abundantly clear is that either the present system or the lottery is distinctly inferior to an all-voluntary military force. Yet, by reducing the decibel level of protest to the draft, enactment of the lottery might delay or even prevent the introduction of this fundamental reform.

Higher calls

The lottery shares the key defect of the present system: compulsory service by a minority of the young men of the relevant age. It requires one out of three or four young men to serve, regardless of their willingness to do so and often at great sacrifice, while their fellows pursue their careers.

[1At long last, in mid–1972, the policy of sending no draftees to Vietnam has been established by President Nixon. The declining number of American troops in Vietnam has removed the difficulties I discussed.]

By comparison with the present system, an obvious disadvantage of the lottery is that it makes service in the military subject to Lady Luck. It reduces the solemn obligation to serve one's country to the level of the Las Vegas gaming tables. The present system at least purports to select on the basis of rational criteria.

A less obvious yet far more basic disadvantage of the lottery is that it would increase sharply the number of young men who would have to be conscripted—possibly to more than double the roughly 200,000 a year who are now conscripted. The lottery would raise draft calls because it would reduce the number of volunteers. Many men now volunteer partly in order to avoid the uncertainty involved in present draft procedures. The new plan would largely remove this uncertainty. Hence many men who now volunteer would not do so. Their places would have to be filled by conscripts even more reluctant to serve—as demonstrated by their unwillingness to volunteer even reluctantly under present arrangements.

If the lottery were the only alternative to the present system, the choice would be very difficult indeed. The number of young men who would gain from the lottery is much greater than the number who would lose—but the gain to most of the gainers would be small, while the loss to many of the losers would be large. There is no problem in the human calculus that is more difficult than to balance quality against quantity. Nonetheless, if this were the only alternative, I would probably prefer the lottery.

A better alternative

Fortunately, there is a third alternative. We can start immediately to move toward an all-volunteer armed force by improving *substantially* the conditions offered to new recruits. The entering pay is disgracefully low—about $50 a week including cost of food, clothing and housing. Other conditions of service—quality of food and housing, the matching of skills to tasks and so on—are deplorable. Every other consideration aside, simple humanity demands a major improvement in the compensation and other conditions of military service. Such an improvement would convert many reluctant volunteers into true volunteers and many who are now drafted or who do not now serve into volunteers of either category.

These measures would not only reduce the residual number of young men who would still have to be conscripted but they would also provide invaluable information on how responsive the supply of volunteers is to the conditions offered. President Nixon has committed himself to moving to an all-volunteer force once the demands of Vietnam have eased. Perhaps experience would show that his object can be achieved even sooner.

Whether that be so or not, a major step toward a system of military recruitment fully consistent with our traditions and values is greatly to be preferred to a minor improvement in a system of compulsory service that denies the very basis of our existence as a society of free men.

THE END OF THE DRAFT?
March 16, 1970

At long last, the end of the draft is in sight.

Two months after his Inauguration, President Nixon appointed a commission "to develop a comprehensive plan for eliminating conscription and moving toward an all-volunteer armed force." That commission has now unanimously recommended a plan that it believes would permit conscription to end on June 30, 1971, when the present legal authority expires. It would retain only a standby draft to be put into effect in case of emergency by action of Congress on the recommendation of the President.

As a member of the President's commission, I was much impressed by the emergence of unanimity out of initial disagreement. As our deliberations proceeded, and especially as our knowledgeable staff developed a growing body of factual evidence, it became ever clearer to all of us how superficial are most arguments in favor of conscription and how inefficient conscription is both as a method of taxation and as a method of recruiting manpower.

Mostly volunteers now

The often hysterical claims that an all-volunteer force is undesirable because it would be all black or all this or all that or because it would strengthen militarism or because . . . all these claims are contradicted by one simple yet overwhelmingly important fact: *our armed forces today consist predominantly of true volunteers.*

Many men "reluctantly" volunteer for a first term of service because of the threat of the draft. But we know that all men beyond the first term of service are true volunteers, and they alone number nearly 40 per cent of the total forces. In addition, our best estimates are that at least one-third of the first-termers are also true volunteers. In all, therefore, at least 60 per cent of the armed forces are true volunteers. A change in the method of recruiting the remaining 40 per cent—mostly enlisted men in the very lowest ranks—cannot produce drastic changes in either the composition or character of the armed forces.

Enforced service by a conscript is a tax imposed on him no less than the check you send to Internal Revenue is a tax imposed on you. The size of his tax is the difference between the sum of money for which he would have served voluntarily and the pay he actually receives. Currently, this tax amounts to about 50 per cent of the potential civilian income of draftees. So unfair a tax imposed on so small a minority would never be passed explicitly by Congress. It persists only because it is hidden.

The tax is not only unfair, it is also inefficient. Every tax involves costs in addition to the amount of the tax itself. For conscription, these indirect costs are the heavy burdens imposed on actual and potential draftees, their families, universities, employers—and most important, on all of us through the weakening of the political fabric of society.

Most of these costs cannot be assigned a money value. But for those that can, the commission estimates that "for each $1 in tax-in-kind collected, an average of $2.50 is foregone by the public"—i.e., that it costs $1.50 to collect $1. That is one reason why, when the books are kept properly to show all costs and all returns, a volunteer force is far less costly than a mixed force of conscripts and volunteers. But it is not the only reason.

A young man is conscripted for two years. He spends the first six months or so being trained, the last few months being processed for his discharge. We are lucky if he spends one year in active service. In addition, the time of other men must be used to train him and move him in and out of service.

To man a mixed conscript-volunteer force of 2.5 million men (the middle of the range of force levels considered by the commission) requires recruiting each year about 440,000 enlisted men (excluding officers). Even with today's low first-term pay and conditions of service, at least 250,000 would be true volunteers, leaving 190,000 who would have to be conscripted or induced to volunteer by threat of the draft.

An all-volunteer force of equal effectiveness has less turnover and uses manpower more efficiently. As a result, it requires recruiting each year about 325,000 enlisted men, or only 75,000 in addition to the present number of true volunteers.

The real alternatives

Compel 190,000 men per year to serve. Or improve pay and conditions of service to attract an additional 75,000 volunteers out of the 1.5 million who each year turn 19. These are the real alternatives.

THE DRAFT UNCOMPROMISE
September 6, 1971

The bill to extend the draft and pave the way for an all-volunteer armed force was tied up in a House-Senate conference for many weeks. The conference reported just before the Congressional recess. Its recommendations were accepted by the House but were not voted on in the Senate. This delay is fortunate because the conference report contains a "compromise" on armed-force pay scales that is a far greater threat to achievement of the bill's objectives than the much-publicized Mansfield amendment. Yet it might have been overlooked in the rush to adjourn.

2 + 2 = 3

The House bill provided a pay raise totaling $2.7 billion on a full year basis; the Senate bill a pay raise totaling $2.8 billion; the conference a pay raise totaling $2.4 billion.

How can $2.4 billion be a compromise between $2.7 billion and $2.8 billion? The answer is easy—if you are an expert at parliamentary maneuvering. First, you note that the House $2.7 billion consisted of an increase of $1.8 billion in basic pay and of $0.9 billion in supplements (housing and subsistence allowances, etc.), while the Senate $2.8 billion consisted of $2.7 billion in basic pay and only $0.1 billion in supplements. You now take each part separately. You compromise between $1.8 billion and $2.7 billion in basic pay at $1.8 billion. You compromise between $0.9 billion and $0.1 billion in supplements at $0.5 billion. You add the compromise $1.8 billion to the compromise $0.5 billion and, presto chango, with the help of a bit of rounding off, you have $2.4 billion as a compromise between $2.7 billion and $2.8 billion.

This seemingly minor reduction is critical because, compared with the Senate bill, the reduction is entirely at the expense of first-term enlisted men and officers. Here are the House, Senate and conference proposed annual pay levels for the grades that are relevant for first-termers.

Proposed Military Compensation

Pay Grade	House	Senate	Compromise
Enlisted Men			
E-1	$ 5,036	$ 5,320	$ 4,872
E-2	5,484	5,530	5,311
E-3	5,893	5,831	5,663
E-4	6,457	6,329	6,189
Officers			
O-1	8,985	9,611	8,659
O-2	11,474	11,138	11,045

These are the grades for which the draft has provided recruits—either conscripts or "reluctant volunteers," i.e., men induced to enlist by the threat of being drafted. For higher career grades, the conference recommendation is between the amounts proposed by the House and Senate, though generally closer to the more generous House scale.

Because of the draft, first-termers have consistently been shortchanged. From 1952 to 1965 there were *no* pay raises at all for enlisted men in the first two years of service. As a result, first-term enlisted men now receive not much more than half the amount that they could earn as civilians. In sharp contrast, enlisted men with more service and officers above the first two grades receive as much as or more than they could earn. This was and is a glaring and completely unjustifiable inequity. It was and is a major obstacle to recruiting volunteers.

The Senate bill went farther than the House bill in removing this inequity by adopting the pay increases recommended by the Gates commission as required to achieve an all-volunteer armed force. The conference proposal is worse than either in this crucial respect. Its adoption would seriously hamper the achievement of an all-volunteer force.

It is not too late

Senator Allott (Republican of Colorado), the author of the Senate pay amendment, plans to lead a fight in the Senate when it reconvenes to return the bill to the conference with the request that it submit a true compromise. There is every reason to expect that he will succeed. His amendment was adopted by a decisive majority—51 to 27—while an earlier amendment incorporating the House pay scale was decisively defeated. Clearly, the Senate wanted a pay raise concentrated on first-termers. Yet the conference proposal slights precisely this group.

Few matters are more important for the political, social and moral health of this country than ending compulsory military service and returning to this nation's long tradition of relying on the voluntary services of patriotic Americans to maintain a loyal and effective armed force. It will be a tragedy if legislative legerdemain is permitted to frustrate the achievement of this objective.

Chapter Seven
SOCIAL SECURITY AND WELFARE

The two programs discussed in the columns of this chapter are part of a much more extensive set of programs enacted in the name of alleviating poverty. These programs include, in addition, farm price supports, public housing, urban renewal, model city programs, the assorted projects in President Johnson's mislabeled "war on poverty," and much else besides, some of which are discussed in later chapters.

Of all these programs, the welfare program is the only one that clearly transfers money to people who are at lower income classes than those who pay the taxes to finance the program—and perhaps for that reason is the program that is most widely regarded as a "mess" and failure.[1] As the columns on Social Security indicate, that program very likely does precisely the opposite—that is, transfers income from lower to higher income classes. For many other so-called poverty programs (like farm price supports and urban renewal), "very likely" can be replaced by "certainly." I hasten to add that in addition to transferring income from some persons to others, all these programs involve much pure waste, so that the "benefit" to the recipient, whoever that may be, is far less than the cost to the taxpayer.

How misleading is the poverty label is sharply etched by the calculation in the final item in Chapter 8 that total governmental expenditures (federal, state, and local) on programs justified on grounds of alleviating poverty exceeded $75 billion in 1969–1970. If this money were really going to the "poor," they would be among the well-to-do! But of course, most of it is going to people who by no stretch of the imagination can be regarded as "poor." The label is "poverty." The contents are waste and subsidy to special interests.

SOCIAL SECURITY
April 3, 1967

Social security has become a sacred cow that no politician can afford to criticize—as the reaction by Republicans and Democrats alike to President Johnson's proposed rise in benefits has again made clear. Yet there is much to criticize.

1 In the past fifteen years, maximum old-age benefits have doubled. *But* the maximum tax assessed on a worker's wages has quintupled.
2 Retired persons currently enjoy a bonanza. *But* youngsters currently entering the system are getting a raw deal.

[1]See M. Friedman and Wilbur Cohen, *Social Security: Universal or Selective*, American *Enterprise Institute*, Washington, 1972, pp. 48–49.

3 The benefit scale in the law is designed to favor the relatively poor. *But* the law has important indirect effects that favor the well-to-do.

The first two facts have a common origin: the aging of the social-security program. At its start in 1937, many workers became taxpayers, no one a beneficiary. It was all intake, no outgo. As time passed, workers who retired began to qualify for benefits. But for some time, the number was so small that outgo still fell far short of intake, even though retired workers received benefits that were many times as large as the equivalent of the taxes once paid on their wages. This situation has been changing rapidly. From 1950 to 1965, the number of retired workers receiving benefits grew more than sixfold, while the number of taxpayers less than doubled.

Benefits and taxes

To finance the excess payments to the growing number of retired, taxes assessed on wages have had to be raised repeatedly. As a result, the benefits promised younger workers are much smaller than the equivalent of the taxes paid on their wages.

The third fact—that social security has indirect effects that discriminate against the poor—is much more subtle. Note a few.

1 The poor generally begin working earlier than the well-to-do. So, on this score, they pay taxes for more years. Yet benefits, once eligibility is established, do not depend on number of years for which taxes are paid.

2 The well-to-do tend to live longer than the poor. They are therefore more likely to survive to receive benefits and also to receive benefits for more years. (This effect is partly offset by the greater value of survivors' benefits to the poor.)

3 Working wives get little for their taxes.

4 Men or women who do not pay taxes for enough quarters to qualify for benefits get nothing whatsoever in return for their taxes.

5 A man between 65 and 72 who works and earns more than a small amount per month loses part or all of his social-security benefits. To add insult to injury, taxes are still assessed on his wages! Property income, on the other hand, whatever its amount, does not affect benefits received.

Clever packaging

Though labeled "insurance," the system of old-age benefits is no such thing. It is a welfare program that transfers income from some to others—notably from the young, rich and poor, to the old, rich and poor. Few of those who support the present system would favor either the structure of taxes by itself—a flat percentage tax on the first $6,600 of earnings and a zero tax on higher earnings—or the structure of benefits by itself—indiscriminate benefits based on age, sex, marital status and previous employment, with no attention to need. Tying the two together and labeling the combination insurance was a masterpiece of clever packaging.

In a recent article (The Wall Street Journal, Dec. 20, 1966), Prof. James Buchanan and Colin Campbell propose a sensible and ingenious method for converting present arrangements into a true insurance system—which could be voluntary—while at the same time fully honoring existing commitments. They propose that current liabilities—which they estimate at the staggering total of $400 billion—be openly recognized, funded and made an explicit charge on general tax funds and that the taxes imposed on younger workers be reduced to the level required solely to pay for the benefits they are being promised. The workers could then be permitted to purchase equivalent retirement benefits elsewhere if they so chose, without endangering the financial soundness of the government system. Their plan—and others for achieving the same objective—deserves prompt and serious consideration.

NEGATIVE INCOME TAX—I
September 16, 1968

The negative income tax, as Paul Samuelson remarked in one of his recent columns (NEWSWEEK, June 10), is a striking example of an idea whose time has come. First suggested decades ago, it has attracted widespread interest only in the past few years as the defects of present methods of assisting the poor have become more obvious and more flagrant.

The widespread interest is remarkable. But the appearance of growing agreement—of support for a negative income tax by the right and the left, by businessmen and professors, by Republicans and Democrats—is highly misleading. In large part, it reflects the use of the same term to describe very different plans. For example, some months ago, more than 1,200 economists from 150 different colleges and universities signed a petition favoring a negative income tax. Despite my longtime advocacy of a negative income tax, I found it impossible to join in sponsoring the petition or even to sign it because I did not agree with the plan it advocated or the arguments it presented.

A specific plan

The basic idea of a negative income tax is to use the mechanism by which we now collect tax revenue from people with incomes above some minimum level to provide financial assistance to people with incomes below that level.

Under present law, a family of four (husband, wife and two dependents) is entitled to personal exemptions and minimum deductions totaling $3,000 ($2,400 personal exemptions, $600 deductions).

If such a family has an imcome of $3,000, its exemptions and deductions just offset its income. It has a *zero taxable* income and pays no tax.[1]

If it has an income of $4,000, it has a *positive taxable income* of $1,000. Under current law, it is required to *pay* a tax of 15.4 per cent, or $154. Hence it ends up with an income after tax of $3,846.

If it has an income of $2,000, it has a *negative taxable income of*—$1,000 ($2,000 minus exemptions and deductions of $3,000 equals—$1,000). This negative taxable income is currently disregarded. Under a negative income tax, the family would be entitled to *receive* a *fraction* of this sum. If the negative tax rate were 50 per cent, it would be entitled to receive $500, leaving it with an income after tax of $2,500.

If such a family had no private income, it would have a negative taxable income of —$3,000, which would entitle it to receive $1,500. This is the minimum income guaranteed by this plan for a family of four.

Let me stress the difference between the *break-even income* of $3,000 at which the family neither pays taxes nor receives a subsidy and the *minimum guaranteed income* of $1,500. It is essential to retain a difference between these two in order to preserve an incentive for low-income families to earn additional income.

Let me stress also that these numbers are all for a family of four. Both the break-even income and the minimum guaranteed income would be higher for larger families and lower for smaller families. In this way, a negative income tax automatically allows for differences in need because of differences in family size—just as it does for differences in need because of differences in income.

This plan is intended to replace completely our present programs of direct relief—aid to dependent children, public assistance, and so on. For the first year or two, it might cost slightly more than these programs—because it is so much more comprehensive in coverage. But, as the incentive effects of the plan started to work, it would begin to cost far less than the present exploding direct-assistance programs that are creating a permanent class of people on welfare.

Alternative plans

By varying the break-even income and the negative tax rate, by adding the negative income tax to present programs rather than substituting it for them, it is possible to go all the way from the rather modest and, I believe, eminently desirable plan just outlined to irresponsible and undesirable plans that would involve enormous redistribution of income and a drastic reduction in the incentive for people to work. That is why it is possible for persons

[1]The no-tax income has since been raised. For 1971, it was $3,750 for a family of four.]

with so wide a range of political views to support one form or another of a negative income tax.

In my next column, I shall try to answer some of the objections to a negative income tax that I have encountered most frequently in the more than two decades since I first began recommending its adoption.

NEGATIVE INCOME TAX—II
October 7, 1968

The proposal to supplement the incomes of the poor by paying them a *fraction* of their unused income-tax exemptions and deductions, which I termed a *negative income tax* years ago, has many advantages over present welfare programs:

1 It would help the poor in the most direct way possible.
2 It would treat them as responsible individuals, not as incompetent wards of the state.
3 It would give them an incentive to help themselves.
4 It would cost less than present programs yet help the poor more.
5 It would eliminate almost entirely the cumbrous welfare bureaucracy running the present programs.
6 It could not be used as a political slush fund, as so many current programs—notably in the "war on poverty"—can be and have been used.

In the course of advocating a negative income tax like the one outlined in my preceding column (NEWSWEEK, Sept. 16), I have repeatedly encountered the same objections time and again. Let me try to answer a few of them.

1 *By removing a means test, the negative income tax establishes a new principle in the relation between citizens and the government.* This is simply a misunderstanding. The negative income tax retains a means test —the straightforward numerical test of income rather than the present complex and demeaning test. It uses the same means test to decide who shall receive assistance from the government as the one we now use to decide who shall pay the expenses of government.

True, it guarantees a minimum income to all. But that is not a new principle. Present welfare arrangements guarantee a minimum income in practice, and in some states, even in law. The trouble is that these present welfare programs are a mess.

2 *The minimum levels of income proposed are too low.* We are talking about a Federal program and a *nationwide* minimum. The levels of assis-

tance are decided higher than current levels in most states. They are decidedly lower than current levels in states like New York, Illinois, California. It would be absurd to enact such high levels as national standards. But there is every reason to encourage the more affluent states to supplement the Federal negative income tax out of state funds—preferably by enacting a supplementary state negative income tax.

3 *The poor need regular assistance. They cannot wait until the end of the year.* Of course. The negative income tax, like the positive income tax, would be put on an advance basis. Employed persons entitled to negative income tax would have supplements added to their paychecks, just as most of us now have positive taxes withheld. Persons without wages would file advance estimates and receive estimated amounts due to them weekly or monthly. Once a year, all would file a return that would adjust for under- or over-payments.

4 *The negative income tax destroys incentives to work.* Under present programs, persons on welfare who obey the law generally lose a dollar in relief for every additional dollar earned. Hence, they have no incentive whatsoever to earn the dollar. Under the negative income tax plan that I propose, such a person would keep 50 cents out of every additional dollar earned. That would give him a far greater incentive than he now has.

One additional point. A welfare recipient now hesitates to take a job even if it pays more than he gets on welfare because, if he loses the job, it may take him (or her) many months to get back on relief. There is no such disincentive under a negative income tax.

5 *The negative income tax will foster political irresponsibility.* If we adopt an open and aboveboard program for supplementing the incomes of people below some specified level, will there not be continued political pressure for higher and higher breakeven incomes, for higher and higher rates on negative income? Will the demagogues not have a field day appealing to have-nots to legislate taxes on haves for transfer to them?

These dangers clearly exist. But they must be evaluated in terms of the world as it is, not in terms of a dream world in which there are no governmental welfare measures. These dangers are all present now—and have clearly been effective. The crucial question is, how do we get out of the mess into which these pressures have driven us? The negative income tax offers a gradual and responsible way to work ourselves out of this mess. No other way of doing so has as yet been suggested.

WELFARE: BACK TO THE DRAWING BOARD
May 18, 1970

I have long supported and worked for the general principles of the welfare-reform bill that is now making its way through Congress. Yet I would vote against the bill in the form in which it passed the House; I have testified to that effect before the House Ways and Means Committee, and I applaud the Senate Finance Committee's recent suspension of hearings on the bill until Secretary Finch submits a new version. The bill in its present form is a striking example of how to spoil a good idea.

The key idea of the proposed reform is to give people on welfare both the opportunity and the incentive to become self-supporting. As outlined by President Nixon in his TV talk of August 8, 1969, this was to be done primarily by making certain that a family'on relief would always gain by working. To this end, he proposed that a family of four with no other income receive $1,600 a year from the Federal government; that the first $60 of earnings a month not affect the amount received, and that each additional dollar earned reduce the amount received by 50 cents. The Federal payment would become zero when the family had earnings of $3,920 a year.

The trouble is that the bill proposed by the Administration and passed by the House does not conform to this design. On the contrary, it gives most persons on relief even less incentive than they have under the existing system of welfare.

This is the unintended result of the way that other programs are linked with the basic Family Assistance Plan. The chief culprits are food stamps and state supplements.

Food stamps

Initially, the Family Assistance Plan was to replace food stamps. Under political pressure, the Administration added food stamps to the basic plan, recommending that as income rose, the food-stamp subsidy be reduced by 30 per cent of additional income. This means that the family would have only 70 cents instead of $1 available to spend out of each of the first $60 of earnings a month; and only 35 cents instead of 50 cents out of every dollar beyond that.

Under present law, persons on relief may earn $30 a month without a reduction in benefits and keep one-third of additional earnings. So just food stamps alone reduce incentives under the House bill to roughly their present level.

State supplements

In eight states, the proposed Federal family allowance exceeds the amount that is now paid by the state. For these states, the Family Assistance Plan would replace the state program entirely. For the other 42 states, the House bill requires that the state supplement Federal payments to maintain present maximum levels of benefits. It permits a state to phase out its supplement as the other income of the family rises. As drafted, this provision reduces still further, and sometimes drastically, the extra amount that a family has available to spend for each additional dollar it earns.

Indeed, if account is taken of still other quirks in the drafted bill, and also of Federal income and social-security taxes, state and local income taxes, and Federal programs like public housing and medicaid, many families would be better off to earn less than to earn more.

The accompanying table illustrates the effect of some of these items. If the illustrative family increased its earnings from $2,280 a year to $5,003 a year, or by $2,723, it would end up with only $357 extra available to spend! It could raise its extra spendable income to $401 by keeping its earnings down to $3,920! How absurd can you get?

This is a travesty on the original intention. A negative income tax—which is what the Family Assistance Plan is—makes sense only if it replaces at least some of our present rag bag of programs. It makes no sense if it is simply piled on other programs.

What's wrong with the house welfare bill

The welfare bill in its current form would lower the work incentive of most persons on relief. This is how it would affect a family of four in a typical state.*

ANNUAL INCOME	$0	$720	$2,280	$3,600	$3,920	$5,003
Receipts from						
Family assistance plan	$1,600	$1,600	$ 820	$ 160	$ 0	$ 0
State supplement	1,400	1,400	1,140	920	867	0
Food stamps	372	156	0	0	0	0
Earnings	0	720	2,280	3,600	3,920	5,003
TOTAL	$3,372	$3,876	$4,240	$4,680	$4,787	$5,003
Minus						
Social security tax	0	35	109	173	188	240
Federal income tax	0	0	0	0	67	275
SPENDABLE INCOME	$3,372	$3,841	$4,131	$4,507	$4,532	$4,488
Amount left out of extra dollar		65.2¢	18.5¢	28.5¢	7.5¢	−4.1¢

*The state is assumed for this illustration to be giving maximum benefits now of $3,000 a year for such a family. Eighteen states, including the most populous, now give about that amount or more. The income levels shown are those at which various benefits cease or start phasing out.

The minimum changes in the House bill required to give a real incentive for work instead of welfare are:

1   The food-stamp plan should be abolished. It is defended in the name of preventing hunger. But that is a smoke screen. The right way to help

the poor is to give them real money to spend on food, not funny money in the form of stamps. The political pressure for food stamps comes from the well-fed farm bloc, not from hungry welfare recipients. The farm bloc senses that the public's willingness to shell out billions a year to keep up the price of foodstuffs is running thin and it sees food stamps as a new gadget to keep the subsidies flowing.

2 The method of phasing out state supplements must be modified to keep the maximum marginal rate to 50 per cent. This means that states should not be permitted to reduce their supplements until the Federal payments end, and then by not more than 50 per cent of additional earnings. To ease the problem for the states, they should be permitted to lower the maximum levels of assistance to which they are now committed.

It is long past time that we reversed the relentless climb of the welfare rolls, that we gave the unfortunate people on welfare a chance to work themselves off welfare and to become independent and responsible citizens. It will be a tragedy if the present opportunity is wasted by either administrative incompetence or political log-rolling.

WELFARE REFORM AGAIN
September 7, 1970

In an earlier column (NEWSWEEK, May 18), I applauded the Senate Finance Committee for asking the Administration to redraft the Family Assistance Act of 1970, which passed the House in April. "The bill in its present form," I wrote, "is a striking example of how to spoil a good idea."

The primary defect of the House bill was that a person on welfare could not add much to his income by going to work. Any extra earnings were largely offset by reductions in welfare payments and other benefits, and in some cases more than offset, so that going to work actually lowered total income.

Too little incentive

The revised version, on which the Senate Finance Committee is now holding hearings, is free from most of the egregious anomalies of the House bill, but unfortunately it does not come much closer to redeeming the bold promise of the President's initial TV speech—to end the relentless rise of the welfare rolls by giving people on welfare both opportunity and incentive to become self-supporting.

The provisions are incredibly complex. However, their incentive effects can be summarized simply without serious inaccuracy: a person on relief who goes to work has about 60 cents left for himself out of each dollar of the first $720 of earnings per year, but only about 20 cents out of each additional dollar until he is entirely off relief (which occurs for a family of four at $3,920 of earnings in some states but not until $7,000 of earnings in New York). For most levels of income, and particularly at the lower levels, this is a smaller incentive to work than exists under the present law—which is uniformly, and correctly, regarded as a mess.

How is it that such a promising initiative has fizzled out? The reason is that the Administration has tried to implement a bold idea without seriously disturbing any existing program. If food stamps, state supplements to existing Federal welfare, medical and housing assistance, and the entrenched welfare bureaucracy are all to remain largely undisturbed, there is no way to construct a sensible family-assistance program.

President Nixon's bold initiative can still be rescued but it will take equally bold action by the Senate Finance Committee to do so. The key objectives of welfare reform should be:

1 To establish a minimum national welfare standard, reducing the incentive for poor people to move in order to qualify for higher welfare.

2 To give persons on relief a strong incentive to work themselves off relief.

3 To end the present division of the nation into two classes—welfare recipients and taxpayers—by treating all alike and all impersonally. This requires a single objective test—best provided by income—to determine who pays taxes and who receives benefits; and cash payments to recipients to eliminate the present paternalistic welfare bureaucracy.

The minimum changes in the present bill required to achieve these objectives are:

1 ELIMINATE FOOD STAMPS. The bill now provides a maximum Federal payment of $1,600 in cash plus $820 in funny-money food stamps to a family of four which has no other income. Both components are reduced as the other income of the family rises. This is one major reason why so little is left out of additional dollars earned. Relief recipients and taxpayers would both benefit if the minimum payment were raised to, say, $2,100 in cash with no food stamps, and the combined payment were reduced by 50 cents for every dollar of earnings after the first $720. The farm bloc, not the poor, are the real political force behind food stamps.

2 ELIMINATE THE PROVISIONS ABOUT THE SUPPLEMENTARY PAYMENTS THAT STATES MUST PAY TO WELFARE FAMILIES. These provisions are a second major reason why so little is left out of additional dollars earned. Instead, let the Federal government fix definite dollar grants to each state on the basis of present commitments. Let these grants taper off over a period of years to fixed future levels. Then leave every state free to do whatever it wishes about supplementing Federal family-assistance payments. Each state separately will have an interest in maintaining work incentives. We need more true federalism as part of the New Federalism.

3 ASSIGN ADMINISTRATION OF THE PROGRAM TO INTERNAL REVENUE AND NOT TO HEW. This will be a step to a single integrated tax system covering both those who pay taxes and those who receive benefits.

Radical surgery, not face-lifting, is required to end the welfare mess.

TRUTH IN ADVERTISING
June 14, 1971

I recently came across an egregious example of misleading advertising. Yet that watchdog of truth in advertising, the Federal Trade Commission, has issued no complaint and is not likely to. Why not? Because the culprit is the U.S. Department of Health, Education and Welfare.

Doublethink

A widely circulated booklet, Your Social Security, begins:

"The basic idea of social security is a simple one: During working years employees, their employers, and self-employed people pay social security contributions which are pooled in special trust funds. When earnings stop or are reduced because the worker retires, dies, or becomes disabled, monthly cash benefits are paid to replace part of the earnings the family has lost."

This is Orwellian doublethink:

Payroll taxes are labeled "contributions" (or, as the Party might have put it in the book "1984," "Compulsory is Voluntary").

Trust funds are conjured with as if they played an important role. In fact, they are small (less than $35 billion) and consist simply of promises by one branch of the government to pay another branch. A decade ago, the Social Security Administration estimated that the present value of the pensions already promised to persons covered by social security (both those who had retired and those who had not) was more than $300 billion. The corresponding sum must be far larger today. That is the size of the trust fund that would justify the words of the booklet. ("Little is Much.")

The impression is given that a worker's "benefits" are financed by his own "contributions." The fact is that currently collected taxes are being used to pay current benefits. No trust fund in any meaningful sense is being accumulated. ("I am You.")

What assurance do current workers have that they will receive the benefits promised? Solely the confidence that our children will be willing to impose taxes on themselves to pay benefits being promised by us to ourselves. This one-sided "compact between the generations," foisted on generations that literally cannot give their consent, may be sufficient assurance, but it is a very different thing from a "trust fund"—a "chain letter" would be a more accurate designation.

The booklet goes on: "Nine out of ten working people in the United States are now building protection for themselves and their families under the social security program."

More doublethink.

What nine out of ten working people are now doing is paying taxes to finance benefits to persons who are not working. An individual working person is in no sense building his own protection—as a person who contributes to a private vested pension system is building his own protection. Persons now receiving benefits are receiving much more than the actuarial value of the taxes that were paid on their behalf. Young persons are now being promised much less than the actuarial value of the taxes that are being paid on their behalf.

More fundamentally yet, the relationship between taxes paid and benefits received is extremely loose. Millions of people will never receive any benefits attributable to their taxes because they have not paid for enough quarters to qualify, or because they receive benefits as spouses rather than on their own account. Two persons may receive the same benefit, yet have paid very different taxes over their working lives because they worked different numbers of years. Conversely, two persons may have paid precisely the same taxes at the same times yet receive very different benefits because one is married and the other is single. A man who continues working after age 65 will be required to pay additional taxes, yet may receive no benefits at all.

Imaginative packaging

Social security is not in any meaningful sense an insurance program in which individual payments purchase equivalent actuarial benefits. It is a combination of a tax—a flat-rate tax on wage income up to a maximum—and a program of transfer payments, in which all sorts of considerations other than the amount paid determine the amount received.

The tax is almost surely far and away the most regressive element in our tax system. The benefits are capricious and inequitable. Hardly any student of social security approves of either part separately. Yet the two combined have become a sacred cow. I know of no greater triumph of imaginative packaging and Madison Avenue advertising.

Chapter Eight
GOVERNMENT VS. THE PEOPLE

This chapter and, to a considerable measure, also the two that follow deal with the difference between the intentions of disinterested persons who support specific government interventions and the outcome of those interventions. The range of cases in which noble intentions produce ignoble results gives reason to believe that this outcome is not accidental, as I try to suggest in the final item in this chapter.

Why is it that well-intentioned reformers so often end up as front men for special interests they would never knowingly represent? The underlying reason is the difference between the way the market operates and the way a political mechanism operates. In a market, I can get command over your money only if you agree. You are free to buy or to refuse to buy what I have to sell. It is therefore in my interest to try to figure out what you are willing to pay for and make it available to you. Of course, if I can, it is also in my interest to prevent other people from competing with me in providing whatever it is that I have to sell. But unless I can get the government to help me, it is very difficult for me to succeed. I may for a time get some other producers to join an agreement to fix at a high level the prices we charge, but the more successful we are, the greater the incentive for participants in the agreement to "chisel," or for outsiders to go into the business. In short, the market makes it in the interest of other people to serve me. I am protected from being overcharged not only by my own efforts but also by the efforts of other customers whose threat, implicit or explicit, to divert their custom induces sellers to keep prices down. I am protected even more effectively by the efforts of other sellers, who have a real interest in letting me know if I am being overcharged. In highly simplified form, this is the essence of Adam Smith's famous passage: although "every individual . . . intends only his own gain, . . . he is in this, as in many other cases, led by an invisible hand to promote an end which was no part of his intention. . . . By pursuing his own interest he frequently promotes that of the society more effectively than when he really intends to promote it."

A political mechanism is very different. It is a means for exercising power, including getting money, without the case-by-case agreement of the person over whom the power is exercised or whose money is being spent. I am required by law to buy specified "safety" equipment on cars "for my own good" whether I want to or not. Some of my money is spent by the National Traffic Safety Agency. I would rather not spend my money that way, yet I have no way to opt out. You may say that I had the choice to vote for it or not. But that is a very different choice than I have in the market. If I vote in the market for a belt, I get the belt I vote for; if I vote in the market not to buy a belt, I don't get the belt. If I vote in the polling booth for auto-safety legislation, and my side wins, I get the seat belt that the National Traffic Safety Agency specifies. If I vote against auto-safety legislation and my side loses, I still get the seat belt that the NTSA specifies. Clearly the connection between what I vote for in the polling booth and what I get is far looser than between what I vote for in the market and what I get.

This difference introduces a very clear bias into the results. Since there is in general little relation between my vote or my political action and the outcome, it only pays me to give much attention to the matter if I have an unusually large interest in it. To shift examples, let me vote as a public-spirited citizen for "public housing" because I have an interest in the poor and am willing to see some of my taxes go to benefit the poor. Once I have voted, I have done my duty, I have a clear conscience, and can enjoy the pleasing glow of rectitude. I can and will now go about my business. I have little incentive to monitor the outcome, to keep close tabs on how the money is spent. But people who have property that they would like to sell or improve are in a different position. To them, activity has just begun. Here is a plush source of revenue available—and available without having to persuade individuals to part with their own money. They have a strong incentive to go after the public funds, to see that it is spent to benefit themselves. Who is going to stop them? The poor? In considerable part they are poor because of limited ability to carry through such activities, and they are likely to be even more disadvantaged in politics than in the market—where they can benefit more directly from other people's greed and ability.

If the misuse of the housing money becomes particularly blatant, an ambitious politician may find it an effective issue to arouse public indignation and support. He may even be able to generate enough interest to get a change in the law or the program. But once the interest dies down, the basic pressures will resume and the changed program will again be dominated by special interests.

This is the fundamental reason why governmental agencies set up to regulate a particular industry are inevitably dominated by that industry; why program after program set up to help the "poor," or to promote "safety," or to raise "standards," ends up doing the opposite. There is an invisible hand in politics that operates in the opposite direction to the invisible hand in the market. In politics, individuals who seek to promote only the public good are led by an invisible hand to promote special interests that it was no part of their intention to promote.

MINIMUM-WAGE RATES
September 26, 1966

Congress has just acted to increase unemployment. It did so by raising the legal minimum-wage rate from $1.25 to $1.60 an hour, effective in 1968, and extending its coverage. The result will be and must be to add to the ranks of the unemployed.

Does a merchant increase his sales by raising prices? Does higher pay of domestic servants induce more housewives to hire help? The situation is no different for other employers. The higher wage rate decreed by Congress for low-paid workers will raise the cost of the goods that these workers produce—and must discourage sales. It will also induce employers to replace such workers with other workers—either to do the same work or to produce machinery to do the work.

Some workers who already receive wages well above the legal minimum will benefit—because they will face less competition from the unskilled. That is why many unions are strong supporters of higher minimum-wage rates. Some employers and employees in places where wages are already high will benefit because they will face less competition from businessmen who might otherwise invest capital in areas that have large pools of unskilled labor. That is why Northern manufacturers and unions, particularly in New England, are the principal sources of political pressure for higher legal minimum-wage rates.

It's anti-negro

The groups that will be hurt the most are the low-paid and the unskilled. The ones who remain employed will receive higher wage rates, but fewer will be employed. As Prof. James Tobin, who was a member of President Kennedy's Council of Economic Advisers, recently wrote: "People who lack the capacity to earn a decent living need to be helped, but they will not be helped by minimum-wage laws, trade-union wage pressures or other devices which seek to compel employers to pay them more than their work is worth. The more likely outcome of such regulations is that the intended beneficiaries are not employed at all."

The loss to the unskilled workers will not be offset by gains to others. Smaller total employment will result in a smaller total output. Hence the community as a whole will be worse off.

Women, teen-agers, Negroes and particularly Negro teen-agers will be especially hard hit. I am convinced that the minimum-wage law is the most anti-Negro law on our statute books—in its effect not its intent. It is a tragic but undoubted legacy of the past—and one we must try to correct—that on the average Negroes have lower skills than whites. Similarly, teen-agers are less skilled than older workers. Both Negroes and teen-agers are only made worse off by discouraging employers from hiring them. On-the-job training—the main route whereby the unskilled have become skilled—is thus denied them.

Who is helped?

The shockingly high rate of unemployment among teen-age Negro boys is largely a result of the present Federal minimum-wage rate. And unemployment will be boosted still higher by the rise just enacted. Before 1956, unemployment among Negro boys aged 14 to 19 was around 8 to 11 per cent, about the same as among white boys. Within two years after the legal minimum was raised from 75 cents to $1 an hour in 1956, unemployment among Negro boys shot up to 24 per cent and among white boys to 14 per cent. Both figures have remained roughly the same ever since. But I am convinced that, when it becomes effective, the $1.60 minimum will increase unemployment among Negro boys to 30 per cent or more.[1]

Many well-meaning people favor legal minimum-wage rates in the mistaken belief that they help the poor. These people confuse wage *rates* with wage *income*. It has always been a mystery to me to understand why a youngster is better off unemployed at $1.60 an hour than employed at $1.25. Moreover, many workers in low wage brackets are supplementary earners—that is, youngsters who are just getting started or elderly folk who are adding to the main source of family income. I favor governmental measures that are designed to set a floor under *family income*. Legal minimum-wage rates only make this task more difficult.

The rise in the legal minimum-wage rate is a monument to the power of superficial thinking.

THE BANK DEPOSITOR
November 7, 1966

Do you have a bank deposit? If so, I trust you are aware of how solicitous Congress has been of your welfare. Over 30 years ago, Congress made it illegal for banks to pay you any interest at all on your checking deposits and gave the Federal Reserve System power to fix the maximum interest rate that member banks may pay you on your savings or time deposits. Needless to say, the Fed promptly exercised this power.

However, there was a loophole in the law. Savings-and-loan associations and banks that were not members of the Federal Reserve System were free to pay any rate on savings deposits. As these associations and banks, anxious to exploit the helpless depositor, offered higher and higher interest, the Fed reluctantly raised the ceiling on the rates member banks could pay in order to keep them from losing their time deposits.

This loophole has now been closed. A month ago, Congress authorized the Federal Reserve, the Federal Deposit Insurance Corp. and the Federal

[1 The rate exceeded 30 per cent in early 1971.]

Home Loan Board to fix maximum rates for all banks and savings-and-loan associations and these agencies promptly exercised their power. So you are now fully protected against being induced to save too much by the lure of high interest or to spend too much out of ill-gotten interest.

Small man protected

Of course, the small man needs the most protection. Aware of this, Congress gave the Fed power to discriminate among depositors. The Fed promptly set a lower ceiling for small than for large deposits. If you can deposit more than $100,000, or buy a certificate of deposit for more than that sum, banks may offer you up to 5.5 per cent. But for the rest of us, the most they are now permitted to offer is 5 per cent.

The new law is a tribute to the social conscience of the banking fraternity, especially the men who run savings and loans. It was they who pressed Congress to protect the small saver—and, incidentally, their own deposits from the competition of commercial banks. To my knowledge, no small depositor even testified in favor of the bill, let alone lobbied for it. Perhaps this is not surprising. Bankers clearly know best what depositors need to be protected from.

One flaw remains in the protective ceiling. The new powers were granted for only one year. However, you need have no concern. I have little doubt that a year from now, Congress will see its duty plain and renew these powers so that you will continue to be protected from the temptation of high interest rates on your saving deposits.[1]

Cupidity curbed

Federal and state governments have been vigilant to protect your welfare not only as bank depositor but also as consumer. Are you a milk drinker? Federal milk marketing authorities set minimum prices at which farmers can sell milk and thereby protect you from the temptation to carry this good habit too far. Do you imbibe hard liquor? State liquor commissioners perform a similar service for you. Only the soft-drink addict has so far been overlooked.

State fair-trade laws curb the cupidity of retailers by keeping them from cutting prices to you on branded items price-fixed by manufacturers—indeed, men have gone to jail for selling headache remedies at too low a price. The Federal Trade Commission makes it hard for chain stores to offer you bargains by using their buying power to get quantity discounts. The Interstate Commerce Commission sees to it that railroads do not undercharge you for riding on their trains—when you can find one—and that truckers do not cut prices when they move your goods. Airlines must get permission from the Civil Aeronautics Board to cut fares—and the CAB has not been easy to persuade.

The protecting hand of the law extends to some items most of us have

[1]As, of course, did occur.]

never heard of. The other day, a newspaper story reported that "American Telephone said it won't appeal a U.S. Court of Appeals decision holding that it is charging too little for its 'Telpak' service." Public spirited of Mother Bell, isn't it?

Do you recall The New Yorker cartoon in which the blowzy blonde in the back seat of a cab tells her butter-and-egg companion as he hands her a glittering bauble, "You're so kind to me, and I'm so tired of it all."

AUTO-SAFETY STANDARDS
June 5, 1967

Now that the furor over car safety has subsided, it is instructive to consider some little-noticed aspects of the Federal legislation it produced.

1 COST The recently issued safety standards will raise the cost and hence the price of new cars. According to some estimates, consumers will pay about $1 billion a year extra.

Suppose Congress had been asked to appropriate this sum for the identical safety equipment, raising the money by a special excise tax on automobiles. Would Congress have enacted this proposal as readily as it enacted the safety legislation? Yet the two are identical except in form.

2 DELEGATION OF POWER TO TAX Congress has been jealous of its prerogative to impose taxes. Time and again it has rejected proposals that the President be granted discretion to alter tax rates. Yet in this case, as in other similar cases, Congress has delegated to an administrative official near-absolute power to decide how large a tax to impose.

3 FAILURE TO COMPARE ALTERNATIVES The basic issue before Congress was safety, not requiring automobile manufacturers to build their cars in specified ways. Yet, so far as I know, there was no discussion whether $1 billion a year would contribute more to safety if spent in this way than if spent in other ways—on improved highways, or driver education, or better enforcement of speed limits, or more intensive investigation of causes of auto accidents.

4 WHO WILL SET THE STANDARDS? The National Traffic Safety Agency has already been criticized for yielding to the demands of manufacturers in drawing up its final safety standards for 1968 cars. Mr. William Stieglitz resigned as consultant to the agency on roughly these grounds. Such complaints will be even more justified in the future—though the complaints themselves may become less shrill.

How else can it work out? Safety standards are a peripheral matter to most car owners. A Ralph Nader may get them or the politicians aroused enough to pass a law; but once the law is passed, the consumers will return to somnolence, from which only an occasional scandal will reawaken them. The car manufacturers are in a very different position. They have billions at stake. They will assign some of their best talent full-time to keep tabs on the standards. And who else has the expertise? Sooner or later they will dominate the agency—as, despite well-publicized tiffs, railroads and truckers have dominated the ICC; radio and TV networks, the FCC; physicians, state medical licensure boards; and so on.

5 EFFECT ON COMPETITION Several small specialty-car manufacturers have already complained that compliance with the new safety requirements would put them out of business—the 1931 Ford that one company replicates has less glass in total in its windshields than the windshield wiper standards require the wipers to clear! No doubt, special exemptions will be granted to these companies. But how shall we ever know about the innovations that might have been made, or the companies that might have been established, without this additional handicap?

The effect on foreign producers will be even more important. Any extra cost will be more of a burden on them than on U.S. producers because they sell a much smaller fraction of their output in the U.S. Beyond this, it will become clear to the agency—staffed as it must be by men trained in the U.S. industry and in daily touch with it—that our cars are really safer and that the way to promote safety is to require foreign cars to meet American specifications.

The result will be a sheltered market for U.S. producers—and higher costs to U.S. consumers that have little to do with safety requirements.

6 THE EFFECT ON SAFETY To begin with, the standards may well make cars safer. But, as administrative rigor mortis sets in, they will soon slow up product improvement, so that a decade from now cars may well be less safe. Reduced competition will reinforce this tendency. In addition, the higher price of new cars will raise the average age of cars on the road.

7 AN OFT-TOLD TALE Time and again, laws passed to protect the consumer have ended up by restricting competition and so doing the consumer far more harm than good. Is it too much to hope that one of these days we shall learn this lesson before we enact a new law rather than after?

MOONLIGHTING
September 18, 1967

Far away in the backwoods where the writ of the unions does not run, workers and employers have been fashioning ingenious arrangements under the spur of Federal wages-and-hours legislation.

The legislation requires that any worker who is employed for more than

40 hours a week must be paid time-and-a-half for hours in excess of 40 (with some exceptions for a few occupations that are subject to a highly volatile demand—like longshoremen). Employers are understandably reluctant to employ men more than 40 hours a week—though many of their workers would prefer to work extra hours at straight time if they could.

The ten-hour day

One somewhat surprising reaction has been a move to a ten-hour day. This enables workers to put in their 40 hours in four ten-hour days, leaving them a long three-day weekend. Another is to separate the number of hours worked from the number paid for. Workers are paid for 40 hours each week but actually work five ten-hour days a week for four weeks and then take a full week off. This device may not be strictly within the letter of the law but it seems clearly consistent with the spirit of the law—and besides, it is mutually advantageous to employer and employee.

To many a worker, the three-day weekend, or the one week off in five, is more leisure than he desires, except in hunting and fishing season—given the state of his finances and the demands of his wife and children. So he moonlights by taking on additional jobs.

Mostly, I have been told, the moonlighting is catch-as-catch-can, arranged by individuals on an individual basis. But I have every confidence that this situation will change. There is ample evidence that imagination and innovation are not stilled by restrictive legislation—only diverted to figuring out ways around it.

The obvious development to be expected is what might be dubbed "cooperative moonlighting"—and, for all I know, it may already be in operation. Let two employers use the same work force, each worker working four ten-hour days for one employer and two ten-hour days for the other. This will put the matter on a regular basis, for both employer and employee, and fully satisfy the law. Moreover, it will have the advantage for the employers that the division of time between the two employers can readily be varied. They can thereby jointly achieve flexibility of hours worked without having to pay time-and-a-half.

As this practice spreads, the law will no doubt cooperate by reducing straight-time hours still further—say to 30 hours a week. That would permit the employers to share men equally and so remove one problem that might now be a source of friction.

Of course, the men may not want to work 60 hours a week, but that could easily be arranged. The cooperative arrangement permits wide variation to suit every taste. And, of course, the hunting season does come and fishing is often excellent. But that too can readily be handled. The law does not prevent men from taking vacations—it seeks only to prevent them from taking non-vacations.

Needless to say, it might be more efficient for the men to work longer hours for the same employer than to straddle two employers to stay inside the letter of the law. But that is a subversive thought that you must stifle at birth lest it undermine our whole system. Start on this line, and soon you will be spoiling all the fun.

Perish the thought!

Eliminate restrictions and simplify laws, and what will happen to all the lawyers now busily engaged in plugging loopholes on the one side and opening them on the other? To all those accountants employed in keeping the records required for compliance, or in advising clients how to keep their books to reduce the costs of compliance? To those business advisory services that regularly issue fat volumes codifying government regulations in various areas, and giving the latest information about how the Administration and courts have interpreted them?

To come closer to home, what would this cooperative moonlighter have left to write about? Perish the thought!

"The state," said Frédéric Bastiat, in 1848, "is that great fiction by which everyone seeks to live at the expense of everyone." Were Bastiat alive today, he would see no reason to alter this definition but he might be led to add to it—"and everyone can be employed either imposing legislative restrictions on his fellows or figuring out how to get around them."

THE NEGRO IN AMERICA
December 11, 1967

NEWSWEEK's remarkable cover story on the Negro in America (Nov. 20) is depressing for what it reveals about the present position and attitudes of the Negro minority in these United States. It is more depressing for what it reveals about the views of well-intentioned liberals.

Negroes have made great progress in the past century, thanks to their own efforts and to the opportunities offered them by a market system—and despite widespread prejudice and governmentally enforced discrimination. Liberals have generally disparaged this progress, encouraged Negroes to look primarily to government for relief, and assured them that the white community, by waving its magic legal wand and opening its purse, could and shortly would eliminate their disabilities and drastically raise their standard of living.

In my opinion, this liberal view is tragically wrong. Many of the problems that the Negro faces in America today were produced or aggravated by governmental measures proposed, supported and executed by liberals holding the views that dominate the NEWSWEEK story. The drive for further legislative measures, and particularly the techniques adopted, have awakened the sleeping giant of racial prejudice among the whites in the North.

The encouragement of unrealistic and extravagant expectations has produced frustration, outrage and a sense of betrayal among the Negroes in the North. Unwittingly, the liberals have set race against race.

Government programs

Let me turn to specifics. Says Newsweek, "welfare, jobs and housing are the three main spokes of the wheel of poverty." Consider each.

1 WELFARE We have adopted paternalistic governmental arrangements for dispensing more than $7 billion a year that impair the freedom, independence and dignity of the recipients, and demean the social workers administering the program. These arrangements have weakened family structure and have produced a permanent class of persons on relief.

2 JOBS Unemployment among Negro teen-agers is running around 25 per cent or more. Why? Largely because minimum-wage legislation has declared that it is better for a youngster to be unemployed at $1.40 an hour than employed at $1 an hour (see my column, Sept. 26, 1966). In the absence of legal minimum wages, unemployment among Negro teen-agers would now be under 10 per cent, not over 25 per cent. Other governmental measures—particularly those favoring unions—have restricted the job opportunities of Negroes.

3 HOUSING Public housing and urban renewal programs have destroyed more dwelling units than they have constructed. Concentration of the poor, many of them broken families, in public housing has reinforced despair and fostered juvenile delinquency. Urban renewal has destroyed viable neighborhoods, driven the poor from their homes to even less satisfactory and more expensive housing and created slums where none existed before. It deserves the insidious label of a "Negro removal program."

4 SCHOOLS To Newsweek's three spokes, I would add a fourth, schooling. Inferior slum schools help to perpetuate the Negroes' present disabilities. Yet these are wholly provided by government.

And private alternatives

Government programs have shackled the forces of self-reliance, independence and private enterprise that alone can produce a permanent solution. Progress toward our common objective requires less government intervention, not the major expansion Newsweek calls for.

In welfare, we could substitute a negative income tax for present welfare arrangements. This would reduce government interference in the lives of the poor yet help them more.

In jobs, we could set free the most effective machine for eliminating low incomes that the world has ever seen—competitive private enterprise.

In schooling, parents who choose not to use public schools could be given a voucher for an equivalent sum of money to be used to purchase schooling. This would give slum children a real alternative. And competition would force improvement in public schools.

It is not an accident that government measures have produced results that are the opposite of those intended by their well-meaning sponsors. I am tempted to address to my liberal friends Oliver Cromwell's plea to his enemies: "I beseech you, in the bowels of Christ, think it possible that you may be mistaken."

BOOK BURNING, FCC STYLE
June 16, 1969

The Federal Communications Commission, which now requires radio and TV stations to provide time to anti-smoking ads at no cost, has voted to go still further and prohibit entirely the advertising of cigarettes on radio and television—if the present Congressional ban on such action is not renewed. The Federal Trade Commission favors strengthening the present required health-hazard warning on cigarette packages. The U.S. Public Health Service and other Federal agencies spend sizable sums on campaigns against smoking.

As it happens, I am an ex-smoker. I quit some dozen years ago when the evidence started piling up on the adverse effects of smoking. That evidence persuaded me that I was paying too high a price for the dubious pleasure of smoking. Like most ex-es, I can be counted on to recite the dreary statistics at the drop of an ash.

Nonetheless, I object strongly to the government's measures because I believe that they are hostile to the maintenance of a free society. Government censorship and thought control are no less censorship and thought control when they are exercised for purposes that I approve of.

Individual decisions

The evidence on the harmful effects of smoking, though certainly strong, is not conclusive. Reasonable men who have studied the evidence believe that the statistical association between smoking and a shorter life may have a more subtle explanation than that smoking shortens life. But even if the evidence were conclusive, that would not justify present policies. Every time we take an automobile ride—or cross the street—we knowingly risk our lives because we think that the gain from the ride or from crossing the street justifies the risk. Just so, a smoker may view the pleasures of smoking as justifying the cost in length of life. We may wish to cajole him, plead with him, try to change his tastes. Do we have the right to do more? To use his money, extracted in taxes, to persuade him that he has reached the wrong decision?

Marx's "Das Kapital" and Hitler's "Mein Kampf" have caused far more deaths than all the cigarettes ever smoked. Should we therefore ban their sale? Should we prohibit their being advertised over the radio and TV? Should we require them to carry a warning: READING IS DANGEROUS TO MENTAL HEALTH AND MAY CAUSE DEATH FROM REVOLUTION AND OTHER DISTURBANCES? Should we spend millions of taxpayers' money to "educate" the public to the viciousness of the doctrines they spread?

In a free society, a government has no business using the power of the law or the taxpayers' money to propagandize for some views and to prevent the transmission of others. Freedom of speech includes the freedom to preach for or against Communism, for or against Fascism—and also for or against smoking. Freedom of speech includes freedom to promote particular views out of religious zeal or altruism or humanitarianism—or plain selfishness. Freedom of speech is for the listener as well as the speaker—to enable him to make his own choice among as wide an assortment of views as his fellows are inclined, for whatever reasons, to set forth.

Collective decisions

But, you will say, where do you draw the line? How can we justify imposing taxes on opponents of the Vietnam war to pay for that war? The answer is that the one decision—to smoke or not to smoke—is divisible and affects us individually. Each person can have what he wishes without preventing others from having what they wish. The other decision is indivisible and affects us collectively. The country is at war. There is no way some of us can be at peace, others of us at war. Unfortunately, one or the other group must be overruled. Just because many collective decisions are unavoidable, it is all the more important that we lean over backward to preserve individual choice where we can, that we decide borderline cases in favor of individual freedom.

Part of the duty of elected officials is to lead and not simply to follow—to try to persuade the rest of us that the policies they favor are in the national interest. Yet, let them go too far in that direction, and the threat of government indoctrination, financed by the taxes we pay, becomes very real indeed, held in check only by the division of powers, the multiplicity of governmental units and the offsetting pressures of different groups.

If we are to preserve a free society, we must reinforce these fragile checks with the unremitting pressure of an enlightened citizenry.

DEFENSE OF USURY
April 6, 1970

In 1787, Jeremy Bentham published a lengthy pamphlet entitled, "Defense of Usury; Shewing the Impolicy of the Present Legal Restraints on the Terms of Pecuniary Bargains." The pecuniary bargains he was concerned with were loans between individuals or business enterprises. The legal restraints were limits on interest rates paid or received. Usury was and is the popular term for charging interest rates in excess of legal limits.

Bentham makes an overwhelmingly persuasive case for the proposition he sets forth at the beginning of the pamphlet, "viz. that *no man of ripe years and of sound mind, acting freely, and with his eyes open, ought to be hindered, with a view to his advantage, from making such bargain, in the way of obtaining money, as he thinks fit: nor* (what is a necessary consequence) *any body hindered from supplying him, upon any terms he thinks proper to accede to."*

Conviction versus practice

During the nearly two centuries since Bentham's pamphlet was published, his arguments have been widely accepted by economists and as widely neglected by politicians. I know of no economist of any standing from that time to this who has favored a legal limit on the rate of interest that borrowers could pay or lenders receive—though there must have been some. I know of no country that does not limit by law the rates of interest—and I doubt that there are any. As Bentham wrote, "in great political questions, wide indeed is the distance between conviction and practice."

Bentham's explanation of the "grounds of the prejudices against usury" is as valid today as when he wrote: "The business of a moneylender . . . has no where, nor any time, been a popular one. Those who have the resolution to sacrifice the present to future, are natural objects of envy to those who have sacrificed the future to the present. The children who have eat their cake are the natural enemies of the children who have theirs. While the money is hoped for, and for a short time after it has been received, he who lends it is a friend and benefactor: by the time the money is spent, and the evil hour of reckoning is come, the benefactor is found to have changed his nature, and to have put on the tyrant and the oppressor. It is an oppression for a man to reclaim his own money: it is none to keep it from him."

Bentham's explanation of the "mischief of the anti-usurious laws" is also as valid today as when he wrote that these laws preclude "many people, altogether, from the getting the money they stand in need of, to answer their respective exigencies." For still others, they render "the terms so much the worse . . . While, out of loving-kindness, or whatsoever other motive, the law precludes a man from *borrowing*, upon terms which it deems too disadvantageous, it does not preclude him from *selling*, upon any terms, howsoever disadvantageous." His conclusion: "The sole tendency of the law is to heap distress upon distress."

Who is hurt?

Developments since Bentham's day have increased the mischief done by usury legislation. Economic progress has provided the ordinary man with the means to save. The spread of banks, savings-and-loan associations, and the like has given the ordinary man the facilities for saving. For the first time in history, the working class may well be net lenders rather than net borrowers. They are also the ones who have fewest alternatives, who find it hardest to avoid legal regulations, and who are therefore hardest hit by them.

Under the spur of Wright Patman and his ilk, the Federal Reserve now limits the interest rate that commercial banks may pay to a maximum of 4½ per cent for small savers but to 7½ per cent for deposits of $100,000 or more. And the deposits of small savers have been relatively stable or growing, while those of large depositors have been declining sharply because they have still better alternatives.

That is the way the self-labeled defenders of the "people" look after their interests—by keeping them from receiving the interest they are entitled to. Along with Bentham, "I would . . . wish to learn . . . why the legislator should be more anxious to limit the rate of interest one way, than the other? Why should he set his face against the owners of that species of property more than of any other? Why he should make it his business to prevent their getting *more* than a certain price for the use of it, rather than to prevent their getting *less?* . . . Let any one that can, find an answer to these questions; it is more than I can do."

MIGRANT WORKERS
July 27, 1970

The old saw is that the Quakers went to the New World to do good and ended up doing well. Today, well-meaning reformers go to Washington to do good and end up doing harm.

A recent Wall Street Journal story gives a striking example—the effects in Michigan of stricter Federal and state standards for housing migrant farm workers. The intent: to improve the conditions of a group of low-paid workers. The result: to hurt the workers, the farmers and consumers.

"Higher labor costs," says the story, "have prompted many growers . . . to switch to mechanized harvesting in recent years, lessening demand for migrant workers. That trend has intensified in the last two years, as government agencies have implemented stricter housing regulations for growers participating in their migrant-worker placement programs . . .

"State and Federal officials estimate that mechanization could eliminate from 6,000 to 10,000 jobs in Michigan this summer that were previously done by migrants . . . License applications [for migrant camps] are down 11 per cent so far this summer . . .

"Nonetheless, approximately 50,000 migrant workers, mostly Mexican-Americans from Southwest Texas, are expected to come into Michigan looking for work this summer. That's about the same number that came through last year."

Mechanization is a good thing if it is a response to a decline in the number of persons seeking jobs as migrant workers at low wages. That would mean that the former migrant workers have found better employment opportunities. Mechanization is a bad thing if it is a response to higher labor costs imposed arbitrarily from the outside. That simply wastes capital to replace people who are forced into unemployment or even less desirable jobs.

Who is helped, who hurt?

Migrant workers are clearly hurt. It is small comfort to an unemployed migrant worker to know that, if he could get a job, he would have better housing. True, the housing formerly available may have been most unsatisfactory by our standards. However, the migrant workers clearly regarded it, plus the accompanying jobs, as the best alternative available to them, else why did they flock to Michigan? It is certainly desirable that they have better alternatives available to them, but until they do, how are they helped by eliminating alternatives, however unsatisfactory, that are now available? That is simply biting off their noses to save our faces.

Farmers are clearly hurt. The cost of migrant labor has been raised. That is why they are mechanizing. The machines limit the rise in cost but do not eliminate it. Costs would be lower if farmers could hire migrant labor on *terms that would be mutually satisfactory to them and the laborers.* But they are not permitted to do so.

Consumers are clearly hurt. At the higher costs, less food will be harvested, so making food prices higher than they otherwise would be.

Producers of mechanized farm equipment are helped by having a larger market. But in the main, they simply produce harvesting equipment instead of other equipment.

The only other people who are helped are the do-gooders responsible for this type of legislation and for these effects. They have the highminded satisfaction of promoting a noble cause. The good intention is emblazoned forth for all to see. The harm is far less visible, much more indirect, much harder to connect with the good-hearted action. Besides, the harm is mostly to someone else.

Is this case unique?

This case is not in any way unique, except that it happens to be more obvious than most. I know hardly any do-gooder legislation of this kind—

whether it be minimum-wage laws or rent control or urban renewal or public housing or fair-employment legislation—which, on examination of its full consequences, does not do more harm than good—and more harm as judged by the intentions of the well-meaning people who sponsor such legislation.

Will the liberals ever learn this lesson of experience? So far, the clear failure of government program after government program to achieve its objective has simply led to a clamor for still larger, still more expensive, still more far-reaching programs—to do still more harm. It is about time that the liberals asked themselves whether the fault may not be in the system they favor—doing good at other people's expense—rather than in the way the system is operated. It is about time that they appealed to their heads as well as their hearts.

ROOFS OR CEILINGS
March 22, 1971

In 1946, George Stigler and I published a pamphlet attacking the legal ceilings that had been imposed on rents during World War II and were then still in effect. We argued that the ceilings, by keeping rents artificially low to those persons who were fortunate enough to live in controlled dwellings, encouraged the waste of housing space and, at the same time, discouraged the construction of additional dwellings. Hence our title, "Roofs or Ceilings."

Nationwide ceilings were subsequently abolished. However, localities were given the option to continue them. New York City—with that unerring instinct for self-destruction that has brought it to its present condition—is the only major city still controlling rents under this option.

A recent article by Richard Stone in The Wall Street Journal, "Shortage of Housing in New York Gets Worse Every Day," brought this ancient pamphlet vividly back to mind. At a time when there is so much talk about imposing new price controls, this cautionary tale is worth pondering.

The New York story

Reports Stone: "The dimensions of the New York shortage are vast. The rental vacancy rate is below 1 per cent . . . Private building is at near-paralysis . . . Increasing numbers of landlords simply give up, abandoning buildings they can neither afford to maintain nor sell at any price. Tenants, left with no heat, water or electricity vacate such buildings in a matter of days. When that happens, blight swallows up whole neighborhoods, almost overnight."

"Every day there are fewer housing units available in New York City than the day before."

"New York's archaic rent-control law keeps the marginally poor whose fortune is improving from moving out of slum neighborhoods."

Others go to great lengths to find a rent-controlled apartment, including keeping "track of obituaries to divine what deaths are creating rent-control vacancies."

"Partly because of rent control, rents on private housing built since 1947—housing that doesn't come under the law—skyrocketed over the past decade . . . After fierce public outcry, the city last summer passed a law holding annual increases to 5 per cent. To no one's surprise, several major builders responded by withdrawing from the city."

Or, as we wrote in our 1946 pamphlet: "Rent ceilings cause haphazard and arbitrary allocation of space, inefficient use of space, retardation of new construction. The legal ceilings on rents are the reason there are so few places for rent. Because of the excess of demand over supply, rental property is now rationed [in New York] by various forms of chance and favoritism. As long as the shortage created by rent ceilings remains, there will be a clamor for continued rent controls. This is perhaps the strongest indictment of ceilings on rent. They, and the accompanying shortage of dwellings to rent, perpetuate themselves, and the progeny are even less attractive than the parents."

Housing and grapefruit

Do not suppose that this sad tale reflects anything special about housing. During World War II, when price control was nearly universal, black markets, and rationing by chance, favoritism, and bribery developed in steel, meat, bananas—you name it. Since World War II, there have been major crises in gold and foreign exchange—because governments have tried to fix the prices of both. When the price of the dollar was fixed too low in terms of other currencies, there was a "dollar shortage"; more recently, when it has been fixed too high, there has been concern about balance-of-payments deficits. The price system is a remarkably efficient system for bringing buyers and sellers together; for assuring that the quantities some people want to buy will match the quantities other people want to sell. Immobilize the price system and something else—if only chaos and queues—must take its place.

Would you like to see a shortage of grapefruit in New York that will get worse with every day? Let New York impose and effectively enforce a ceiling price on grapefruit below the market price. Let Washington do so, and the shortage will be nationwide. And you can substitute any product you wish for "grapefruit," provided you add the qualification that the ceiling price be "effectively enforced." That is the direction in which the well-meaning people who are talking about legal price-and-wage control are pushing us. They should be condemned to hunting for an apartment in New York.

WHAT IS KILLING THE CITY?
March 20, 1972

In two remarkable columns, Stewart Alsop has explored "The City Disease" that is killing the South Bronx area of New York City (NEWSWEEK, Feb. 28 and March 6). He summarized his findings as follows: "Well-intentioned and liberal-minded people (including this writer) have assumed that the way to cure conditions like those in the South Bronx is to spend a lot of money in the slums. A lot of money has been spent in the South Bronx and other New York slums. New York's expenditures for 'social services' have tripled since John Lindsay became mayor, and Federal spending for social purposes has also vastly increased. All the time, the city disease has got worse —and worse and worse."

Paradox?

This result seems a paradox. How can it be that more spending is accompanied by worse results?

One standard explanation is that the disease has gotten worse despite the increase in spending, that it would have gotten still worse if there had been less spending, and that we need still more spending by New York City and the Federal government. Though this explanation has produced a massive and continuing increase in Federal, state and local government spending for "social services," its plausibility has worn thin as spending has mounted and the disease has continued to get worse.

A second explanation is that the fault is not with the amount of government spending but with the way government has spent the money. In housing, this explanation has led to stress on rehabilitation instead of new construction, on small-scale scattered public housing instead of gigantic housing projects, on rent supplements instead of public housing. Unfortunately, despite the great fanfare and extravagant promises that accompany each new program, still the city disease marches on.

The right explanation, I submit, is very different. Mr. Alsop is simply wrong when he says, "New York's expenditures for 'social services' have tripled." They may not have changed at all—or may even have declined. What has happened is that expenditures by the *government* of the City of New York have tripled. But where has the money come from? Primarily from the people in New York City. Where else can it come from? The money may take a detour via Albany or Washington—which will, of course, take their cut —but that only conceals, it does not change, the ultimate origin of the money. The citizens of New York City have spent more through their government and therefore have had less to spend themselves.

No. To be expected.

The total amount available for spending has not been increased by Lindsay's programs. On the contrary, it has been decreased as the deterioration of the city and ever-higher taxes have encouraged people and business to move out. Is it really a paradox that we get less for our money when government bureaucrats spend our money for our supposed benefit than when we spend our own money on our own needs?

But, you may say, government spending is for the poor; the money government spends comes from the well-to-do; hence private spending would benefit different people.

Wrong on both counts. The government program may be labeled "welfare for the poor," but that does not mean that very much of the money spent benefits the poor. Much of the money goes to buy land or buildings or services from the not-so-poor—as, most notably, in urban renewal programs—to provide amenities for the not-so-poor. Some of the rest goes to pay excellent salaries to bureaucrats. Even the part that does trickle down to the poor is largely wasted because it encourages them to substitute a handout for a wage.

As to who pays, the possibility of taxing the rich is strictly limited, especially in a city like New York. It is too easy for the rich to move. Whatever the rhetoric, the poor pay their full share of the taxes.

Government spending is the problem, not the solution. We do not need new government programs. We need to abolish the old programs and let people spend their own money in accordance with their own values. The city would then get better—and better and better.

For New York City, it is probably too late for this cure because so large a part of the voting population already consists of city employees and welfare recipients. But it is not too late for other cities to learn from New York's disease.

PROHIBITION AND DRUGS
May 1, 1972

"The reign of tears is over. The slums will soon be only a memory. We will turn our prisons into factories and our jails into storehouses and corncribs. Men will walk upright now, women will smile, and the children will laugh. Hell will be forever for rent."

This is how Billy Sunday, the noted evangelist and leading crusader against Demon Rum, greeted the onset of Prohibition in early 1920. We know now how tragically his hopes were doomed. New prisons and jails had to be built to house the criminals spawned by converting the drinking of spirits into a crime against the state. Prohibition undermined respect for the law, corrupted the minions of the law, created a decadent moral climate—but did not stop the consumption of alcohol.

Despite this tragic object lesson, we seem bent on repeating precisely the same mistake in the handling of drugs.

Ethics and expediency

On ethical grounds, do we have the right to use the machinery of government to prevent an individual from becoming an alcoholic or a drug addict? For children, almost everyone would answer at least a qualified yes. But for responsible adults, I, for one, would answer no. Reason with the potential addict, yes. Tell him the consequences, yes. Pray for and with him, yes. But I believe that we have no right to use force, directly or indirectly, to prevent a fellow man from committing suicide, let alone from drinking alcohol or taking drugs.

I readily grant that the ethical issue is difficult and that men of goodwill may well disagree. Fortunately, we need not resolve the ethical issue to agree on policy. *Prohibition is an attempted cure that makes matters worse—for both the addict and the rest of us.* Hence, even if you regard present policy toward drugs as ethically justified, considerations of expediency make that policy most unwise.

Consider first the addict. Legalizing drugs might increase the number of addicts, but it is not clear that it would. Forbidden fruit is attractive, particularly to the young. More important, many drug addicts are deliberately made by pushers, who give likely prospects their first few doses free. It pays the pusher to do so because, once hooked, the addict is a captive customer. If drugs were legally available, any possible profit from such inhumane activity would disappear, since the addict could buy from the cheapest source.

Whatever happens to the number of addicts, the individual addict would clearly be far better off if drugs were legal. Today, drugs are both incredibly expensive and highly uncertain in quality. Addicts are driven to associate with criminals to get the drugs, become criminals themselves to finance the habit, and risk constant danger of death and disease.

Consider next the rest of us. Here the situation is crystal-clear. The harm to us from the addiction of others arises almost wholly from the fact that drugs are illegal. A recent committee of the American Bar Association estimated that addicts commit one-third to one-half of all street crime in the U.S. Legalize drugs, and street crime would drop automatically.

Moreover, addicts and pushers are not the only ones corrupted. Immense sums are at stake. It is inevitable that some relatively low-paid police and other government officials—and some high-paid ones as well—will succumb to the temptation to pick up easy money.

Law and order

Legalizing drugs would simultaneously reduce the amount of crime and raise the quality of law enforcement. Can you conceive of any other measure that would accomplish so much to promote law and order?

But, you may say, must we accept defeat? Why not simply end the drug traffic? That is where experience under Prohibition is most relevant. We cannot end the drug traffic. We may be able to cut off opium from Turkey—but there are innumerable other places where the opium poppy grows. With French cooperation, we may be able to make Marseilles an unhealthy place to manufacture heroin—but there are innumerable other places where the simple manufacturing operations involved can be carried out. So long as large sums of money are involved—and they are bound to be if drugs are illegal—it is literally hopeless to expect to end the traffic or even reduce seriously its scope.

In drugs, as in other areas, persuasion and example are likely to be far more effective than the use of force to shape others in our image.

LEGISLATING UNEMPLOYMENT
July 3, 1972

Congress is at it again. Once more it is in the process of legislating an increase in unemployment. Of course, the legislation is not labeled "A Bill to Create Unemployment." After all, Congress can teach big business a thing or two about deceptive labeling. No, the bill is labeled "A Bill to Increase the Minimum-Wage Rate."

The true minimum-wage rate is zero—the amount that an unemployed person receives from his nonexistent employer. This minimum-wage rate will not be affected by the new law. Rather, the law will increase the number of persons who receive a wage rate of zero. Here is a person with limited skill whose services are valued at $1.60 an hour (the existing legal minimum) by a potential employer. The new law would make it illegal for the employer to hire that person. He could give him charity—pay him $1.80 or $2 for services that he values at only $1.60—but he could not legally hire him for the market value of his services. It is a mystery why anyone would suppose that a person is better off unemployed at $2 an hour than voluntarily employed at $1.60.

Ignorance?

The economic expansion now under way promises to reduce the extremely high rates of unemployment of teen-agers, blacks, and women—the groups with lowest skills. A higher legal minimum-wage rate will have precisely the opposite effect—as every prior rise in the legal minimum has had.

The House has recognized the adverse effect of a rise in the legal minimum-wage rate on teen-age unemployment by enacting a two-step minimum—the present $1.60 an hour for youths under 18 and students under 21, and a higher rate for most other nonagricultural workers ($1.80 this year, $2 a year from now). The Senate has not yet acted, but its Labor committee has reported a bill that would simply raise the rate to $2 this year and to $2.20 next year.

The two-step rate is better than a one-step rate. At least, it would reduce the harm done by raising the minimum. But a no-step rate would be better than either.

When a minimum-wage rate was first enacted in 1938 and, to a lesser extent, even when it was last raised in 1966, it was not unreasonable for legislators to dismiss the possible effect on employment. While economists have always recognized that high minimum-wage rates create unemployment and so reduce the take-home pay of poor people—which is what buys food, clothing, and other necessities—empirical studies documenting this effect were scattered and appeared inconclusive.

The situation today is different. Scattered studies have been brought together, additional studies made and some earlier studies re-evaluated. The evidence is now overwhelming that the unemployment predicted by economic analysis is confirmed by economic experience.[1]

Or conflicting interests?

As matters now stand, if Congress enacts a higher minimum-wage rate, it will do so knowing that one effect will be to raise unemployment—as the action of the House documents.

Why would Congress do such a thing? Because the adverse effect on the poor is diffuse and its source misunderstood and hence produces little political pressure. Effective pressure is exerted by organized groups that welcome the effect of a high minimum-wage rate in strengthening unionized and skilled workers vis-à-vis nonunionized and unskilled workers and in protecting employers in high-wage areas (the North) from the competition of employers in low-wage areas (the South). These organized groups find ready allies in the liberal reformers whose lack of understanding of economics misdirects their sincere concern for the disadvantaged.

My first column in this space (NEWSWEEK, Sept. 26, 1966) was on the then recently passed rise in minimum-wage rates. I wrote, "I am convinced that the minimum-wage law is the most anti-Negro law on our statute books—in its effect, not its intent. It is a tragic but undoubted legacy of the past—and one we must try to correct—that, on the average, Negroes have lower skills than whites. Similarly, teen-agers are less skilled than older workers. Both Negroes and teen-agers are only made worse off by discouraging employers from hiring them. On-the-job training—the main route whereby the unskilled have become skilled—is thus denied them."

This remains the unpalatable truth.

[1] For an excellent, though not fully up-to-date, summary of these studies, see John M. Peterson and Charles T. Stewart Jr., "Employment Effects of Minimum-Wage Rates" (American Enterprise Institute, 1969).

DOING GOOD[1]

There is an old saw to the effect that the Quakers came to the New World to do good and ended up doing well. My theme today is how varied are the results that can follow the attempt to do good. Sometimes, it succeeds magnificently, sometimes, the results are innocuous, but sometimes, the results are positively evil.

This uncertain outcome is worth stressing, particularly for you young men and women who are today commencing your life's work, because of your natural tendency to take the will for the deed, to ask what a man's motives and intentions are rather than whether the measures he proposes will in fact achieve the end he professes to seek.

This tendency has idealistic roots. But its flower is cynicism. Working it backward, you see what you interpret as evils—the coexistence of poor and rich; idle men and idle machines; slums, pollution, and the rest of the familiar litany. If the will is the deed, then is the deed not the will? How tempting to conclude that evil men are responsible for what we see as evils, to blame the bloated and heartless capitalists for gleefully grinding the poor under their heels.

This way is the cynical view that society is not merely flawed but corrupt, that the only solution is to throw the rascals out, to clap them in jail as criminals.

This way also is intolerance, smugness, and arrogance. If what matters is only the will, if the solution to our problems is simply to have good men in charge, then anyone who disagrees with me about what should be done must have different motives—and mine of course are noble, so his must be ignoble. It is far easier for me to question his motives than to examine his arguments, to undertake the difficult and tantalizingly elusive task of seeing how my policy and his policy will in fact work. And if his motives are evil, is not the proper response invective and scorn rather than reasoned argument and patient discourse?

The view that evil motives explain social evils is simple-minded. Fortunately, it is also false. There are real evils and it is important that we seek to correct them, but not everything that at first sight appears to be an evil is one and we should not let myopic concentration on the real evils blind us to the accomplishments and achievements of society that we take for granted. More important, few of the real evils in our society today are the product of evil men. Many evils simply reflect limited resources—not everybody's wants can be satisfied. Many evils reflect the cussedness of other men in putting their interests above mine. Some evils, and those I especially want to talk about, are the result of good men trying to do good.

This great University, like my own University of Chicago, is a monument

[1]Talk given at Commencement of University of Rochester, June 6, 1971. A condensed version was published in *Readers Digest*, October, 1971.

to successful attempts to do good. So, also, are the voluntary hospitals, the public libraries, the great museums, and, on a different level, the local charities, orphanages, and other eleemosynary institutions that are spread throughout our country. These are shining tributes to what men can accomplish when they use their own energies and their own wealth to serve interests that go beyond narrow self-interests, that go to causes and values and beliefs.

Some attempts to do good have failed simply because, as Robert Burns put it, "the best laid schemes o' mice and men gang aft a–gley." In such cases, the will is to be honored even if the deed did not follow.

The Spanish Inquisition exemplifies another face of doing good. The men who tortured their fellows were not evil men. They were trying to do good—to save the souls of their victims. Heaven preserve us from the sincere fanatic who knows what is good for us better than we do, and who knows that it is his duty and his obligation to make us do what is good for us—whether his name be Torquemado, Lenin, or Hitler, or on a minor scale, Marcuse, or Nader.

The sincere fanatic has done vast harm in the course of human history. But in our time and our country, the major flaw that has converted doing good into doing evil is very different: it is the temptation to solve every problem by spending somebody else's money. Only government has the power to do that on a large scale. So the standard cliche for every social ill has become—more government spending, more government manpower. The result has almost always been that the money ends up being spent for very different purposes than those intended by the do-gooders, and makes the problem worse rather than better.

Consider our urban slums. Housing for the poor is bad; there is urban blight; what shall we do about it? Men seeking to do good promoted public housing and urban renewal. The result. More dwelling units torn down than constructed; negro removal rather than urban renewal; worse slums and poorer housing conditions. Why? Because the do-gooders returned to their homes in a pleasing glow of rectitude once the laws were passed, leaving the field to the sustained efforts of persons who could benefit directly from the new programs. Evil special interests? No. Naive do-gooders trying to do good with someone else's money.

This story is repeated in area after area. We are now spending on programs ostensibly directed at alleviating poverty some $75 billion a year. If this were spread over those classified as "poor" by the arbitrary Social Security definition, it would come to something like $3,000 per man, woman, and child, or to $12,000 per family of four. This is roughly the average income of the population as a whole. If this money were going to the poor, they would be among the well-off and poverty would be a thing of the past. Obviously it is not. The label on the legislation is "poverty." But the content is waste and special interest—and by special interest, I include yours and mine. The truly poor would be better off if we taxed them less and erected fewer slush funds in their name.

As Thoreau wrote in 1854—around the time the University of Rochester was founded—"There is no odor so bad as that which arises from goodness tainted. It is human, it is divine, carrion. If I knew for a certainty that a man was coming to my house with the conscious design of doing me good, I should run for my life."

I am more of a reformer than he. I propose simply that we add an eleventh amendment to the Bill of Rights. Every person shall be free to do good—at his own expense.

Chapter Nine
GOVERNMENT AND THE INTERESTS

The ability of special interests to get legislation enacted in their favor or to take over control of governmental bodies set up to regulate them, which is exemplified in this chapter as well as in Chapters 8 and 10, has led many social critics on both the left and the right to conclude that there is a "ruling class" that runs the government and through the government the society. On this view, the ruling class is able to use its control of government to line its own pockets at the expense of the rest of the country.

Fortunately for the chances of preserving and extending freedom, the conclusion is false. True enough, we have a mass of special-interest legislation and of regulating agencies dominated by the industries that they are supposed to regulate. True enough, the apparent beneficiaries of each such piece of legislation or of such regulating bodies are generally in the upper income groups, or at least in groups above the average. However—and here is the fallacy in the "ruling class" view—the special interests that are served are fragmented and each gets its benefits largely at the expense of other special interests. It is likely that the special interest groups as a whole and possibly each one separately would benefit if the special-interest legislation as a whole were abolished.

Consider a simple illustration. Air fares would be roughly 60 per cent of their present level if they were not controlled as they now are by the C.A.B. We know this because two states (Texas and California) are large enough to support substantial intrastate carriers that are free from C.A.B. control because they do not engage in interstate travel. (They are controlled by state bodies, but that has apparently not been very restrictive). Their fares are about 60 per cent of the controlled fares on comparable runs (compare the Los Angeles–San Francisco fare on PSA with the Los Angeles–Reno or Los Angeles–Phoenix fares on the C.A.B. regulated carriers). This means that regulation costs air travellers 40 per cent of the total amount they pay as fares to the regulated carriers.

Who benefits? Mostly no one. The profits of the airline industry have been notable for their thinness not their abundance. Because the regulated lines cannot effectively compete on price, they compete through offering frills and extra service. As a result, their rate of use of space is decidedly lower than that of the intrastate lines, and their costs per passenger mile is much higher. Their profits are, if anything, lower measured either relative to capital or revenue. Clearly most of the 40 cents cost to travellers per dollar of air fare simply pays for economic waste. But suppose some, say 4 cents, seeps through to profits.

Who travels by air? Mostly high-income people. Who owns airline stocks? Mostly high-income people. So high-income people are taking $1 out of their left pocket in their capacity as passengers to put 10 cents in their right pocket in their capacity as owners of airline stock. Smart ruling class.

The reason for this nonsense is not an all-wise–all-powerful ruling class, but precisely the same phenomenon described in the introduction to Chapter 8—the invisible hand in politics. The interests of the passengers is diffuse. Travelling is but one of many ways that the rich spend their money. The interests of the owners of airlines and their managers is concentrated. This is *the* way, or a major way, that they get their income. In the political process, therefore, the producer wins and the consumer is exploited. In the economic process, the diffused interest of the consumer receives its proper attention.

OIL AND THE MIDDLE EAST
June 26, 1967

Few U.S. industries sing the praises of free enterprise more loudly than the oil industry. Yet few industries rely so heavily on special governmental favors.

These favors are defended in the name of national security. A strong domestic oil industry, it is said, is needed because international disturbances can so readily interfere with the supply of foreign oil. The Israeli-Arab war has produced just such a disturbance, and the oil industry is certain to point to it as confirmation of the need for special favors. Are they right? I believe not.

The main special favors are:

1 PERCENTAGE DEPLETION This is a special provision of the Federal income tax under which oil producers can treat up to 27½ per cent of their income as exempt from income tax—supposedly to compensate for the depletion of oil reserves.[1] This name is a misnomer. In effect, this provision simply gives the oil industry (and a few others to which similar treatment has been extended) a lower tax rate than other industries.

2 LIMITATION OF OIL PRODUCTION Texas, Oklahoma and some other oil-producing states limit the number of days a month that oil wells may operate or the amount that they may produce. The purpose of these limitations is said to be "conservation." In practice, they have led to the wasteful drilling of multiple wells draining the same field. And the amount of production permitted has been determined primarily by estimates of market demand, not by the needs of conservation. The state regulatory authorities have simply been running a producers' cartel to keep up the price of oil.

3 OIL IMPORT QUOTAS The high domestic prices enforced by restriction of production were threatened by imports from abroad. So, in 1959, President Eisenhower imposed a quota on imports by sea. This quota is still in effect.

[1This rate was reduced in the Tax Reform Act of 1969 to 22 per cent.]

Currently, it is slightly more than 1 million barrels a day (under one-fifth of our total consumption).

Foreign oil can be landed at East Coast refineries for about $1 to $1.50 a barrel less than the cost of domestic oil. The companies fortunate enough to be granted import permits are therefore in effect getting a Federal subsidy of this amount per barrel—or a total of about $400 million a year.

These special favors cost U.S. consumers of oil products something over $3.5 billion a year (Gilbert Burck, Fortune, April 1965). This staggering cost cannot be justified by its contribution to national security.

The following points indicate the basis for this judgment:

1 Restricting imports may promote the domestic industry but why pay a $400 million subsidy to oil importers? A tariff of $1.25 a barrel would restrict imports just as much—and the U.S. Government rather than the oil importers would get the revenue. (I do not favor such a tariff but it would be less bad than a quota.)

2 Oil from Venezuela—after the U.S., the largest oil producer in the world—is most unlikely to be cut off by international disturbances threatening our national security. Yet it too is covered by the import quota.

3 Restrictions on domestic oil production at least have the virtue that domestic production could be expanded rapidly in case of need. But such restrictions are an incredibly expensive way to achieve flexibility.

4 The world oil industry is highly competitive and far-flung and getting more so. The Mideast crisis has left large oil-producing areas undisturbed. Moreover, the Arabian countries themselves cannot afford to refuse to sell for long. Only World War III is likely to produce severe disruptions of supply—and then the emergency is likely to be brief.

5 If all the special favors to the oil industry were abandoned, prices to the consumer would decline sharply. Domestic production also might decline—but then again, if the industry were freed of all the artificial props that raise costs and stifle initiative, production might rise rather than decline. In either event, a vigorous and extensive domestic industry would remain, protected by the natural barrier of transportation costs.

If domestic output did decline, we might want to insure against an emergency by stockpiling oil, paying for holding reserve wells in readiness, making plans for sharp reductions in nonessential consumption, or in other ways. Measures such as these could provide insurance at a small fraction of the $3.5 billion a year the U.S. consumer is now paying.

The political power of the oil industry, not national security, is the reason for the present subsidies to the industry. International disturbances simply offer a convenient excuse.

WHAT'S IN A NAME?

November 20, 1967

Consider an imaginary conversation between Roger Blough, chairman of the board of U.S. Steel, and Senators Everett Dirksen of Illinois and Vance Hartke of Indiana.

Mr. Blough: Gentlemen, I seek your assistance. The steel industry is in serious straits. Our costs are rising and our profits are falling.

Senator Dirksen: At a time like the present, when the country is faced with the grave danger of inflation, it would be most unfortunate to have steel prices rise. Yet even that would be better than to let the steel industry founder.

Mr. Blough: Unfortunately, we cannot raise our prices. We would lose too much business to steel producers in Japan and Europe. We would have to cut back sharply on our operations.

Senator Hartke: That would be serious for my constituents in Gary. What can we do?

Mr. Blough: Introduce a bill to impose an excise tax on steel.

The Senators (*in unison*): But surely that would hurt, not help, the steel industry!

Mr. Blough: By itself, it would. But I suggest that the proceeds from the tax be used to pay a subsidy of like amount to steel producers.

Senator Hartke: You puzzle me. Wouldn't the tax and subsidy just cancel?

Mr. Blough: Not quite. The tax would be on all steel, whether produced in this country or abroad. The offsetting subsidy would go only to domestic producers. The effect would be a higher price to domestic steel producers without the fear of inroads into our markets by foreign producers.

Senator Dirksen: What about the excess of the taxes over the subsidy? Should we use that to reduce the frightening deficit we face?

Mr. Blough: Oh, no. The proposed tax and subsidy would affect adversely the firms now engaged in importing steel. I suggest that we use the excess tax revenue to compensate them for the burden we are asking them to bear in the national interest.

Such a conversation never has taken place and never would. Mr. Blough would not make such a proposal. If he did, Senators Dirksen and Hartke would not take it seriously.

Yet the limitation on imports urged by the steel industry and sponsored by Senators Dirksen and Hartke, among others, is identical in substance to the imaginary proposal. Limiting the amount of steel that may legally be imported would enable the industry to raise prices without fear of foreign competition. It would make the price at which steel sells in the U.S. higher than the price at which it can be purchased abroad—precisely the result that the excise tax would achieve.

Subsidies or competition

The recipients of permits to import steel will receive a subsidy equal to the difference between the price of domestic and foreign steel—just as under the hypothetical excise tax. Such permits will be valuable and no doubt will be bought and sold, as are currently permits to import oil and other products subject to quotas. A recipient of a permit would then be able to get his subsidy by selling the right to import steel rather than by exercising it.

The difference between the imaginary excise-subsidy and the actually proposed import quotas is political, not economic. In the one case, the subsidy by the government to the steel industry is open and aboveboard, in the other, it is disguised.

The U.S. can acquire steel by producing steel itself—or by producing other goods, selling them abroad, and using the proceeds to buy steel. If steel can be purchased at a lower price from foreign than from domestic producers, then the U.S. steel industry has failed the market test. It is best for the nation that some of the men and capital resources devoted to producing steel be devoted to more useful pursuits—perhaps producing some of the products we shall then export in return for the steel we import.

The steel industry professes to be a friend of free enterprise. In speech after speech, its leaders extol the superiority of capitalism over socialism. They stress the virtues of private initiative, free markets, competition, the discipline of profits and losses. Yet as soon as that discipline affects the wrong column of their ledgers, they run to Washington for help.

It is tempting to berate the steel industry for hypocrisy. But the real fault is with the rest of us. It is up to us to see to it that business enterprises can promote their own interests only by serving their customers, not by having the law corral customers.

HOW TO FREE TV
December 1, 1969

In his powerful attack on TV news coverage, Vice President Agnew accurately described the present lack of diversity, but touched only lightly on causes and cures.

The causes are not to be found in the character of the men who present the news or who run the networks. Both groups try to present the news fairly. Yet, with the best of intentions, three collections of men breathing the same intellectual atmosphere and with a strong incentive to appeal to the same audience in the same way will inevitably present a one-sided point of view.

Causes

This narrow range of views has its origins in two related features of TV: first, the requirement of a government license in order to operate a TV station; second, the effective stifling of pay-TV for well over a decade by the Federal Communications Commission under the pressure and influence of the networks.

To see the importance of the second feature, suppose that it were made illegal for any reading matter to be sold directly to the public. Reading matter could be distributed only if it were given away to all comers, financed, as TV programs now are, by advertising, philanthropy or government subsidy.

What would happen to our present variety of reading matter—to which Mr. Agnew referred so aptly? Would advertisers finance newspapers and magazines of the kind we now have? Perhaps a few, but surely not many, and hardly any that would take a strong, independent and unpopular position, or that, like the New Republic, National Review, Harper's, Atlantic Monthly, would appeal to very limited audiences.

What kind of books would be published? Some time ago, I bought a magnificent collection of reproductions of Andrew Wyeth's paintings, which sells for $75. Can you conceive of an advertiser finding it in his interest to use so expensive a book with such limited appeal as a vehicle for selling his product? No, the books published would be mostly the kind that are now printed by the millions in paperback—the kind we "effete snobs" call "trash."

The books published would appeal to the masses—in this sense the advertisers could say that they were giving the public what it wants, just as the TV networks now claim. Yet the public would not get what it wants in the meaningful sense of getting everything that it was willing to pay for. It would get only those items that could be produced cheaply enough to serve as fillers between the advertisements.

This is precisely the situation in TV today. The insistence that programs must be "given away"—that is, paid for by the public through its purchase of advertised products—has led to precisely the results that it would lead to with reading matter: deadening uniformity; limited choice; low-cost, low-quality programs. It has also fostered the dominance of networks and their geographical concentration, because their special advantage is in merchandising nationwide advertising. That is why they have bitterly opposed pay-TV.

The networks have been able to maintain their monopoly position because of the requirement of a government license to operate a TV station. Without this requirement, it would have been impossible for them to have prevented the development of pay-TV on a large scale—and, for all I know, of still other alternatives to present-day commercial TV.

The FCC supposedly regulates the radio and TV industry in the public interest. But like just about every other regulatory agency—ICC, CAB,

FPC, and so on through the dreary alphabet—it has in fact become an instrument of the industry it supposedly regulates. It has been used by that industry to preserve monopoly and to prevent competition. Its abolition is essential if we are to have truly free TV.

Cure

But, you will say, the number of TV channels is limited —not to three but to a fairly small number. Surely, government must decide who is to use them. That is a non sequitur. Gold mines are limited. Must the government therefore decide who is to operate them? Land is limited. That may call for zoning requirements, but does it require the licensing of the use of particular parcels to particular people? Precisely the same solution is available for the allocation of TV channels as for the allocation of land. Just as the U.S. sold much of its public land a century ago, let the FCC sell now to the highest bidder the rights now covered by a license (to broadcast at a specified frequency and power in a specified way during specified hours of the day, from a particular location). And then let it go out of business.

The owners of these rights would have private property in them, which they would protect from trespass as you and I protect our land from trespass, through the courts. They could buy and sell the rights, subdivide them, recombine them, as you and I do with our land.[1] They would have the full protection of the Bill of Rights just as the press now does.

Monopolies, if any developed, would be subject to the antitrust laws, not, as now, protected by a government agency. And they would be far less likely to develop because advertisers and networks would be denied the special privileges that they are now granted.

Consequences

What kind of TV system would emerge from the free and unfettered operation of market forces? No one can say in detail. The market is most ingenious and always produces surprises. But certain things are clear. First, there would still be programs supported entirely by advertising—as giveaway newspapers are now. Second, there would be many programs supported partly by advertising, partly by fees—as many newspapers and magazines are now. Third, there would be many programs supported entirely by fees—as so many books and other publications are now. Fourth, the TV bill of fare would be far richer than it now is. It would cater to all viewers, not just those influenced by advertising. It would provide expensive programs for limited audiences as well as low-cost programs for mass audiences.

---

[1] The technical feasibility of this proposal is examined and demonstrated in R. H. Coase, "The Federal Communications Commission," Journal of Law and Economics, October 1959, and in Arthur S. DeVany, Ross D. Eckert, Charles J. Meyers, Donald J. O'Hara, Richard C. Scott, "A Property System for Market Allocation of the Electro-magnetic Spectrum: A Legal-economic-engineering Study," Stanford Law Review, June 1969.

Here, Mr. Agnew, is a far better road to a cure than asking listeners to write and telephone TV stations. Give the viewer the power that makes the consumer the boss in other areas, the power to buy from whom he wants what he wants to buy. That is the way to a truly free TV.

HOW TO END GIVEAWAYS
February 23, 1970

Would you like to become a millionaire overnight? Just persuade the Federal Communications Commission to grant you a license for a radio or TV station. You pay a nominal fee but the license will immediately have a high market value. For the sake of protocol, it will be best not to try to convert your well-gotten gain into cash at once, but if you wait a reasonable time, and if you sell to a "reputable" buyer, experience indicates that the FCC will not object.[1]

You're not in the radio or TV business? Then persuade the Interior Department to grant you a permit to import foreign oil. You pay nothing for the permit but it enables you to purchase oil for about $1.25 a barrel cheaper than you can buy domestic oil.

Perhaps you are in the airline business. Then persuade the Civil Aeronautics Board to grant you the right to fly a lucrative route.

A permit to run a liquor store in California and in many other states costs little, if you can get one, yet may be worth $100,000 or more. The right to set up a savings-and-loan association, or to convert one from a mutual to a stock company, or to start a commercial bank is worth a substantial sum in many states. In New York City, a medallion to operate a taxicab, granted initially at a nominal fee, is today worth more than $20,000.

Conferring privileges

In all of these examples—and the many others that I have not mentioned or do not know about—a government agency creates privileges by restricting the number of persons who may engage in a particular activity or the amount of business they may do, and then grants these privileges to a lucky few.

Most of these restrictions should be abolished completely. As I argued in a recent column (NEWSWEEK, Dec. 1), the government should go out of the business of regulating and controlling TV and radio. Oil import quotas should be eliminated. We should buy the oil where we can get it at the lowest price, not subsidize high-cost domestic producers. Free competition should be permitted on the airlines, subject only to objective safety standards. There were sixteen scheduled domestic trunk airlines in 1938, when

[1]The most recent case in the news is the agreement by Dun & Bradstreet to buy Corinthian Broadcasting for stock valued at $134 million. Corinthian has five TV stations plus publishing enterprises.

CAB control was introduced. The number has shrunk, primarily through merger, to eleven. Not a single new line has been granted permission by the CAB to operate—and not for lack of applicants. Similarly, anyone who wants to set up a liquor store, or a commercial bank, or drive a cab should be free to do so, provided he can satisfy objective minimum standards of responsibility or competence. His freedom to sell a product or service should not, as now, depend also on a bureaucrat's judgment whether additional units are "necessary" to serve the public. Let the market decide.

Auctioning rights

Suppose, however, that the government, in its infinite wisdom, decides to limit the number who may engage in any activity to a smaller number than wish to do so. The least it can do is to avoid giveaways. It can adopt the method Alaska used to assign oil leases: decide how many people it is going to permit in an activity, specify the terms and conditions, announce these publicly, and hold an open auction to decide which particular persons will engage in the activity.

This is a simple and direct way to end giveaways. TV licenses can be auctioned off instead of assigned without charge. So can rights to import oil. Alternatively, a tariff can be levied on oil and importers permitted to bring in as much oil as they wish at that tariff. (This alternative is apparently being considered by the Cabinet committee investigating oil import quotas.) Rights to particular air routes, to establish one of a limited number of liquor stores, to operate one of a limited number of cabs—each and every one of these can be auctioned off. The public will still suffer from governmentally created monopoly, but at least it will recover some of its loss in the form of revenue.

The general principle works both ways. The argument for selling limited rights to the highest bidder and not giving them away is precisely the same as the argument for buying resources that government needs rather than commandeering them—whether those resources be land for public buildings, or the services of policemen, or the services of soldiers. Giveaways and conscription are two sides of the same counterfeit coin.

A SILVER LINING?
February 1, 1971

It takes much searching to find the silver lining in some clouds. To this believer in free markets and in the iniquity of government intervention into private decisions about prices and wages, that is the situation with the recent jawboning by President Nixon in response to rises in oil and steel prices. But congenital optimism will out. So I herewith report a thinly plated silver lining.

Oil

Despite speeches and advertisements in praise of free enterprise that flow from the oil industry as profusely as the black gold from its wells, the oil industry has been enormously successful in getting government to intervene in its behalf. Percentage depletion, prorationing of oil (i.e., limitation of domestic production) by Texas and other states, quotas on the import of oil from abroad—these measures of government beneficence have raised the cost of oil to the American public by billions of dollars.

The one recent break in this pattern was President Nixon's response to a rise in the price of oil. He proceeded to assert Federal authority over many offshore wells, thereby ending output limitations on such wells by state regulatory bodies. He also liberalized regulations to encourage greater oil imports from Canada. Small steps, but at least steps in the right direction toward a freer market and more plentiful supplies of oil.

Steel

The recent steel episode is similar. Like oil, the steel industry has welcomed government intervention. "Protected" by tariffs for well over a century, it recently staged a major campaign for the enactment of steel-import quotas. Fortunately, the campaign did not succeed. But it did produce so-called "voluntary" agreements by steel producers in other countries to limit exports to the U.S.

When Bethlehem Steel recently announced a dramatic price rise on some products, President Nixon raised the possibility of suspending the "voluntary" limitation on imports. A gentle hint by Secretary Rogers to his foreign counterparts is all that it would take—the foreign steel producers would be delighted to oblige. Here again, this would be a step in the right direction.

But the silver lining is, I fear, paper-thin. In the first flush of reaction, there was talk of liberalization of imports. That talk has now died down, following the announcement of a smaller price increase by U.S. Steel and a retreat by Bethlehem. Indeed, Bethlehem's initial price increase may well have been as large as it was to prepare the ground for a smaller increase. This apparent success will encourage the Administration to go further in the direction of jawboning and arm-twisting. This too may, as Eliot Janeway has speculated, be part of Bethlehem's aim. Negotiations with the United Steelworkers are looming, and the steel companies would be delighted to have the President in their corner to bring pressure on the union. How better to get him there than by first tempting him to strike out against price increases, then withdrawing the increases in whole or part, and thereby shifting some responsibility to him for bearing down on unions in turn? Machiavelli did not write about his time alone.

Reality

The President is being urged on all sides to intervene in price and wage decisions to protect the consumer against business and unions. The fact is that government intervention almost always ends up—whatever the initial aim—strengthening business and labor monopoly and gouging the consumer. Jawboning will, I fear, be no exception.

The reason I oppose government intervention so strongly is because I am persuaded, as Adam Smith wrote in 1776, that "people of the same trade seldom meet together, even for merriment and diversion, but the conversation ends in a conspiracy against the public, or in some contrivance to raise prices. It is impossible indeed to prevent such meetings, by any law which either could be executed, or would be consistent with liberty and justice. But though the law cannot hinder people of the same trade from sometimes assembling together, it ought to do nothing to facilitate such assemblies; much less to render them necessary."

Business can and does serve the consumer and serve him well—when we force it to compete and when we deny it special governmental favors. Vigorous competition, from home and abroad, will do far more to keep business in line than will any amount of exhortation from Washington.

SOCIAL RESPONSIBILITY OF BUSINESS*

When I hear businessmen speak eloquently about the "social responsibilities of business in a free enterprise system," I am reminded of the wonderful line about the Frenchman who discovered at the age of 70 that he had been speaking prose all his life.

The businessmen believe that they are defending free enterprise when they declaim that business is not concerned "merely" with profit but also with promoting desirable "social" ends; that business has a "social conscience" and takes seriously its responsibilities for providing employment, eliminating discrimination, avoiding pollution and whatever else may be the catchwords of the contemporary crop of reformers.

In fact they are—or would be if they or anyone else took them seriously—preaching pure and unadulterated socialism. Businessmen who talk this way are unwitting puppets of the intellectual forces that have been undermining the basis of a free society these past decades.

But what does it mean?

The discussions of the "social responsibilities of business" are notable for their analytical looseness and lack of rigor. What does it mean to say that "business" has responsibilities?

A corporation is an artificial person and in this sense may have artificial responsibilities, but "business" as a whole cannot be said to have responsibilities, even in this vague sense. The first step toward clarity in examining the

*Reprinted from The New York Times Magazine Section, September 13, 1970.

doctrine of the social responsibility of business is to ask precisely what it implies for whom.

Presumably, the individuals who are to be responsible are businessmen, which means individual proprietors or corporate executives. Most of the discussion of social responsibility is directed at corporations, so in what follows I shall mostly neglect the individual proprietor and speak of corporate executives.

In a free-enterprise, private-property system, a corporate executive is an employee of the owners of the business. He has direct responsibility to his employers.

That responsibility is to conduct the business in accordance with their desires, which generally will be to make as much money as possible while conforming to the basic rules of the society, both those embodied in law and those embodied in ethical custom.

Of course, in some cases his employers may have a different objective. A group of persons might establish a corporation for an eleemosynary purpose—for example, a hospital or a school. The manager of such a corporation will not have money profit as his objective but the rendering of certain services.

In either case, the key point is that, in his capacity as a corporate executive, the manager is the agent of the individuals who own the corporation or establish the eleemosynary institution, and his primary responsibility is to them.

Judging is not easy

Needless to say, this does not mean that it is easy to judge how well he is performing his task. But at least the criterion of performance is straightforward and the persons among whom a voluntary contractual arrangement exists are clearly defined.

Of course, the corporate executive is also a person in his own right. As a person, he may have many other responsibilities that he recognizes or assumes voluntarily—to his family, his church, his clubs, his city, his country.

He may feel impelled by these responsibilities to devote part of his income to causes he regards as worthy, to refuse to work for particular corporations, even to leave his job, for example, to join his country's armed forces.

If we wish, we may refer to some of these responsibilities as "social responsibilities." But in these respects he is acting as a principal, not an agent; he is spending his own money or time or energy, not the money of his employers or the time or energy he has contracted to devote to their purposes.

If these are "social responsibilities," they are the social responsibilities of individuals, not of business.

What does it mean to say that the corporate executive has a "social responsibility" in his capacity as businessman? If this statement is not pure rhetoric, it must mean that he is to act in some way that is not in the interest of his employers.

Choosing between alternatives

For example, that he is to refrain from increasing the price of the product in order to contribute to the social objective of preventing inflation, even though a price increase would be in the best interests of the corporation.

Or that he is to make expenditures on reducing pollution beyond the amount that is in the best interests of the corporation or that is required by law in order to contribute to the social objective of improving the environment.

Or that he is to hire "hard-core" unemployed instead of better-qualified available workmen to contribute to the social objective of reducing poverty.

In each of these cases, the corporate executive would be spending someone else's money for a general social interest. Insofar as his actions in accord with his "social responsibility" reduce returns to stockholders, he is spending their money. Insofar as his actions raise the price to customers, he is spending the customers' money. Insofar as his actions lower the wages of some employees, he is spending their money.

The stockholders or the customers or the employees could separately spend their own money on the particular action if they wished to do so. The executive is exercising a distinct "social responsibility," rather than serving as an agent of the stockholders or the customers or the employees, only if he spends the money in a different way than they would have spent it.

But if he does this, he is in effect imposing taxes, on the one hand, and deciding how the tax proceeds shall be spent, on the other.

This process raises political questions on two levels: principle and consequences. On the level of political principle, the imposition of taxes and the expenditure of tax proceeds are governmental functions.

We have established elaborate constitutional, parliamentary, and judicial provisions to control these functions, to assure that taxes are imposed so far as possible in accordance with the preferences and desires of the public—after all, "taxation without representation" was one of the battle cries of the American revolution.

We have a system of checks and balances to separate the legislative function of imposing taxes and enacting expenditures from the executive function of collecting taxes and administering expenditure programs and from the judicial function of mediating disputes and interpreting the law.

Here the businessman—self-selected or appointed directly or indirectly by stockholders—is to be simultaneously legislator, executive, and jurist. He is to decide whom to tax by how much and for what purpose, and he is to spend the proceeds—all this guided only by general exhortations from on high to restrain inflation, improve the environment, fight poverty and so on and on.

The whole justification for permitting the corporate executive to be selected by the stockholders is that the executive is an agent serving the interests of his principal. This justification disappears when the corporate executive imposes taxes and spends the proceeds for "social" purposes.

He becomes in effect a public employee, a civil servant, even though he remains in name an employee of a private enterprise. On grounds of political principle, it is intolerable that such civil servants—insofar as their actions in the name of social responsibility are real and not just window dressing— should be selected as they are now.

Involves Socialist view

If they are to be civil servants, then they must be selected through a political process. If they are to impose taxes and make expenditures to foster "social" objectives, then political machinery must be set up to guide the assessment of taxes and to determine through a political process the objectives to be served.

This is the basic reason why the doctrine of "social responsibility" involves the acceptance of the socialist view that political mechanisms, not market mechanisms, are the appropriate way to determine the allocation of scarce resources to alternative uses.

On the grounds of consequences, can the corporate executive in fact discharge his alleged "social responsibilities"? On the one hand, suppose he could get away with spending the stockholders' or customers' or employees' money. How is he to know how to spend it?

He is told that he must contribute to fighting inflation. How is he to know what action of his will contribute to that end?

He is presumably an expert in running his company—in producing a product or selling it or financing it. But nothing about his selection makes him an expert on inflation.

Will his holding down the price of his product reduce inflationary pressure? Or, by leaving more spending power in the hands of his customers, simply divert it elsewhere? Or, by forcing him to produce less because of the lower price, will it simply contribute to shortages?

Even if he could answer these questions, how much cost is he justified in imposing on his stockholders, customers and employees for this social purpose? What is his appropriate share and what is the appropriate share of others?

And, whether he wants to or not can he get away with spending his stockholders', customers', or employees' money? Will not the stockholders fire him? Either the present ones or those who take over when his actions in the name of social responsibility have reduced the corporation's profits and the price of its stock. His customers and his employees can desert him for other producers and employers less scrupulous in exercising their social responsibilities.

Compare wage restraint

This facet of "social responsibility" doctrine is brought into sharp relief when the doctrine is used to justify wage restraint by trade unions. The conflict of interest is naked and clear when union officials are asked to subordinate the interest of their members to some more general social purpose.

If the union officials try to enforce wage restraint, the consequence is likely to be wildcat strikes, rank-and-file revolts and the emergence of strong competitors for their jobs. We thus have the ironic phenomenon that union leaders—at least in the United States—have objected to government interference with the market far more consistently and courageously than have business leaders.

The difficulty of exercising "social responsibility" illustrates, of course, the great virtue of private competitive enterprise—it forces people to be responsible for their own actions and makes it difficult for them to "exploit" other people for either selfish or unselfish purposes. They can do good—but only at their own expense.

Many a reader who has followed the argument this far may be tempted to remonstrate that it is all well and good to speak of government's having the responsibility to impose taxes and determine expenditures for such "social" purposes as controlling pollution or training the hard-core unemployed, but that the problems are too urgent to wait on the slow course of political processes, that the exercise of social responsibility by businessmen is a quicker and surer way to solve pressing current problems.

Aside from the question of fact —I share Adam Smith's skepticism about the benefits that can be expected from "those who affect to trade for the public good"—this argument must be rejected on grounds of principle.

What it amounts to is an assertion that those who favor the taxes and expenditures in question have failed to persuade a majority of their fellow citizens to be of like mind and that they are seeking to attain by undemocratic procedures what they cannot attain by democratic procedures.

In a free society, it is hard for "good" people to do "good," but that is a small price to pay for making it hard for "evil" people to do "evil," especially since one man's good is another's evil.

Here's another facet

I have, for simplicity, concentrated on the special case of the corporate executive, except only for the brief digression on trade unions. But precisely the same argument applies to the newer phenomenon of calling upon stockholders to require corporations to exercise social responsibility [the recent G. M. crusade, for example].

In most of these cases, what is in effect involved is some stockholders trying to get other stockholders [or customers or employees] to contribute against their will to "social" causes favored by the activists. Insofar as they succeed, they are again imposing taxes and spending the proceeds.

The situation of the individual proprietor is somewhat different. If he acts to reduce the returns of his enterprise in order to exercise his "social responsibility," he is spending his own money, not someone else's. If he wishes to spend his money on such purposes, that is his right, and I cannot see that there is any objection to his doing so.

In the process, he, too, may impose costs on employees and customers. However, because he is far less likely than a large corporation or union to have monopolistic power, any such side effects will tend to be minor.

Actions may be rationalized

Of course, in practice the doctrine of social responsibility is frequently a cloak for actions that are justified on other grounds rather than a reason for those actions.

To illustrate, it may well be in the long-run interest of a corporation that is a major employer in a small community to devote resources to providing amenities to that community or to improving its government.

That may make it easier to attract desirable employees, it may reduce the wage bill or lessen losses from pilferage and sabotage or have other worthwhile effects.

Or it may be that, given the laws about the deductibility of corporate charitable contributions, the stockholders can contribute more to charities they favor by having the corporation make the gift than by doing it themselves, since they can in that way contribute an amount that would otherwise have been paid as corporate taxes.

In each of these—and many similar—cases, there is a strong temptation to rationalize these actions as an exercise of "social responsibility." In the present climate of opinion, with its widespread aversion to "capitalism," "profits," and "soulless corporation," this is one way for a corporation to generate goodwill as a by-product of expenditures that are entirely justified in its own self-interest.

It would be inconsistent of me to call on corporate executives to refrain from this hypocritical window-dressing because it harms the foundations of a free society. That would be to call on them to exercise a "social responsibility"!

If our institutions, and the attitudes of the public make it in their self-interest to cloak their actions in this way, I cannot summon much indignation to denounce them.

At the same time, I can express admiration for those individual proprietors or owners of closely held corporations or stockholders of more broadly held corporations who disdain such tactics as approaching fraud.

Whether blameworthy or not, the use of the cloak of social responsibility, and the nonsense spoken in its name by influential and prestigious business-men, does clearly harm the foundations of a free society.

I have been impressed time and again by the schizophrenic character of many businessmen.

They are capable of being extremely farsighted and clear-headed in matters that are internal to their businesses. They are incredibly short-sighted and muddle headed in matters that are outside their businesses but affect the possible survival of business in general.

This short sightedness is strikingly exemplified in the calls from many businessmen for wage and price guidelines or controls or incomes policies. There is nothing that could do more in a brief period to destroy a market system and replace it by a centrally controlled system than effective govern-mental control of prices and wages.

Are profits wicked?

The shortsightedness is also exemplified in speeches by businessmen on social responsibility. This may gain them kudos in the short run. But it helps to strengthen the already too prevalent view that the pursuit of profits is wicked and immoral and must be curbed and controlled by external forces. Once this view is adopted, the external forces that curb the market will not be the social consciences, however highly developed, of the pontificating executives; it will be the iron fist of government bureaucrats. Here, as with price and wage controls, businessmen seem to me to reveal a suici-dal impulse.

The political principle that underlies the market mechanism is unanim-ity. In an ideal free market resting on private property, no individual can coerce any other, all cooperation is voluntary, all parties to such cooperation benefit or they need not participate.

There are no "social" values, no "social" responsibilities in any sense other than the shared values and responsibilities of individuals. Society is a collection of individuals and of the various groups they voluntarily form.

The political principle that underlies the political mechanism is confor-mity. The individual must serve a more general social interest—whether that be determined by a church or a dictator or a majority. The individual may have a vote and a say in what is to be done, but if he is overruled, he must conform. It is appropriate for some to require others to contribute to a general social purpose whether they wish to or not.

Unfortunately, unanimity is not always feasible. There are some respects in which conformity appears unavoidable, so I do not see how one can avoid the use of the political mechanism altogether.

But the doctrine of "social responsibility" taken seriously would extend the scope of the political mechanism to every human activity. It does not differ in philosophy from the most explicitly collectivist doctrine. It differs only by professing to believe that collectivist ends can be attained without collectivist means.

That is why, in my book *Capitalism and Freedom*, I have called it a "fundamentally subversive doctrine" in a free society, and have said that in such a society, "there is one and only one social responsibility of business—to use its resources and engage in activities designed to increase its profits so long as it stays within the rules of the game, which is to say, engages in open and free competition without deception or fraud."

Chapter Ten
GOVERNMENT AND EDUCATION

Some years ago, when Charles E. Wilson, former head of General Motors, was testifying before Congress in connection with confirmation for a high Government post, he remarked "What is good for General Motors is good for the United States." My colleagues in the universities sneered at this remark, pointed to it as showing how small-minded, how self-interested, how blind our business leaders are. Simultaneously, they and their colleagues were trooping down to Washington testifying in favor of "federal aid" to higher education, i.e., government subsidies. One after another in effect said, "What's good for higher education is good for the country." Never did I see one even smile when he said it, or recognize in any way any inconsistency between his sneers at Mr. Wilson and his testimony in Washington.

All of us—you and I not excepted—are far more aware of our own interests than that of other people's. We all know that what is good for us is good for the country. That is why the "devil" theory of special-interest legislation is wrong. The men who urge Congress to pass laws that you and I regard as benefitting their special interests seldom do so out of devil motives. They are generally completely sincere when they urge that the measure is in the public interest. As the Bible says, we see the mote in the other man's eye, not the beam in our own.

As you have read my animadversions against special interests in prior chapters, you have probably been sympathetic to my view in most cases because the special interests I have been inveighing against are not yours. In this chapter, I come closer to home for many readers, particularly those who are college students or on college faculties.

I believe one of the great scandals in the United States is government subsidization of higher schooling. There is no other policy I know of which so clearly and on so large a scale imposes costs on low-income people to provide subsidies to high-income people. Some academic people have recognized the evil and spoken out against governmental subsidy. But their number is pitifully and shamefully small. A larger number have recognized the evil without speaking out against it or have proposed that it be solved by still larger governmental expenditures so that still more extensive subsidies to youngsters from low-income families would offset the subsidies to youngsters from high-income families. (This is in effect the recommendation of the Carnegie Commission on Higher Education headed by Clark Kerr, former President of the University of California.) But most have simply been smugly self-righteous, taking exactly the same stand as the oil industry people who defend oil-import quotas, the chemical producers who defend tariffs, and so on *ad nauseam*.

The columns in this chapter offer alternatives to the present relation between government and schooling: at the level of higher schooling, loans to students to repay costs rather than subsidies, scholarships at institutions chosen by the student rather than direct provision of schooling by state institutions; and at the level of elementary and secondary schooling, a voucher scheme which would enable parents to choose schools for their children.

These proposals are still very poor bets. They go against the narrow self-interest of most teachers and educational administrators—at least as they are likely to view that self-interest—and hence are likely to be viewed unfavorably by intellectuals as a class. Yet the growing dissatisfaction with the present system at all levels and by many different segments of our society offers some hope for change.

"FREE" EDUCATION
February 14, 1967

Gov. Ronald Reagan has stirred up a hornet's nest by proposing that students who attend state colleges and the University of California be required to pay tuition of $150 to $250 a year in addition to present student fees of $90 to $275 a year. Professors and students have risen almost as one man in protest at such an outrageous suggestion. Make the students pay for their own schooling? Preposterous. "Free" education is an ancient tradition in California, and this is one tradition that even the campus rebels are disposed to defend with all their might and main—after all, their pocketbooks are at stake.

Unfortunately, low-income taxpayers and youngsters not in college are much less effective than students and professors in presenting their case to the public. "Free" tuition is highly inequitable to them. In addition, it lowers the quality of higher education. Governor Reagan's proposal is long overdue and unduly modest, not only for the state of California, but for other states as well.

Equity

The cost of higher education to the state of California is roughly $2,000 per student per year. The youngster admitted to a state school automatically gets a scholarship of that amount. By reason of this subsidy, he can expect to earn a higher income for the rest of his life than youngsters of equal ability who do not go to college. He will repay a small part of the subsidy himself—in the form of taxes on the increase in his income. But the greater part of the subsidy is paid by the rest of the taxpaying public, including his fellow citizens who are not able to take advantage of the "free" education.

Despite the rhetoric to the contrary, state colleges and universities serve mainly the well-to-do. For California, more than half the students in 1963 came from the top quarter of families—whose incomes exceeded $10,000 a year. At the other end of the scale, only 5 per cent or so of the students came from the 18 per cent of the families with incomes less than $4,000. Yet, the idealistic students march in the name of social justice.

It is eminently desirable that every youngster, regardless of his or his parents' income, social position, residence or race, have the opportunity to get higher schooling—*provided he is willing to pay for it either currently or out of the higher income the schooling will enable him to earn.* There is a strong case for providing generous *loan* funds to assure opportunity to all. There is a strong case for disseminating information about the availability of such funds and for urging the underprivileged to take advantage of the opportunity. There is no case for subsidizing those who get higher schooling at the expense of those who do not.

Educational quality

California in effect says to its high-school graduates: "If you are in the top half or so of your class, you automatically qualify for a scholarship of $2,000 a year—provided you attend a state-run school. If you are so foolish as to go to Stanford or Claremont, let alone Harvard or Yale or Chicago, not a penny for you." If California is going to give scholarships, it would be far better to give them to the youngsters directly and let them decide which schools to attend—as under GI educational benefits. State-run institutions would then finance themselves by tuition fees and would compete on more even terms with private institutions. If they were more attractive to students, they would flourish; if not, they would decline.

The need to compete for students would force colleges to be more responsive to student interests. Berkeley is justly famed for the quality of its research faculty—not for the quality of undergraduate teaching. As California is demonstrating, state schools have developed to a high pitch the art of appealing to the legislature and influencing public opinion—that is the way now to get funds—while all the time demanding independence from political influence. Far better that they develop to a high pitch the art of schooling youngsters—that would make them truly independent of politics.

When the smog clears, perhaps California will have shown other states how to broaden educational opportunity, raise the quality of college training and simultaneously relieve the budget—all by exploiting the insight that people value what they pay for and will pay for what they value.

'PUBLIC' EDUCATION
March 13, 1967

"Does money bring happiness?" is a recurrent theme in movie, short story and novel. Yet the corresponding question is seldom asked about government expenditures. It is simply taken for granted that more government spending means more of whatever the spending is for.

Take the debate over the financing of higher education in California. Educators from all parts of the country have not hesitated to proclaim without detailed study that the proposed cuts in state appropriations jeopardize the quality and quantity of higher education in California. Apparently they regard this proposition as in a class with the proposition that 2 plus 2 equal 4. Yet, while California is at or near the top of the country in per capita *government* expenditures for higher education, it appears to be backward in the quality and quantity of higher education—despite the many boasts to the contrary.

Some depressing facts

In the Financial Barrier to Higher Education in California, a study prepared for the California State Scholarship Commission and published in 1965, well before the present furor, Edward Sanders and Hans Palmer point out:

1 Dropouts are massive. "Only 27 per cent of the first-time freshman enrollees graduated four years later"; in the U.S. as a whole, 54 per cent do.
2 "A smaller percentage of the number of high-school graduates actually complete a four-year program than in the U.S. as a whole"—23 per cent of high-school graduates receive a bachelor's degree in California, 28 per cent, in the U.S. as a whole.
3 "California appears to be considerably less successful than the remainder of the nation in bringing students from low-income groups into college."

Perhaps California educators should take a brief recess from patting themselves on the back and grapple with these depressing facts—or, if they are wrong, refute them.

Could it be that California lags in higher education because of—and not despite—its leadership in *government* spending? After all, the "public" is served not only by government schools but also by private schools, ranging from junior colleges to major universities like Stanford and the University of Southern California.

The government financing of "free" state schools has starved private schools. How easy would you find it to sell books or houses or cars if the government were giving them away? It is a tribute to the quality of the private schools and the generosity of private donors—as well as to the defects of state schools—that the private schools account for as much as 12 per cent of total enrollment in California institutions of higher learning, 16 per cent of full-time enrollment, and 26 per cent of bachelor's degrees.

Some possible causes

Though large government spending may reduce private spending, must it not raise total spending? Clearly, it would, if government simply gave individuals money to spend on schooling but did not itself run schools.

However, once government runs schools, it is by no means certain that even total spending, let alone total results, will be higher. We are all more reluctant to vote taxes on ourselves for general benefits than we are to pay directly for benefits we ourselves receive. Yet once tax-supported facilities are available "free," we are also reluctant to spend "our own money" for private alternatives. Many a parent might be willing to spend an extra sum to get better schooling for his child—but if he dispenses with "free" schools, he must pay not only the extra cost but the whole cost. Thus, paradoxical as it may seem, total spending on higher education in California might be larger today than it is, if government spending were smaller. And even if total spending were not larger, total *results* would almost surely be better if the smaller government spending were directed more toward encouraging and aiding the poor to take advantage of educational opportunities and less toward providing facilities for the well-to-do.

The right question—not only in education but in many other areas as well—is: how can the community get the most—in quality and quantity—for the money it spends? *Not,* how can the taxpayer, legislature and governors be persuaded to increase government appropriations?

DECENTRALIZING SCHOOLS
November 18, 1968

The Ocean Hill-Brownsville dispute is dramatic evidence of how deeply concerned about their children's schooling are the parents—Negro, Puerto Rican and white—in that low-income district. Whoever is to blame for the confrontation that has kept most schools in New York City closed most of the time since the beginning of the school year, the parents are surely right on the central issue of quality. Their children have been getting inferior schooling, and the parents have had no control over the schooling. It is an encouraging sign that so many low-income parents both know and care.

The Board of Education of New York City has responded to mounting dissatisfaction by experimenting with decentralization—the Ocean Hill-Brownsville dispute grew out of such an experiment. This is a move in the right direction—not only in schooling, I may add, but also in other important civic functions. The tragedy is that decentralization of the kind now envisaged will not give the parents effective control over their children's schooling.

Political control

The key to the present problem is that schooling is not only financed by government but also mainly administered by government. As a result, parents can exercise control over schools only through the political process. If a consumer does not like the service he gets at a department store, he can withdraw his custom and go elsewhere. He does not first have to persuade 51 per cent of the customers of the store (plus many who do not shop at the store at all) that the service is so bad that they should change the management.

The problem is exacerbated in the slums because the poor cannot afford private alternatives and yet have been largely impotent politically. They have many votes, but the very qualities that make or keep them poor limit even more sharply their political power. Their votes simply help to determine which faction of the middle or upper class exercises power. Political decentralization that involved a real dispersal of power from the center to separate areas would help, but unfortunately the main result would simply be to transfer power from one set of bureaucrats to another. The new bureaucrats would be more responsive to local demands—but this would still deny effective individual choice to the creative minorities that, in the slums as elsewhere, are the true breeders of progress.

A far better alternative is to introduce competition in schooling, to give parents a real choice. Why not say to every parent: "The community is committed to spending X dollars a year on schooling your child. If you do not send your child to our public school, you relieve us of this cost. In return, the community will give you a voucher for X dollars a year per child. You can use this voucher to purchase schooling at any other approved school, public or private, but for no other purpose."

Parental control

This would enable parents to exert economic pressure individually on the school, as on the department store, without having to go through a cumbrous political mechanism. It would establish a large market that does not now exist for medium-priced private schools. Supply would rapidly develop to meet the demand. If public schools met the new competition by improving their quality, they would keep their custom, if not, they would decline.

This is the right way to decentralize schooling, to give parents more effective control over schools, and to open up opportunities for children in the slums. It is the right way to meet the growing problem of organized teachers battling political bodies to divide up the spoils. It is the right way to get a more sensible salary structure for teachers —one that pays higher salaries to good teachers and lower salaries to bad teachers in place of a rigid civil service structure that fixes salary mainly by seniority and degrees rather than merit.

It is also the right way to stimulate variety and diversity—in the suburbs as well as the cities—and to end the present discrimination against families who send their children to parochial schools—while keeping church and state separate.

This plan would harness the enormous potential of a free market to improve the quality of schooling and to broaden the range of alternatives open to our children—black and white, rich and poor, gifted and slow. As in other areas, we can all benefit by using the market: parents, students, taxpayers and teachers.

POLICE ON CAMPUS
April 14, 1969

The disruption this winter at my university—the University of Chicago—was handled brilliantly and effectively by president Edward Levi and the administration, *given the attitude of the faculty*. But this attitude undermines our defenses against the intolerant radicals who are seeking to destroy all universities. We must do some drastic rethinking if we are to preserve the university as the home of reason, persuasion and free discussion.

At Chicago, nonviolent passive resistance by the university plus the steady, undramatic application of university disciplinary procedures finally brought a sit-in at our administration building to an end without force and violence and without any concession by the university to the "demands" of the students. But the cost in damage, vandalism and interruption of vital university functions was enormous—all because fewer than 5 per cent of the students permitted themselves to be inveigled into the adoption of coercive tactics.

The university a sanctuary . . .

President Levi's approach was the right one because of the widespread belief among the faculty that the university is a sanctuary and that calling on the civil authorities—i.e., the police—must be a very last resort. Given this attitude, the use of police on campus can only divide, fragment and embitter both faculty and students.

In the Middle Ages in Europe, universities were very nearly city-states and did provide sanctuary against often hostile external political units. More important for the U.S., the university has regarded itself, and has been regarded by students and parents of students, as *in loco parentis*, and hence as having an obligation to control its "children" within the family. Neither of these reasons for the faculty attitude is any longer valid. A more relevant reason is that the university can perform its true function only if it is a community whose members share common values and have a common commitment to free and untrammeled inquiry. The need to use outside force to maintain discipline undermines this sense of community and hence should be avoided—provided that it can be avoided without tolerating modes of discourse (confrontation, force, coercion) that are fundamentally inconsistent with the basic values of the university.

Whatever the desirability of avoiding outside force, I have become increasingly impressed with how ineffective university disciplinary procedures are for offenses such as trespass, destruction of university property and interference with the civil rights of others. If a student were to break and enter my apartment, I would, if I could, call the police at once. If he were arrested and convicted, it would never occur to me to submit him to a university disciplinary procedure.

Should it be different for a student who breaks and enters a dean's office? In that case should we, who are ill-equipped and ill-trained for the job, turn ourselves into police officers, force ourselves into the student mob, get fellow professors to identify the participants, pass out summonses, and then use suspension or expulsion or the like to punish such offenses? I believe not.

. . . Or part of the community?

The university is part of the community at large. We should tend to our business—which is to teach the young and to conduct scholarly analysis. We should rely on the civil authorities to protect us from coercion by other people, whether that coercion takes the form of seizure of property or interference with the civil rights of other students or faculty. If this coercion interferes seriously with the university's task we may also want to deny persons committed to such tactics access to the university—not to punish them, but to preserve the university.

If this distinction between the proper domain of the university and of the civil authorities were widely accepted by the faculty, it might be possible to nip incipient disruptions in the bud by calling in the police at once. Indeed, if it were widely accepted, the occasion for calling in the police would be unlikely to arise.

As it is, we have the worst of both worlds. Time and again, unwillingness to have the police on campus has permitted a disruption to grow to a scale that has made mass force and violence inevitable when police were finally called—Columbia, San Francisco State and Berkeley bear tragic testimony. Thanks to wise leadership and an eventually united faculty, the University of Chicago was able to avoid that outcome—this time. Next time—who knows?

THE IVORY TOWER
November 10, 1969

Moratorium Day was marked by attempts to get universities, as institutions, to take a stand on the war in Vietnam. These attempts have met with surprising success. A few universities officially suspended classes on October 15. Many others approved the suspension of classes by individual faculty members. Some faculties have voted to take a political position on the war—most notably, at Harvard. Seventy-nine college presidents signed a public letter expressing disagreement with our policy in Vietnam.

The actions and the statements have typically been accompanied by a disclaimer that they involved the taking of a political position by the university as an institution. For example, the letter of the college presidents starts with the admirable sentiment, "We speak as individuals . . . The universities and colleges which we serve take no positions as institutions on the Vietnam war; these are pluralistic communities where men speak for themselves alone on off-campus issues." But why then a statement signed only by *college presidents?* Why do these men not issue statements as individuals; or add their names to statements signed by citizens from varied walks of life? However sincere the college presidents are in their protestations, the very fact that college presidents and only college presidents signed the statement cannot help but give the impression that their institutions as institutions have taken a political position.

Dangerous trend

This is a dangerous trend. If continued, it will destroy the university as the home of free inquiry and the uninhibited search for truth. This conclusion has nothing to do with the merits or demerits of the position taken by the faculties and the presidents on the particular issue of Vietnam. The basis for the conclusion was stated lucidly by my colleague Prof. George J. Stigler of the University of Chicago, in an unpublished memorandum written some years ago in connection with very different issues.

1 "The university," wrote Professor Stigler, "is by design and effect the institution in a society which creates discontent with existing moral, social and political institutions and proposes new institutions to replace them. The university is, from this viewpoint, a group of philosophically imaginative men freed of any pressure except to please their fellow faculty, and told to follow their inquiries wherever they might lead. Invited to be learned in the institutions of other times and places, incited to new understanding of the social and physical world, the university faculty is inherently a disruptive force . . .

2 The instrument of criticism and dissent is the individual faculty member, not the university in some group sense . . . This *individualiza-*

tion of the university is the feature which allows universities to have so privileged a position in society: a professor may become an unmitigated nuisance, or even, with great luck, a serious threat to powerful political or social groups in the population, but the university as a community is no part of this professor's school or party. In fact, if the university is properly staffed with active and independent minds, some of this professor's colleagues will deny the validity of his ideas and many will deny the primacy or significance or applicability of them . . .

3 Should the university as an institution enter moral, social, or political movements, it then becomes an instrument of oppression against the individual professor. If the university endorses idea X, any opponent of idea X in the university community has been censured. It matters not whether X is a nearly universal moral conviction—such as that the dignity of man must be defended—or the most transitory and partisan endorsement of a man or scheme. If there were an absolutely certain truth, the university community could endorse it with small cost; however, the very first of these certain truths has yet to be determined.

4 The university as an institution discharges its moral responsibility to society when it provides the conditions for free inquiry, and it violates this responsibility when it sacrifices freedom of inquiry to more immediate goals . . .

5 I place no weight on the objections on grounds of cost or expediency to the intervention by the university as an institution in moral, social, and political movements . . . A university is dedicated to the costly and inefficient enterprise of discovering and improving knowledge. The one, the grave complaint against institutional intervention in social movements is that it constitutes a rejection of the paramount moral goal of a university."

HOMOGENIZED SCHOOLS
February 28, 1972

How a question is asked often determines the answer. For example, if you were asked "Should parents be permitted to spend their income on better schooling for their children?" you would almost surely say "yes." If you were asked "Is it fair and just that children who happen to live in low-income communities should receive poorer schooling than children who live in wealthy suburbs?" you would almost surely say "no"—and that is what courts have said recently in California, Texas and New Jersey in declaring local financing of public schools unconstitutional. Yet clearly the two answers are contradictory. If all children must receive the same schooling, how can parents spend more on their children's schooling?

Enforced equality . . .

The contradiction suggests that it may be worth exploring the implications of the courts' decisions.

If it is wrong for different communities in a state to spend different amounts per child on public schooling (or in some other sense provide unequal schooling), how can it be right for different states to do so? For different countries? Even if we stop at our own borders, the courts' decisions clearly imply Federal financing of schools to assure equal expenditure per child throughout the land. "Control by local school boards of local schools" brought hearty applause from Congress when President Nixon said it in his State of the Union address. But it will be a slogan without content if Washington pays the bill.

Parents could escape a homogenized school system by sending their children to private schools. But surely that would be inconsistent with the courts' answers to the second question. If private schooling is permitted, an obvious escape from the courts' decisions is to starve the governmental school system and encourage private schools. The courts would surely treat that, and properly, as an evasion of the law, just as they did the many attempts to set up private schools in the South that followed court orders to public schools to integrate. Equal spending on schooling per child therefore logically implies the prohibition of private schools—and indeed this answer has been reached by some of the more "advanced" educational reformers.

But why stop with schooling? If it is wrong for different children to have different amounts spent on their schooling, how can it be right to have different amounts spent on their food? Housing? Clothing? Etc.?

Translating into practice the appealing negative answer to the second question therefore implies seeking the complete equalization of conditions of life—a homogenized society. This is a road that we have been trying to travel for some time. We have not gotten very far, because, fortunately, the ingenuity of men in pursuing their own interests and the interests of their spouses and children keeps defeating the attempts of clumsy bureaucrats egged on by egalitarian sentiment. Yet we have already paid a high price in freedom and efficiency for the attempts.

What is wrong with traveling this road? Is not the vision of a society in which the law requires that all children receive the same amount of schooling, housing, feeding and clothing an inspiring and desirable vision?

. . . Leads to slavery

It certainly is not. Such enforced egalitarianism can be obtained only on a low level. What gain equality at zero? If I cannot use extra income to improve the lot of my children, why should I seek extra income? Even more, if my children (and by extension I myself) will have the same level of living whatever I do, why should I work? If there is no carrot to encourage effort, there will have to be a stick. Enforced egalitarianism also means forced labor; it also means a slave state. It is a horrible, not an inspiring, vision.

Of course, taking one step down this road does not condemn us to travel it to its bitter end. Socialism is not like pregnancy. We can be, as we are, a little or even more than a little socialist without going all the way. Yet it is the ideal that animates our actions. If the ideal is false, perhaps we should reconsider the steps that we have taken, or are prepared to take, in its name.

There is all the difference in the world between the more fortunate among us giving of our substance in order to establish a minimum standard below which no disadvantaged person or child shall be forced to live, and trying to legislate uniformity of condition. The difference is between freedom and slavery.

Chapter Eleven
MONOPOLY

Since the two columns in this chapter which deal with the Post Office were published, a much-ballyhooed "reform" has been effected. The Post Office is no longer a government department; it is now a separate Corporation, the Post Office Service, but still a monopoly, still a government organization. And, as I suggested that it would be in the second column, it has remained "high-priced and inefficient." Postal service continues to deteriorate and deficits to mount.

Both governmental monopoly, like the Post Office, and private monopoly, like the New York Stock Exchange or A. T. & T. are undesirable; but of the two evils, governmental monopoly is much the worse because it tends to be more inefficient. In Britain, both mail and telephone are governmental monopolies; in the United States, mail is a governmental monopoly and telephone a private monopoly. Mail service is better in Britain than in the United States (because the British civil service is more efficient than that of the United States) but phone service is worse. A nice almost controlled experiment.

More important, whereas there are some cases, of which telephone is probably one, where technical considerations enforce monopoly, most private monopoly reflects governmental assistance and support in the form of exclusive franchises or a governmentally administered cartel, as in banking, radio, T.V., airlines, railroads and so on; or special immunities, such as those granted to trade unions; or licensure requirements, as in medicine, dentistry, law, barbering, and so on; or tariffs and quotas. Hence, the problem of monopoly, as a matter of policy, is largely a problem not of getting government to enact and enforce legislation against monopoly but of keeping government from enacting and enforcing legislation strengthening and preserving monopoly.

A favorite parlor question of mine in economic discussions is to say to my partner in conversation: "Suppose you could get one law and only one law enacted for the sole purpose of stimulating competition. What law would you enact?" The answers typically center on strengthening anti-trust laws, occasionally on eliminating regulatory bodies, but hardly ever do I get what almost everyone agrees is the correct answer after he hears it: a law abolishing all restrictions on foreign trade, i.e., enacting free trade. Foreign competition would do far more to promote domestic competition than a manyfold multiplication of the budget of the antitrust division of the Department of Justice.

The three columns in this chapter touch on only a few monopoly issues. Some columns in other chapters (notably those on oil, steel, and TV) could as well have been included in this. Yet even so, I confess that the problem of monopoly is far from adequately treated in this book.

THE POST OFFICE
October 9, 1967

Complaints on postal service sent to the Postmaster General are directed to the wrong address—that is like berating a dog for barking instead of purring. The Post Office is both a monopoly and a government bureau—so it should occasion no surprise that it is costly, inefficient and backward.

Even Postmaster General O'Brien has recognized this fact. He has proposed that the Post Office be converted into a nonprofit government corporation. But that would change only the form not the substance. As a monopoly, it would still be costly; as a government organization, it would still be inefficient and backward.

There is a simpler, more modest, yet more effective solution. Let Congress simply repeal provisions of the present law which prohibit private persons from competing with the U.S. Post Office (presently, private persons may provide mail service, but only if the letters also carry U.S. stamps).

Why monopoly?

The tyranny of the status quo leads most of us to take it for granted that the postal service must be a government monopoly. The facts are very different. There have been many private ventures—including the storied Pony Express, which failed when the telegraph line (also private) reached California and provided an even faster service. Many others succeeded—which was precisely what led postal officials to foster, over many decades, a succession of Congressional enactments to outlaw private mail delivery.

It will be objected that private firms would skim the cream by concentrating on first-class mail and especially local urban delivery—on which the Post Office makes a substantial profit—while leaving to the Post Office the mail on which it loses money.

But this is an argument for, not against, competition. Users of first-class mail are now being overcharged (taxed is the word we use in other contexts) to subsidize the distribution of newspapers, periodicals and junk mail. Similarly, local delivery subsidizes mail for remote areas.

If we want to subsidize the distribution of such material, we should do so openly and directly—by giving the originators of such mail a subsidy and letting them buy the services of distributing it as best they can. And we should finance the subsidy in accordance with the general canons of taxation, not by a special levy on the users of first-class mail.

Nonetheless, the argument is politically powerful. It explains why many a newspaper and periodical—even some staunch defenders of free markets in other connections—will defend the Post Office's monopoly. They will defend it because they favor subsidizing dissemination of information and educational matter—but doubt that they can persuade the public to do so directly and openly. They will be overimpressed by the importance of the subsidy to their pockets—because they will not allow fully for the improvements that competition would bring. It would be expensive for them to pay the full cost of the present inefficient delivery service—but the cost will be cut sharply by the more efficient service that would spring up.

In any event, I see no reason myself why readers of newspapers and periodicals, and distributors of junk mail, should not bear the full cost of distribution, whatever it may turn out to be—and I, for one, hope that it does not turn out to be so low as to encourage still more junk mail.

Why not competition?

One obstacle to introducing competition is a lack of imagination. Our minds are not fertile enough to envisage the miracles that unfettered enterprise can accomplish, in mail service as in other areas—rapid delivery within a city by pneumatic tubes and between cities by facsimile wire, much more extensive use of traveling post offices instead of monuments to the political pull of the Postmaster General and the local congressman, and so on *ad infinitum*.

A more important obstacle to introducing competition is the nature of the political process. Competition would benefit the general public. But the general public has no effective lobby. It would benefit men and women who would find new business and employment opportunities. But few of them have any idea that they would be benefited, so they have no effective lobby. Competition might harm postal employees and big users of subsidized mail. As concentrated special-interest groups, they are well organized and do have an effective lobby. Their special interest, not the general interest, is therefore likely to shape the course of postal legislation. An oft-told tale.

THE PUBLIC BE DAMNED
August 5, 1968

A Presidential commission has just made official what you and I have long known from experience. The Post Office "each year . . . slips further behind the rest of the economy in service, in efficiency and in meeting its responsibilities as an employer."

The commission recommended that the Post Office be converted from a government department to a nonprofit government corporation. That might improve matters some, but since the Post Office would still be a monopoly and a government organization, it would remain high-priced and inefficient.

A far better solution is one I suggested many months ago (NEWSWEEK, Oct. 9, 1967)—simply repeal the present provision making it illegal for private enterprise to provide mail service. Competition would quickly set modern technology to work in the transmission of mail, and simultaneously lower the cost to the consumer. The government system would have to shape up or ship out.

Pressure groups vs. . . .

But neither the one proposal nor the other will be adopted. The facts of political life that make this prediction a near-certainty were brought home to me when I was writing my earlier column on the Post Office. Why not, I thought, use it to persuade a congressman to introduce a bill to repeal the present prohibition on private delivery of mail? That would have started desirable legislation on its way, made the column more topical, and given the Congressional sponsor some publicity. So I spoke to a number of friends in Congress.

All were favorable to the substance of the bill, yet none was willing to introduce it. As one congressman said to me, "Can you suggest any unions we might conceivably persuade to testify in favor of it?" I could not do so.

Strong pressure groups will oppose changing present arrangements. the postal unions that have become experts in lobbying before Congress; the users of third- and fourth-class mail, who fear that the subsidy they now enjoy would be threatened if Congress no longer finances postal deficits.

No strong pressure groups will favor the proposed changes—which serve only the widespread general interest of the public. If the proposed changes were made—if, for example, private competition were permitted—pressure groups would emerge. Enterprises that succeeded in the new business and their employees and customers would become such groups. But these are only potential, not actual.

A congressman has limited time and influence. It is wise for him to husband that time and influence to promote measures that have some chance of being adopted, or, at least, of bringing him some political support. What can he gain by the purely quixotic gesture of sponsoring a bill to introduce competition into the postal service? Only the active hostility of present special interests. True, many more persons would be benefited than would be harmed and the aggregate benefit would greatly exceed any transitional harm. *But*, and it is a big but, the few persons who believe that they would be harmed will be aware of that fact, and each will expect significant harm, so it will pay them to fight the bill. Most persons who would benefit will not be aware of that fact. Even if they were, the benefit to most would be small. Hence, they are unlikely to devote much effort to promoting the bill—or even to have their vote influenced by its introduction. Their vote is likely to be determined by the matters with respect to which they are members of special interest groups.

. . . Diffused general interest

Many citizens regard it as a paradox that a democratic government, supposed to promote the general welfare, should enact so many measures that promote special interests. It is not a paradox. It is the result to be expected when government engages in activities that have concentrated effects on small groups and widely diffused effects on the rest of the citizens. A majority rules in a political democracy, but the majority that rules is typically a coalition of special interests—not a majority promoting the general interest.

In the heyday of nineteenth-century capitalism, William H. Vanderbilt, a railroad tycoon, is said to have remarked, "The public be damned" to an inquiring reporter. That may have been his attitude but it was never an accurate description of how private enterprise behaved. Competition saw to that. Enterprises that damned the public did not survive for long. But however accurate it may have been then, today the phrase fits Washington to a T.

CUSTOMERS GO HOME
August 26, 1968

You are in a business that is booming. Customers are pounding at your door. Sales records are being set every month. Profits are soaring.

How do you react? You close up shop for one day a week and tell customers to stay home. Impossible? Not at all. That is precisely what firms dealing in securities have been doing some months now. Business is so good, they claim, that they need to shut down one day a week to keep up with the paper work.

Surprise cubed

Perhaps the most surprising thing about this surprising performance is that it has elicited so little comment about how surprising it is. The financial writers all take it for granted that it is an understandable and natural, if regrettable, response to an upsurge of stock-market activity.

It is anything but. In an industry with as many firms as there are in the securities business, such a concerted shutdown would generally be unstable, unnecessary and illegal. It would be unstable because it would pay each firm separately to keep open precisely on the day on which other firms closed down. The firms that first opened for business would force the rest to do the same. It would be unnecessary because the firms would respond to the increase in custom either by hiring more help or by raising prices. Either would be more profitable than slamming the door in customers' faces. It would be illegal because it would violate antitrust laws.

The concerted shutdown is a clear sign that there exists an effective monopolistic agreement to restrain trade in the securities industry. The existence of such a monopoly, not anything special about the process of buying and selling securities, explains how the industry can get away with a four-day week.

The shutdown is not the only evidence of monopoly. The standard schedule of rates for buying and selling securities, recently the subject of extensive investigation by the SEC, is another. The high price of seats on the New York Stock Exchange is a third. On the London market, where seats are not so tightly limited in number, the price of a seat is nominal.

Monopoly is harmful to the public, whether private, as in the securities industry, or governmental, as in the Post Office. Both mean unnecessarily high prices to the consumer. Both are departures from free enterprise.

But there are important differences. Private monopolists have a far stronger incentive than governmental monopolists to be efficient. Each firm dealing in securities will try to keep down its costs in order to keep up its profits. The civil servants administering the Post Office have a private interest in wheedling from Congress as large a budget as they can.

Private monopoly is also more subject to erosion than governmental monopoly. Competition will make itself felt in one way or another whenever the monopoly price is far above the competitive price. The recent stock-market hearings offer a dramatic example. The commission charged on large purchases and sales is clearly exorbitant. As a result, firms executing such orders have been able to get the business only by agreeing to "give up" part, often a large part, of their commissions to other firms designated by the customers—clearly an indirect form of price-cutting. In addition, a third market has developed in which large traders deal directly, bypassing the organized exchanges. A less dramatic but more pervasive example is competition among firms to provide "free" services to customers in the form of investment information and advice, attractive lounges with tickers, and so on.

The Post Office has not been forced in the same way to cut the rate for first-class mail even though the present rate is well above the competitive price. And it certainly has not felt impelled to compete by offering better service. Its legal monopoly on carriage of mail is a far more effective deterrent to competition than any private agreement can possibly be.

Preserving monopolies

Indeed, one can go even farther. Private monopolies seldom last long unless they can get governmental assistance in preserving their monopolistic position. In the stock market, the SEC both provides that assistance and shelters the industry from antitrust action—as the ICC does for railroads and trucking, the FCC for radio and television, the CAB for airlines, and so on through the dreary governmental alphabet. Remove this assistance and, while private monopoly will not disappear, it will be greatly reduced in scope and importance.

Chapter Twelve
CENTRAL PLANNING VS. FREE ENTERPRISE

This chapter covers a wide range of specific issues—from a papal encyclical to the mode of governing the West Bank of the Jordan. Their common theme is the widespread bias against the free market and in favor of central planning, despite the clearly superior performance of the market. This theme has been present in many of the earlier chapters of this book, but in most of these it has been a minor theme. In these columns, it is the major theme.

This general bias against the free market is a puzzling phenomenon, particularly on the part of intellectuals. I have often noted that the two groups that threaten the free market most are businessmen and intellectuals, but for opposite reasons. The businessman is in favor of free enterprise for everyone else but not for himself—he's always a special case, urging that governmental assistance, protection, and subsidy for him are necessary to serve the national interest. The intellectual is just the other way. He is strongly in favor of free enterprise for himself but not for anyone else. He wants no central government planning bureau to tell him what to write, what research to engage in, what to teach. No, he believes in free speech, a free press, and academic freedom. But when it comes to other people, that's a different story. Then he will tell you about the necessity of having central direction to avoid the wastes of competition and duplication of effort and to assure that resources are employed in accordance with the "right" social priorities.

Why is it that intellectuals do not see the inconsistency? Is it only their expectation (which, incidentally is doomed to be disappointed) that in a centrally planned society they will be in the driver's seat? Is it their tendency to overestimate the power of deliberate direction because cerebration is their specialty and to underestimate the power of voluntary cooperation? Is it the subtlety of the argument for a free market by comparison with the simplicity of the argument for passing a law to remedy a supposed ill? All these play a role, I believe, but even together they do not seem to me to offer a satisfactory explanation for the persistent faith in the virtues of central direction despite the enormous accumulation of evidence, particularly in recent decades, that collectivism is the road to tyranny, inequality, and misery; and that a free market is the only feasible road to freedom and plenty.

Resolving this puzzle is of the greatest importance. The free society badly needs, and certainly deserves, the support not the hostility of intellectuals.

PAPAL ECONOMICS
April 24, 1967

"On the Development of Peoples," the encyclical just issued by Pope Paul VI, proceeds on two very different levels. One level is an eloquent and moving statement of needs and objectives—a plea for charity, justice and peace to which all men of good will must say Amen.

The second level is advice about how to improve the lot of "people who are striving to escape from hunger, misery, endemic diseases and ignorance." On this level, men of good will should say Nay—for acceptance of the Pope's advice is likely to hurt, not help, the very people who are the object of his concern.

The kernel of the Pope's advice is: "Individual initiative alone and the mere free play of competition could never assure successful development . . . It pertains to the public authorities to choose, even to lay down, the objectives to be pursued, the ends to be achieved and the means for attaining these, and it is for them to stimulate all the forces engaged in this common activity. But let them take care to associate private initiative and intermediary bodies with this work. They will thus avoid the danger of complete collectivization or of arbitrary planning."

Central planning vs. . . .

Despite the qualifications, the Pope clearly believes that central economic planning is the key to economic development; that free markets and private enterprise have at most a minor role to play.

The Pope has much company. This belief is today widely held by intellectuals, particularly in the underdeveloped countries. Moreover, it has been acted on in country after country. What have been the results? Precisely the opposite of those the Pope anticipates. Wherever the condition of the ordinary man has improved, wherever he has hope for a brighter future, there free markets and private enterprise have considerable play and central planning has been limited in scope. Wherever the authorities have engaged in detailed and extensive central planning, there the ordinary man has remained poor, or his condition has deteriorated.

East and West Germany offer an almost ideally controlled experiment—a single people, with much the same cultural and economic background, torn asunder by the accident of war. On one side of the boundary, a predominantly free market—and prosperity, freedom and hope; on the other side of the boundary, detailed central economic planning—and misery, tyranny and despair.

Or compare Malaya and Singapore with their neighbors India and Indonesia. Malaya and Singapore developed and prospered under largely free trade and free markets, with negligible central planning. The ordinary man has a far more abundant life than he has in India and Indonesia, countries that embarked enthusiastically on detailed and comprehensive central planning, with results as depressing as they are clear.

India, to my mind, is the greatest tragedy of them all. It has tremendous potentialities. Its hundreds of millions of suffering people could create for themselves a rapid and sustained improvement in their standard of life—if only they were freed from the strangling tentacles of widespread intervention and control by governmental authorities.

Today's examples could be multiplied and they are in addition reinforced by earlier experience. Britain, the U.S., Western Europe and even Japan are all equally dramatic examples of the effectiveness of free markets and private enterprise.

. . . The invisible hand

In the face of such evidence, how can the Pope's view be so widely accepted? The intellectual subtlety of the argument for free markets is, I believe, one part of the answer. The advantages of central planning seem obvious. As the Pope says, "A planned program is, *of course*, better and more effective than occasional aid left to individual goodwill" (italics added). The advantages of the free market are more difficult to grasp. It takes a subtle argument to show how an individual who, in Adam Smith's words, "intends only his own gain . . . is . . . led by an invisible hand to promote an end which was no part of his intentions," to show how "by pursuing his own interests he frequently promotes that of society more effectively than when he really intends to promote it."

POLITICS AND VIOLENCE
June 24, 1968

There is no simple, widely accepted explanation for the increasing violence that is disfiguring our society. That much is clear from the public soul-searching renewed by the tragic assassination of Robert Kennedy.

This soul-searching has touched on many plausible contributing factors —from the malaise over Vietnam and racial unrest to the boredom produced by affluence. But it has neglected one factor that underlies many specific items mentioned. That factor is the growing tendency, in this country and throughout the world, to use political rather than market mechanisms to resolve social and individual problems.

The tendency to turn to the government for solutions promotes violence in at least three ways:

1 It exacerbates discontent.
2 It directs discontent at persons, not circumstances.
3 It concentrates great power in the hands of identifiable individuals.

1 *The political mechanism enforces conformity.* If 51 per cent vote for more highways, all 100 per cent will have to pay for them. If 51 per cent vote against highways, all 100 per cent must go without them.

Contrast this with the market mechanism. If 25 per cent want to buy cars, they can, each at his own expense. The other 75 per cent neither get nor pay for them. Where products are separable, the market system enables each person to get what he votes for. There can be unanimity without conformity. No one has to submit.

For some items, conformity is unavoidable. There is no way that I have the size of U.S. armed forces I want while you have the size you want. We can discuss and argue and vote. But having decided, we must conform. For such items, use of a political mechanism is unavoidable.

But every extension —and particularly every rapid extension —of the area over which explicit agreement is sought through political channels strains further the fragile threads that hold a free society together. If it goes so far as to touch an issue on which men feel deeply yet differently, it may well disrupt the society —as our present attempt to solve the racial issue by political means is clearly doing.

2 *If a law, or action by a public official, is all that is needed to solve a problem, then the people who refuse to vote for the law, or who fail to act, are responsible for the problem.* The aggrieved persons will naturally attribute to malevolence the failure of others to vote for the law, or of civil servants to act.

A specific problem often can be resolved by a law —generally one that imposes costs on some to benefit others. But along this road, there is no end to demands. These will inevitably call for more than the total of the nation's resources —however ample they may be.

Circumstances —the fact that resources are limited —make it impossible to meet all demands. But to each citizen it will appear —often correctly —that he is being frustrated by his fellow men, not by nature. Men have always reached beyond their grasp —but they have not always attributed failure to the selfishness of their fellow men.

France is today a striking example —of both escalating demands and the personalizing of discontent.

3 *Political power is not only more visible but far more concentrated than market power can ever be.* The Kennedy family is a harrowing example. Joseph P. Kennedy amassed a fortune of hundreds of millions of dollars. Yet he never had power of a kind to tempt anonymous assassins. Two sons have been assassinated, one at the pinnacle of political power, the other at the beginning of a great political career.

To put it objectively, had the Kennedy fortune never been amassed, the effect on the history of the world would have been trivial —except that it would have been more difficult for the sons to pursue political careers. The assassination of the two sons may well change the history of the world.

A free and orderly society is a complex structure. We understand but dimly its many sources of strength and weakness. The growing resort to political solutions is not the only and may not be the main source of the resort to violence that threatens the foundation of freedom. But it is one that we can do something about. We must husband the great reservoir of tolerance in our people, their willingness to abide by majority rule —not waste it trying to do by legal compulsion what we can do as well or better by voluntary means.

BECAUSE OR DESPITE?
October 28, 1968

"Nixon's whole campaign," wrote James Reston in The New York Times recently, "now is directed to this 'new class' of workers who have moved into the middle class *as a result of* the welfare state and planned economy policies the Republicans have held against Roosevelt for more than a generation." (my italics)

"As a result of" or "despite"? Reston has much company in taking the first for granted. Indeed, this view is so widely held that it will seem to most readers sheer perversity on my part to question it.

There is no doubt that the condition of the ordinary man improved greatly in the past 35 years, There is no doubt that a vast array of legislation was adopted in that period with the announced aim of improving the condition of the ordinary man. Is it not obvious that the first must be the consequence of the second?

Intentions versus results

Far from it. We all know that intentions are hardly a reliable guide to results. We all know that the mere fact that one event precedes or accompanies another does not demonstrate that the one causes the other —*post hoc, ergo propter hoc* is the label for a logical fallacy, not a valid method of reasoning. In the past 35 years, there have also been two great wars, a sharp rise in juvenile delinquency, an explosive growth in the fraction of the world's population living under Communism. Shall we say then that these events are responsible for the improvement in the condition of the ordinary man in the U.S.?

To justify his statement, Reston would at least have to show that a comparable improvement in the condition of the ordinary man has never occurred in the absence of "a welfare state and planned economy policies." He clearly cannot do so.

Consider, for example, the experience of the U.S. between the Civil War and the first world war. During this interval, nearly half a century, the U.S. had neither a welfare state nor planned economy policies. The U.S. came about as close to a laissez-faire, free-enterprise society as one could hope to observe in practice. The only significant exception was that tariffs were imposed on imports of goods. But people could come freely —immigration was unrestricted.

Yet the conditions of life of the masses of the people improved enormously —including the condition of the millions on millions of immigrants who streamed to the U.S. The overwhelming majority of immigrants were impecunious when they came, most with few skills and little wealth beyond the clothes on their backs. History records few if any examples of a comparable transformation of poverty-stricken millions into prosperous workers and an affluent middle class. This remarkable performance owed much to wise governmental policy —the policy of noninterference —but owed nothing to either welfare state or planned economy policies.

Whose welfare state?

The conclusion suggested by this sweeping comparison of historical episodes is confirmed by a detailed examination of the legislation enacted since 1933. Much of that legislation has interfered with productive efficiency while helping hardly anyone —agricultural price-support programs, legislation to regulate business, foreign-exchange controls, for example. Much of the rest, though enacted in the name of welfare, has in fact imposed heavy burdens on persons in the lower-income classes and yielded benefits primarily to persons in the middle- and upper-income classes —public housing, urban renewal, governmental financing of higher education, for example. Still other legislation has directly increased poverty or converted transitory poverty into permanent dependence —legal minimum-wage rates, the special immunities of labor unions, and direct relief, for example. And all of the legislation has involved much sheer waste.

The condition of the ordinary man has improved greatly in the past 35 years —as it did in the prior 35 years and in the 35 years before that. The improvement has throughout, in my opinion, been a product of the enormous opportunities provided to all by a competitive free-enterprise system —the most effective machine yet developed for eliminating poverty and raising the standard of life of the masses. The recent improvement has occurred despite a mass of ill-considered and mischievous legislation. It will continue even if that legislation is retained. But it would proceed more rapidly and its benefits would be spread wider if that legislation were repealed.

INVISIBLE OCCUPATION
May 5, 1969

On a recent visit to Israel, I toured the west-bank territory occupied during the 1967 six-day war. Much to my surprise, there was almost no sign of a military presence. Israeli soldiers were conspicuous only by their absence. The Jordanian Arabs were peacefully going about their business. I had no feeling whatsoever of being in occupied territory.

We crossed and recrossed the frontier between Israel and the west bank without encountering any soldiers and without noticing any obvious barriers to free movement. Traffic in Jenin, one of the major cities in the west-bank territory, was being directed by a Jordanian policeman wearing a gun on his hip. Even Israeli civilian administrators were few and far between. Governmental functions were being carried out by the prewar Jordanian civil servants.

The Dayan policy

The absence of a military presence and the continuity of administration are deliberate. At the outset of the occupation, Moshe Dayan, the charismatic general and Minister of Defense, laid down a policy of laissez-faire—if I may appropriate that much abused economic term to describe a related political phenomenon. Intervention by Israeli authorities was to be held to a minimum—and even that minimum was to be exercised as far as possible by consultation with the appropriate local groups rather than by order.

This wise policy involved almost literal laissez-faire in the economic sphere—and is possible only because it did. Jordanian money is permitted to circulate alongside Israeli money. West-bank farmers may grow whatever they wish and may sell their produce at any price they can command not only in the west bank but also in Jordan itself, so there is active trade across the Jordan River. An agricultural extension service manned by several hundred Jordanian civil servants, plus a literal handful of Israeli experts added after the war, has been galvanized into greater activity and has been extremely effective, so that agricultural output is growing rapidly. To a casual observer, the area appears to be prospering.

The major interferences with economic laissez-faire are restrictions on the export of farm products to Israel and on the movement of labor. Restrictions on exports have been imposed because Israel has adopted a governmental policy of supporting the prices of some farm products (we are by no means the only country that goes in for such foolishness). The importation of these products into Israel from the west bank would tend to force down the fixed prices or require the accumulation of additional surpluses. Restrictions on the movement of labor partly have a similar rationale—preservation of union wage rates —and partly the valid justification of reducing social tension and the danger of disruptive activity.

Trade and aid

These restrictions encourage the west bank to sell to Jordan rather than to Israel. As a result, Israel exports more to the west bank than it imports from the west bank and the west bank exports more to Jordan than it imports from Jordan. Jordan thereby gets foodstuffs and other items partly in return for pieces of paper (Jordanian currency) hoarded by west-bank residents. In effect, Israel is indirectly giving the equivalent of foreign aid to Jordan!

Another surprising consequence is that the military, who generally favor running things by direct orders coming down a chain of command, are in Israel the strongest supporters of free markets and nonintervention. They see by example that the anonymous market frees them from burdensome tasks and eliminates much potential conflict. They see that the elimination of barriers to the movement of goods, men and capital would foster the economic integration of the west bank with Israel without requiring political integration.

Here, on a scale sufficiently small to be readily comprehensible, is a striking illustration of the general principle that the free market enables people to cooperate in some areas to their joint benefit while permitting them to go their own way in other areas of their life. This principle explains why the nineteenth century, when laissez-faire was the ruling philosophy, was an era of international peace and economic cooperation while the twentieth century, when the key words are central planning and government intervention, has been marred by recurrent international strife and discord. Marx to the contrary notwithstanding, trade unites and politics divides.

UP IN THE AIR
July 28, 1969

This column was begun in a jet that had crossed the Atlantic in six hours but had now been circling Kennedy for an hour, stacked up awaiting permission to land.

What waste. A multimillion dollar jet, a marvel of modern technology, manned by a highly skilled and highly paid crew, occupied by nearly 200 passengers, many spending highly valuable time, serviced by a pleasant and attractive complement of hostesses, guzzling fuel as it circled aimlessly high in the sky. The cost was easily thousands of dollars an hour.

How is it that this waste occurs, not only occasionally, which is no doubt unavoidable, but regularly, so that experienced travelers, let alone the airlines, regard it as a routine matter? How is it that the large financial return from eliminating the waste is not an effective prod?

Socialism vs. capitalism

As I sat in the plane, I reflected that the airplane manufacturers seem to be able to turn out these marvelous mechanical miracles in ample number to meet the demand of the airlines for them. The airlines seem to be able to acquire the highly skilled flight crews in ample number (with a real assist, it is true, from the military services, which train most of them). They seem to be able to hire sufficient stewardesses to woman the cabins. Occasionally, a plane is delayed by mechanical trouble, but the airlines generally have been able to acquire the skilled maintenance and ground men to service the planes, so this is seldom a bottleneck. I have heard no stories of planes being delayed by the inability to get ample airplane fuel, or meals to feed the passengers, or liquor to befuddle them.

How is it that it has been possible to attend to all these matters —and yet not to arrange things on the ground so that planes can generally be landed promptly and without delay? Is it somehow inherently more difficult to arrange space for landing planes than to build them and operate them in the air? That seems very dubious indeed.

I believe the answer to the puzzle is much simpler. Every other activity described is mostly private and highly competitive —private enterprise builds the planes, private(or where governmental, highly competitive) airlines fly them, private firms produce and supply the fuel for man and machine. The airports, on the other hand, are a socialized monopoly — financed and run by government. As a result, there is no effective way that the waste involved in airport delays can be converted into effective pressure to eliminate them. The pressure must make its convoluted way through the FAA, the Administration, Congress and local governments.

There is no reason why this need be so. In the heyday of free enterprise, the railroads built and almost wholly financed their own terminals —even when they were "union" terminals servicing a number of lines —and still operate them. Why should airlines not be required to provide their own landing facilities —not necessarily directly but perhaps by paying fees to other private enterprises that run the airports? The airlines doubtless initially welcomed Federal subsidization of landing facilities. I wonder whether they now think they really got a bargain?

President Nixon has proposed a vast expansion of landing facilities to be financed by user charges but to continue to be operated by governmental agencies. The method of finance is the right one. The cost of landing facilities should be borne by those who use them. The method of operation is the wrong one. The right solution is to move toward private operation as well as finance.

Too pat?

Many a reader will regard my explanation as too pat —as simply a knee jerk reaction of an economic liberal (in the original sense of that much-abused term). Maybe so —but I urge them to see whether the shoe does not fit, not only here but elsewhere. Where are the long lines of frustrated drivers? At the doors of the automobile dealers selling cars produced by private enterprise —or on the highways and city streets provided by government? What are the problems plaguing education? A shortage of high-quality desks, chairs, and other educational equipment, including books, produced by private enterprise —or the inefficient organization and conduct of public schools? Where is technology backward and primitive? In the privately run telephone industry (albeit the existence of monopoly does occasionally produce delay and inefficiency) —or in the governmentally run Post Office?

LUNACY
September 29, 1969

"If Apollo was a victory for U.S. engineering genius, it could not disguise American failures at home . . . If we can put men on the moon, why can't we build adequate housing? Or feed all citizens adequately? Or end social and economic injustice?" This particular quotation comes from Time magazine, but it might have been lifted from any of dozens of comments on the spectacular moon landing.

The widespread acceptance and repetition of this cliché is a depressing testimonial to the superficiality and lack of historical perspective in so much that passes for informed commentary on current affairs.

Achievements . . .

Failure at home indeed. Is it failure to have converted an empty continent in two centuries into the most prosperous and thriving area in the world? Is it failure to have absorbed the "refuse" of Europe by the teeming millions and to have converted them into affluent middle-class citizens? Is it failure to have produced the most extensive network of private eleemosynary institutions in the world? The most extensive system of private and governmental higher education? To have a larger fraction of the population go to college than any other nation?

Seldom if ever has there been a success story like ours. Consider the third of a century from 1880 to 1914. Population doubled from 50 million to 100 million, as more than 22 million immigrants came to our shores. Most came with little besides the clothes on their backs —plus two hands and the urge to improve their lot and the lot of their children. Not only were they absorbed but their level of living as well as that of the rest of the population rose by leaps and bounds. And all this —let present-day liberals take note —without any governmental wars on poverty, graduated income taxes and burgeoning bureaucracies. This was a triumph of participatory democracy —the right kind, voluntary cooperation coordinated by a free market.

The story did not end in 1914. The creative drive of our people and the productive potential of free enterprise which could tame a continent were able also to surmount the obstacles imposed by growing government intervention into the private lives of our citizens.

Despite two great wars and two minor wars since 1914, population has again doubled. Average income per capita has risen two and a half fold — even after allowing for the higher prices today than then. This rise in income has been widely shared. Every index of level of living —whether it be the quantity or quality of food, the quantity or quality of housing, the amount of leisure time, years of schooling, vacation travel —all show substantial and widely spread rises.

No class has been left out —certainly not the Negroes. Unquestionably, there has been much discrimination; unquestionably, the economic lot of Negroes has been decidedly less satisfactory than that of whites; unquestionably, widening the opportunities of Negroes remains a major and urgent task. Yet let us not forget the successes —and not only, or even mainly, over the past decade. From 1870 on, there has been continued improvement in the social and economic conditions of the Negro —both absolutely and relative to whites. To cite but one readily available indicator: in 1870, 10 per cent of nonwhite youngsters between 5 and 19 years old were in school, 54 per cent of white youngsters. By 1900, the percentages were 31 and 54; by 1930, 60 and 71; by 1960, 82 and 85.

The income we regard as denoting "poverty" —and properly so by our lights —is above the *average* income of all the families in the Soviet Union. It is above the income of perhaps 90 per cent of the world's population.

. . . And aspirations

The cliché about Apollo is itself ironic testimony to our success at home. That success has raised our aspirations to levels never before dreamed of. In other times and places, the goal of "adequate" housing and food for all and the *end* of social and economic injustice seemed as fantastic as a voyage to the moon. The example of U.S. success has made both goals seem equally attainable.

Yet they are not. We may, and we all hope shall, continue to attain higher incomes, have more and more adequate housing, and reduce social and economic injustices. We must face and meet today's problems and not rest on past glories. But no matter how well we succeed, our aspirations will continue to rise, and will continue to exceed our attainments. "Ah, but a man's reach should exceed his grasp, or what's a heaven for?"

DEVELOPMENT FASHIONS
December 21, 1970

Recently I spent a week in a "developing" country. (A euphemism used to avoid the invidious designation of "underdeveloped." In U.N. language, countries are classified as either "developing" or "developed" despite the fact that most of the "developed" countries are developing faster than the "developing" countries. Semantics, where is thy sting?)

The country I visited is very different in resources and political background from other underdeveloped countries that I have visited. Yet the governmental policies that it is following to foster economic development are identical. I was able to reel them off without being told. Just as every female, whether her legs are slender and beautiful or fat and dumpy, was driven by fashion to hike up her dress, so every "developing" country, regardless of its specific characteristics, is driven by fashion to adopt a uniform set of governmental policies.

The shopping list

Here is a partial list of what every well-dressed "developing" country must have these days.

1 *An international airline.* Hardly a country is so underdeveloped that it does not have a fleet of U.S.-built jet aircraft, often indeed flown by U.S. or other foreign pilots, to show its name in the international airports of the world. Ghana Airways, Korean Air Lines, Turkish Airlines —the list goes on and on. Almost all lose money —but then what woman fusses about the price tag if she can get the money from her husband or father or uncle?

2 *A steel plant for countries that happen to have readily available supplies of ore and fuel may make economic sense.* But every "developing" country wants this symbol of industrialization, regardless of whether it makes sense. Egypt's steel mill is the modern equivalent of Egypt's ancient pyramids—a monument to proclaim the glory of her rulers. The major difference is that the maintenance costs of the modern monuments are far higher than of the ancient monuments—each year, Egypt spends about twice as much in producing steel at home as it would cost to buy it abroad.

3 *Auto-assembly plants.* The cheapest way for most underdeveloped countries to get automobile transportation would be to import the secondhand cars that are a drag on the U.S. and European markets. But this would be demeaning. India, as I once put it, is too poor to afford secondhand cars. So "developing" countries impose high tariffs on secondhand cars, or sharply restrict their import by quotas, in order to induce Ford or American Motors or Fiat or Rootes to set up a local assembly plant producing new cars. The resulting prices for secondhand and new cars strike an American as fantastic (some years ago, after selling an old Buick in the United States for $22, I priced the same model in no better condition in Bombay at $1,500).

A South American expert has estimated that his country would save money if it paid the employees at a local Ford assembly plant their current salaries to stay at home and imported directly from the U.S. the cars now being produced locally.

In 1963, I estimated that the annual cost to India of getting its motor transportation by producing new cars locally instead of by importing new and used cars amounted to more than one-tenth of the foreign aid India was then receiving each year from the U.S.

Why such uniformity?

Free trade in ideas, like free trade in goods, fosters standardization, though neither in ideas nor goods does this go so far as to eliminate all variety —as witness this column.

This tendency toward standardization is greatly reinforced by the jet experts who propagate the current orthodoxy in the economics of development with all the zeal of religious missionaries of an earlier and simpler age. The new missionaries come bearing gifts in the form of "development loans" at low interest rates or outright grants called "foreign aid." The gifts strengthen the government sector relative to the private sector and enable government officials to follow policies and undertake projects that would be politically unacceptable if the people at home had to pay the costs. That is why foreign aid is very far indeed from an unmixed blessing for the ordinary people in the underdeveloped countries.

Women seem to be staging a successful revolt against the fashion experts who decreed the midi. Who would have believed it possible? Maybe the badgered citizens in the underdeveloped countries of the world will yet be inspired to do likewise and to liberate themselves from their fashion experts. That will be the day!

ADDENDUM

The two articles which follow were written after this volume went to press. They appear at the end of this book because of that fact, and have been included at the suggestion of the publisher.

WELCOME TO A FLOATING POUND
July 24, 1972

Public reaction to the recent floating of the British pound has been almost uniformly negative. The press has spoken of "crisis" in the international financial system, "failure" of the Smithsonian agreement, "danger" to the dollar.

This reaction is a mistake. Use of the market instead of government fiat to determine the price of the pound sterling is a major step toward a healthy world monetary system.

Then and now

Compare the present action with Britain's response on earlier occasions when holders of pounds sought to sell more of them for dollars or marks or francs or yen or whatever at the official price than others were willing to buy at that price. The British Government, which perforce became the residual buyer, dug deep into its reserves to meet the run, borrowed additional sums from foreign central banks and governments, and restricted the international movement of money, capital and goods. These measures often served simply to encourage the run. Since the price of the pound was pegged, it was nearly costless to speculate against the pound. If Britain weathered the run, pounds could be repurchased at the same price. If Britain devalued, there was a sure profit.

Sometimes the threat was weathered. When it was not (1949 and 1967), the pound was devalued to a new fixed rate. Because of the crisis pressures, the devaluation was overdone, setting the stage for internal inflation and a new exchange crisis.

This time, the British were more sensible. They met the run with reserves for a few days, and then set the pound free. Speculators no longer had a sure thing. If they sold pounds, they drove down the price, which raised the possibility of a loss when they repurchased the pounds. Moreover, Britain saddled itself with neither unnecessary foreign debts nor an unrealistic pegged exchange rate. The market rate may for a time fall too low, but if so it will rise again. And who knows what the right rate is? Given the present high rate of inflation in Britain and the prospect of still more rapid inflation, any rate that is right now is sure to be too high some time from now. The